AVIATION'S MILLION D

...is not an astronaut, it's you! Although ⟦barcode D1458097⟧ e
a price tag on a real person, if you are cu. ⟍r
instrument proficiency then you are one of thousands of pilots who
account for more than a million dollars spent annually on instruction.
IFR Pocket Simulator Procedures is a complete guide to instrument
flight procedures and techniques and will save you hundreds of dollars
on the cost of your training. Read the following comments about the
"pocket simulator" and learn how it can make flying safer and less expensive for you:

> *IFR Pocket Simulator Procedures* is the most popular "do it yourself" book
> on radio navigation that we have ever featured as a main selection the
> Aviation Book Club. The book is literally a *pocket simulator* and utilizes the
> same "see it on the panel" approach to VOR and ADF problem solving that
> the author, Henry H. Culver, Jr., incorporates into his exciting, new, visual
> training aid: the "Pilot's *Dial-a-Panel* Navigation Trainer."
>
> **Flying Book News**

> Henry Culver's *pocket simulator* is an important adjunct to our ATC 610-J
> Personal Flight Simulator. *IFR Pocket Simulator Procedures* is a book de-
> signed to be *used,* not just read and filed away on the shelf.
>
> **Analog Training Computers, Inc.**

> *IFR Pocket Simulator Procedures* is one of the ten best pilot books in print!
>
> **Jeppesen Editorial Board**

> At last!...a practical and uncomplicated book of in-flight navigational pro-
> cedures for commercial/instrument students. *IFR Pocket Simulator Pro-
> cedures* is an outstanding reference text that covers all phases of advanced
> VFR and IFR navigation in an easy, step-by-step format and will help you
> immeasurably with your personal recurrent training program.
>
> **The Ninety-Nines, Inc.**

> I compliment you on your excellent book...it is very thorough and well
> written. I think that your *pocket simulator* is first rate!
>
> **Guy Murchie**
> author of *Song of the Sky*

> There isn't a more thorough book available to cover the extensive work that
> flight schools put their students through. The author leaves no stone un-
> turned—the procedures are accurate and functional and the quizzes are
> great methods to test your understanding. *IFR Pocket Simulator Procedures*
> is foremost in supplementing any instrument course.
>
> **Air Progress Magazine**

IFR
POCKET SIMULATOR
PROCEDURES

FOR USE IN THE AIRCRAFT, OFFICE OR HOME

Simplified "in-flight" radio navigational procedures, abbreviated attitude instrument flying techniques and fundamentals of radio and instrument operation essential to the safe conduct of an IFR flight.

Henry H. Culver, Jr.
Gold Seal Flight Instructor

PUBLISHERS OF AVIATION BOOKS AND TRAINING AIDS

ST. LOUIS, MISSOURI

Third Edition, Revised

Illustrations by Daniel Pearlmutter
Inside front and back cover drawings are
reproduced with permission of Guy Murchie
from his book, *Song of the Sky*. New York:
Ziff-Davis, 1979.

ISBN: 0-9601062-1-9
Library of Congress Catalogue Card No.: 76-27149

Printed in the United States of America

*To the enthusiastic students at
Culver Military Academy,
Culver Girls Academy,
and the Culver Summer Schools
who are learning to fly.*

About the Author

Henry H. Culver, Jr. is a *Gold Seal* Instrument Flight Instructor with Golden Eagle Aviation, Inc., in St. Louis, Missouri. He holds a Commercial Pilot certificate, with single and multi-engine land ratings and an Advanced Ground Instructor certificate endorsed for instruments. Mr. Culver served as a captain in the United States Air Force and taught flying at the Luke Air Force Base Aero Club in Arizona where he began flying in 1966. Later, he taught flying at the Scott Air Force Base Aero Club in Illinois and at Thunderbird Aviation, Inc., in St. Louis before joining the staff at Golden Eagle Aviation in 1980. Mr. Culver's bestselling book, *IFR Pocket Simulator Procedures* was published in 1976 and his innovative, new training aid, the "Pilot's *Dial-a-Panel* Navigation Trainer" was introduced in 1982. He is an active member of both the Greater St. Louis Flight Instructors Association and the Missouri Pilots Association and is currently designated as an FAA Accident Prevention Counselor in the St. Louis district of the central region.

Contents

APPENDICES

Foreword

The instrument rating is basically a package of navigational procedures and aeronautical disciplines that will improve a pilot's proficiency and expand his aircraft's utility. More than any other rating, it testifies to an airman's competency as a pilot and represents to the aviation world that the holder takes his flying seriously. If some readers consider the instrument rating as just another "paperwork plateau" then it must be regarded as a very lofty and precipitous plateau indeed because every year it challenges, rewards, and frustrates more pilots than all other ratings combined. Although the instrument rating is a formidable objective, most pilots can achieve it easily if they possess the three following ingredients for success: *motivation, time,* and *money.* Those students fortunate enough to possess all three of these key ingredients always seem to succeed; however, the others who are not so endowed, never tend to progress very far and for them the instrument plateau becomes as insurmountable as the fabled glass mountain in Grimm's Fairy Tales. Generally speaking, motivation and time are relatively insignificant problems for most students compared to money, the real culprit. A student can motivate himself as he perceives his own progress and budget his time to accommodate his training schedule but he cannot control the market value of his money. Instrument training has never been cheap, but it is more expensive today than ever before because not only have aircraft rental prices continued to rise at the same alarming rate as the cost of other goods and services, but also, the new FAR Part 61 (see p. 204) now requires applicants for the instrument rating to achieve a higher degree of overall proficiency for the flight test, demonstrated by their ability to "shoot" both the ILS *and* ADF approaches in addition to the basic VOR approach. Although the new regulations are an important contribution to the standardization of instrument training and to the establishment of more realistic proficiency requirements for certification, they do place an additional financial burden on the student who must train to meet these new standards.

Increasing numbers of economy minded pilots are now switching to the use of instrument ground trainers or "simulators" for a portion of their training as an alternative to flying costly rental aircraft. These flight simulators have achieved immense popularity in recent years because they rent for about half as much as an airplane and the Federal Aviation Regulations authorize their use for twenty of the minimum forty hours of instrument time required for certification. Revolutionary advances in simulator technology have enabled enterprising companies like Analog Training Computers, Inc., and Pacer Systems Inc., to manufacture portable "desk-top" simulators that are relatively inexpensive. Most of these compact machines are now equipped with adjustable D.G. headings and VOR courses because the industry recognizes that students need instruments that they can index manually in order to practice, on their own, many of the fundamental navigational procedures (like the ones presented in this book) that may be covered too briefly in the programmed lessons. Other manufacturers like The Singer Company (Link Division), produce sophisticated "walk-in" type simulators that are more expensive; however, they offer additional features like three axis control movement, multi-engine controls, navigation plotting consoles and even wings! There is no question that an instrument ground trainer has tremendous training value, but like an aircraft, it is a very busy classroom and is a far less appropriate place for a new procedure to be *introduced* than a place to apply and reinforce a new procedure previously discussed. Unfortunately for the instrument student, many flight schools generate revenue only when their airplane engines are running or their simulators are humming so many procedures, which could be taught with equal effectiveness in front of a blackboard for less than half the cost of a simulator or a third the cost of an aircraft, are usually presented to the student only after the simulator or aircraft is in operation and costing him money.

I wrote *IFR Pocket Simulator Procedures* to correct this inequity and to bridge the gap between the FAA written exam and the final certification checkride. The book is literally a "pocket simulator" and presents you with every radio navigational procedure and attitude flying technique that most approved schools (see p. 114) require in their instrument flying course curriculums. Contrary to what many beginning commercial/instrument students believe, there is not an unlimited number of in-flight nav procedures available for use in the cockpit. There is only a finite number of practical, commonly used procedures that need to be learned . . . and should be mastered by those pilots who "take their flying seriously." These radio procedures, which are covered in Chapters I through VIII of this book, are the same procedures that I have animated with my new, navigation kit: the "Pilot's *Dial-a-Panel* Navigation Trainer" (see p. 297).

The effectiveness of your flight instruction program depends not only upon how efficiently the course information is presented to you by your instructor, but also upon how quickly you can absorb it; and in this regard, the "pocket simulator" is an invaluable tool. Instead of paying upwards of $75 per hour for an introduction to these nav procedures while flying a well-equipped airplane or simulator, you can now LEARN them economically in the privacy of your home or office and save hundreds of dollars on the cost of your training. By adding a step between the classroom and the cockpit, *IFR Pocket Simulator Procedures* enables you to prepare yourself *at your own pace* for subsequent lessons in an aircraft and/or simulator where you will be able to APPLY your assimilated knowledge and earn your rating with minimum expense.

Since *IFR Pocket Simulator Procedures* was first published in 1976, many pilots that I have met at various airshows and organizational events have asked me why the book doesn't address itself to area navigation (RNAV). Briefly stated, area navigation is a method of point-to-point navigation that allows you to fly a selected course to a predetermined point (way-point), without the need to overfly ground-based, navigational facilities. I believe as most pilots do that area navigation is a valuable tool and I even have an RNAV system in my airplane (p. 170); however, *IFR Pocket Simulator Procedures* does not have a specific chapter dedicated to area navigation because the navigational procedures discussed in Chapters I through VII apply to electronically displaced stations as well as to "real" ones. Once you set a waypoint's bearing and distance from a selected VOR/DME station into the area navigation control panel (see p. ii), you create a *phantom station* that provides you with the same navigational information as a traditional, ground-based station and you may use all of the nav procedures in this book without modification! The "Pilot's *Dial-a-Panel* Navigation Trainer," which teaches you radio navigation through your interpretation of the instruments while you "fly" different in-flight problems, *does* cover area navigation. Because this kit is a visual training aid that allows you to take advantage of the considerable training benefit you achieve from being able to scan a realistic control panel which animates the RNAV display, DME and the other instruments, I feel that the redundancy of having to discuss the same nav procedures twice (i.e., once for a ground-based station and once for an electronic waypoint) is justified.

Wolfgang Langewiesche, author of the flying classic *Stick and Rudder,* recently commented that "an airplane is a chain linkage of various factors: the speed of the airplane, its weight, the thrust and so forth are all connected to each other by iron-clad laws of physics and aerodynamics and because of this, an airplane can only be flown one way . . . only the words and methods used to teach this single way of flying are different." In *IFR Pocket Simulator Procedures,* the "words and methods" that I use to teach navigation are no exception. Using an admittedly "different" approach, I seek to improve your instrument proficiency by providing you with reliable in-flight procedures which are compatible with the radio equipment commonly found in most light, general aviation aircraft. The book employs a functional outline format to achieve this objective because aerial navigation is also a "chain linkage of various factors" and the iron-clad mathematical laws which define the relationships between these factors (distance, speed, time . . . etc.), adapt very readily into concise step-by-step procedures.

For the very reason that an airplane can be flown only one way, it can be *navigated* only one way also and this involves simply the use of proven procedures to determine your position over the earth's surface at any given time. I sincerely hope that the "words and methods" I use to teach this single way of navigating will seem less "different" to you as time goes on and that the procedures I present in this book will be helpful to you in your future flying.

Before reading further, please study the Instrument Flying Course Syllabus in Appendix A (p. 173), and observe that the departure, enroute and arrival operations outlined in the instrument cross-country phase of the course (Phase III) are only directed applications of the radio procedures presented in Chapters I through VIII of this book. In addition, notice that aircraft control, the keystone of attitude flying, which is repeatedly emphasized in Phase I of the syllabus as being a fundamental skill in basic instrument flying, is discussed in Chapter IX. Although *IFR Pocket Simulator Procedures* is primarily oriented to the dissemination of radio navigational procedures, aircraft control is just as essential to a successful IFR flight as unerring navigation and I hope that the "control and performance" procedures presented in Chapter IX will both reaffirm the necessity for learning proper attitude instrument flying techniques and serve as a useful source of reference in the future. Chapter X is a comprehensive review of the entire book in the form of an Instrument Recurrent Training Schedule. It consists of six lessons, one lesson each month for six months and includes both aircraft control techniques and navigation/approach procedures. At the end of the six month period, the schedule is repeated, thus rotating through all of the material every six months.

Refer to the St. Louis Area Chart (p. xx), courtesy of Jeppesen Sanderson Company, to work the problems in Chapters I through VIII. Because this chart and the approach charts that appear in Appendix E are presented for illustration only (not to be used for navigational purposes), they are *not* "time valued" and therefore have not been replaced with current charts. Consult the Glossary of Aeronautical Terms (p. 269) to clarify any abbreviations which are not fully explained in the text.

Henry H. Culver, Jr.

St. Louis, Missouri
June 1982

Notice to Airmen

When Richard Bach, in his recent best-selling story, *Jonathan Livingston Seagull,* quotes the old proverb that "the gull sees farthest who flies highest," he is not speaking literally about altitudes and distances per se, but instead, is speaking ethereally about the higher levels of consciousness which an individual may attain through self-discipline and love. In IFR flight, the highest level of "instrument" consciousness that a pilot may attain is the ability to VISUALIZE his navigation.

IFR Pocket Simulator Procedures blends the traditional "see it on paper" approach to VOR and ADF problem solving that ground school instructors teach in the classroom, with the more functional "see it on the panel" approach that instrument flight instructors teach in the cockpit, to present you with a unique selection of easily understood, quick and accurate in-flight procedures that will help reduce your navigational workload and develop your visualization. These procedures are not intended in any way to substitute for a thorough academic understanding of the basics of VOR and ADF navigation gained by attending an accredited ground school; they are volunteered only to supplement this prerequisite study and to facilitate the translation of your academic knowledge into a more efficient interpretation of the "needles and numbers" displayed on the instrument panel in your airplane.

Although every navigational procedure or rule of thumb in this book serves as a vehicle toward improving your instrument proficiency, *do not* memorize any procedure that you are unable to understand completely and/or subsequently visualize. Unlike Jonathan Seagull, our flying disciplines may only be perfected and enjoyed in this world (level of consciousness) . . . so why foolishly risk passing prematurely on to the next world where the only IFR flight plans that are accepted, can NEVER be cancelled?!

H.H.C.

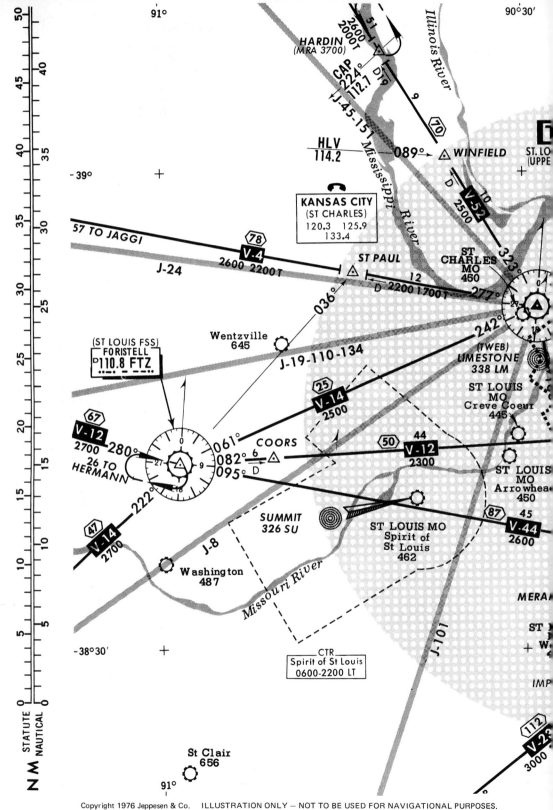

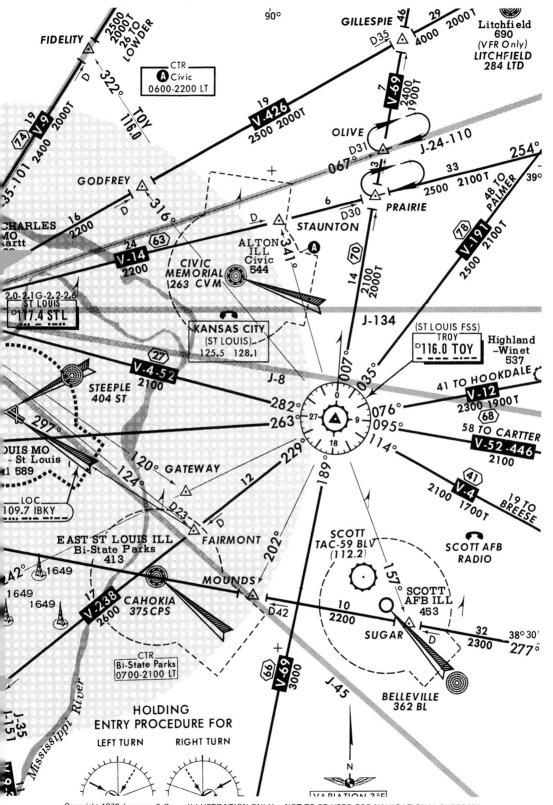

Chapter I
RADIO ORIENTATION

This chapter covers VOR and ADF homing, station passage and position identification procedures. Unlike the radio navigational procedures discussed in subsequent chapters that facilitate your orientation to some specific magnetic course which emanates from a given VOR station or non-directional beacon (NDB), the procedures presented in this chapter facilitate your orientation to the station itself! Homing enables you to proceed to any VOR or NDB that you have tuned and aurally identified; however, it is *not* recommended for IFR flight because it does not incorporate wind drift correction and in a crosswind your aircraft follows a curved path to the station. When maintaining a specific course is required, you MUST track to the station (see Chapter III, p. 37). VOR and ADF station passage procedures enable you to identify when you have crossed the station and for some novice pilots, it may provide their only positive "fix" since passing the previous station. Finally, the position identification procedures enable you to determine your magnetic bearing from any particular station or your exact position over the ground using any two stations. Experienced pilots who "take their flying seriously,"

1

routinely monitor their enroute progress by drawing "lines of position" on their chart that intersect their course. A line of position (LOP) may be a VOR radial, NDB bearing, highway, railroad track, river or anything else that crosses your flight path at an oblique angle. By using any two LOPS, you can "triangulate" a fix (see pp. 7 and 12). Since a line of position does not have to be an electronic course, the position identification procedures may also be used with dead reckoning or DR navigation which is a method of determining (*reckoning*) your present location based upon your heading, time and groundspeed from your last fixed (*dead*) position. Navigation is fun and the more proficient that you become, the less you will depend upon your radios to tell you what your compass and clock can tell you with just a little practice. For example, did you know that you can establish your position with two LOPs (highway/railroad track or river/power lines . . . etc.) that you happen to fly over at different times? This procedure involves establishing a "running fix" and may be obtained by using any two LOPs that are at an oblique angle to your flight path. Simply determine the time that you passed over the first LOP and estimate the distance that you flew until crossing the second LOP, then *advance* the first LOP (parallel to itself) by this distance and observe that you are located at the point where these two LOPs now intersect. As we begin now to explore the subtleties of radio navigation starting with VOR homing, remember that the nav procedures presented in this book are easy and efficient techniques used by thousands of knowledgeable pilots every day to accomplish the various in-flight tasks. Study these proven procedures carefully and stop struggling to draw a course-line between two distant points on your three foot chart with your eight inch plotter . . . learn to crease your chart and connect these points instead!

A.   VOR

1.   VOR HOMING

When an aircraft "homes" to a station, it temporarily flies inbound on some RANDOM magnetic outbound course (radial) until the wind or rough pilot control technique drifts it to another radial. As the aircraft drifts right or left of the course selected, the CDI needle drifts left or right in the opposite direction on the VOR head and informs the pilot that he must rotate the OBS knob again to recenter the CDI needle, and readjust his heading slightly to the new indicated course in order to continue inbound.* The particular radial that the aircraft happens to be flying on, identifies where the aircraft is located in relation to the station and is best determined by rotating the OBS knob until the CDI needle centers with a "From" indication (see p. 6). Alternatively, the aircraft's position may be approximated without "knob twisting" by visualizing the magnetic compass rose that is superimposed over most VOR stations depicted on the various enroute charts. If this circle is divided in half and its diameter is drawn through the station and 90 degrees to any given radial, then the To/From indicator informs the pilot on which side of the station (in which "hemisphere" of the circle) he is flying. If the circle is further subdivided into four equal parts then the CDI needle informs the pilot in which specific "quadrant" within the indicated hemisphere he is located based upon the direction of needle deflection relative to the course (radial) selected; i.e., if he imagines himself flying parallel to the course within both quadrants of the indicated hemisphere then he is located in that quadrant where the CDI needle points toward the course (see Note p.4).

*NOTE: Although a slight heading correction flown toward the needle would probably maintain the aircraft on its course if it were *tracking* inbound, the pilot is *homing* to the station in this instance, and is not attempting to maintain any specific course!

PROCEDURE:

Step 1: Tune the Omni navigation receiver to the proper frequency and aurally identify the VOR station.

Step 2: Rotate the OBS knob to center the CDI needle with a "To" indication.* Turn right or left, whichever is the shorter direction, to the OBS course indicated and fly the corresponding heading.

Step 3: Correct for right or left needle drift by recentering the CDI needle with the OBS knob and turning the aircraft to the new indicated heading.* Repeat this step as necessary until station passage which will be indicated by a complete reversal of the To/From indicator from a "To" to a "From" indication (see p. 5).

NOTE: Anytime the aircraft's heading coincides with the degrees set under the OBS course index, the CDI needle is DIRECTIONAL (points toward the selected course). Thus, when the needle drifts right or left of center while homing, it always swings toward the course that the aircraft was formerly on, and *usually* swings toward the station (see Note 2, p. 50).

Sample Problems

1. If ATC requests that you proceed "direct" to the Troy VOR from your present position, should you home or track to the station?

2. Is it possible for an aircraft to home away from the station?

3. What radial is your aircraft on if the CDI needle is centered, the To/From indicator reads "To," and 315 degrees is under the course index?

4. Whenever the winds aloft are *calm,* the flight path of an aircraft which is homing to a VOR will always be a straight line. True or false?

5. In which of the four quadrants around the station is your aircraft located if:

    a. The course selector is set to 045 degrees, the CDI needle is to the right and the To/From indicator reads "To"? (North, East, South or West)

    b. The course selector is set to 270 degrees, the CDI needle is to the left and the To/From indicator reads "From"? (Northwest, Northeast, Southeast, Southwest)

Answers

1. You would track to the station on whatever course is indicated (under the course index) after rotating the OBS knob to center the CDI needle with a "To" indication.

2. No!

3. 135 degree radial southeast of the station.

4. b. False . . . pilot induced drift (failure to hold a heading) or aircraft induced drift (imbalance in the rigging of the flight controls resulting in a slight, untrimmable slip or skid) will also cause the aircraft to fly a curved flight path to the station.

5. a. West
    b. Northwest

2. VOR STATION PASSAGE

Approaching any VOR station, the sensitivity of the CDI needle will increase because the width of the converging courses (radials) is narrowing (see p. 17). Just before passing over the VOR station, the aircraft enters the cone of confusion where the CDI needle may swing from side to side, the To/From indicator may fluctuate, and the course warning flag may appear. Because the width of the cone varies with altitude, the actual time the aircraft spends in the cone varies according to both its altitude and groundspeed. Station passage occurs when the To/From indicator makes the first positive change to "From."

PROCEDURE:

Correct for needle drift until station passage but don't "chase" the CDI needle when it swings rapidly from side to side; instead, maintain a constant heading until the To/From indicator reverses. After crossing the station, turn immediately to your outbound course and parallel it briefly until the CDI needle settles down, then intercept it at about a 30 degree angle (Chapter II, p. 18).

Sample Problems

1. The cone width over a VOR station narrows with increases in altitude. True or False?

2. A small lateral displacement from the desired course when flying close to the station, causes a large off course indication during VOR navigation. True or False?

3. The To/From indicator reads "Off" when: (1) passing directly over a VOR station, (2) when passing abreast of a VOR station through the CROSS OVER AREA (an area 20 degrees wide *on either side* of the course which is 90 degrees to the one set under the course index), (3) the VOR facility is shut down for maintenance or (4) the signal strength from a distant VOR is too weak to be reliable.

    a. (1) Only.
    b. (1), (3), (4).
    c. All of the above.

Answers

1. False
2. True
3. All of the above

3.   VOR POSITION IDENTIFICATION

PROCEDURE a: Radial Determination

Step 1: Tune the Omni navigation receiver to the proper frequency and aurally identify the VOR station.

Step 2: Rotate the OBS knob until the CDI needle is centered and the To/From indicator reads "From."

Step 3: Read the radial on which the aircraft is located under the course index. Draw this magnetic outbound course (radial) on the chart to describe your "line of position" from the station.

> *NOTE:* Visualize your aircraft's position. If, for instance, you determine that you are south of the station (on the 180 degree radial), and you do not know how far south, then either work a time and distance problem (see Chapter V, p. 59) and solve for the distance variable, or triangulate your distance south by using an intersecting course from another station (see b).

PROCEDURE b: Position Identification by Triangulation

Step 1: Select two VOR stations within receiving distance and tune both frequencies into the aircraft's two VOR navigation (nav) receivers, or successively into the one (if the aircraft has only one VOR receiver).

Step 2: Rotate the OBS knob on each of the VOR nav heads until the CDI needles center with a "From" indication.

Step 3: Note the radials (magnetic outbound courses) under both OBS course indices and plot them from both stations on the chart using the magnetic compass roses provided. The aircraft is located at the point where these two course lines intersect.

Sample Problems

Flying on an "abbreviated" IFR clearance (*local* "tower-to-tower" instrument clearance not routed through the Air Route Traffic Control Center) to the Alton Civic Memorial Airport in Illinois from the Spirit of St. Louis Airport, you are in the clouds on instruments at 4000 feet heading 065 degrees. If you determine that the aircraft is on the 185 degree radial of the St. Louis VOR and the 264 degree radial of the Troy VOR then:

1.   What is your aircraft's position?

2.   What LOM do you expect to fly over within the next few minutes?

3.   You should expect to cross V-4 but not V-44 on your present heading. True or False?

Answers

1.   Your aircraft is over the Creve Coeur Airport.

2.   The Steeple LOM that is associated with the Front Course Rwy 24 approach at Lambert-St. Louis Airport.

3.   True.

B.   ADF

1.   ADF HOMING

When an aircraft "homes" to a non-directional beacon, it temporarily flies inbound on some RANDOM magnetic bearing "To" the beacon until the wind or rough pilot control technique drifts it to another inbound bearing. The reciprocal of the aircraft's inbound bearing at any given time is its magnetic bearing "From" the beacon which like a VOR radial, identifies the aircraft's azimuth from the beacon (see p. 11).

PROCEDURE:

Step 1:   Tune the ADF receiver to the proper frequency and aurally identify the beacon (station).

Step 2:   Turn the shorter direction (left needle: left turn; right needle: right turn) to align the "head" of the ADF needle (bearing pointer) with the nose of the aircraft (the D.G. now indicates the aircraft's magnetic bearing "To" the beacon . . . see Chapter II, p. 27) which is the zero degree relative bearing reference at the top of the ADF dial. The aircraft is now proceeding toward the beacon.

Step 3: Correct for drift of the bearing pointer to the right or left of the zero nose reference (left wind: left drift; right wind: right drift) by turning toward the "head" of the pointer to reposition it on the nose.* Continue readjusting the aircraft's heading as necessary in response to subsequent pointer drift to maintain this zero relative bearing. Station passage occurs when the pointer moves through the wing tip position (see p. 10).

> **NOTE:* Any time the aircraft's heading coincides with the degrees of a given magnetic bearing, the bearing pointer is DIRECTIONAL (points toward the bearing). Thus, when the "head" of the bearing pointer drifts right or left of the zero nose reference it always points toward the magnetic bearing "To" the beacon that the aircraft was formerly on and it *always* points to the beacon.

Sample Problems

1. If ATC requests that you proceed "direct" to the Limestone LOM (ILS Rwy 12R approach at the St. Louis-Lambert Airport) from your present position, should you home or track to the station?

2. Is it possible to home away from the station?

3. If you tune in and identify the Limestone LOM and then turn the aircraft until the "head" of the ADF bearing pointer is on the nose, what is the aircraft's position if your D.G. indicates a heading of 250 degrees and your DME tuned to the St. Louis VORTAC indicates 20 NM?

4. With strong westerly winds aloft, it is unlikely that an aircraft, which is homing to a nondirectional beacon with an initial heading of north, will make station passage on a heading of east. True or False?

5. If you are homing to a beacon, are you drift-
    ing left or right of course if your compass
    heading is increasing?

Answers

1. You would track to the station on whatever
    magnetic bearing "To" the station that the air-
    craft happens to be on.

2. No!

3. The aircraft is east northeast (070 degree mag-
    netic bearing "From") of Limestone and ap-
    proximately over the Alton Civic Memorial Air-
    port.

4. True . . . the aircraft will cross the station on a
    heading nearer to the direction of west.

5. Left.

2. ADF STATION PASSAGE

Approaching any non-directional beacon, the sensitivity of the
bearing pointer increases because the width of the converging
magnetic courses (bearings) is narrowing. When close to the
station, the bearing pointer becomes unsteady and erratic due to
the area of signal confusion. This characteristic increases with
altitude. Also, a small lateral displacement from the desired course
causes a large off course bearing indication. A bearing pointer
deflection of 5 degrees, when the aircraft is 10 miles from the
station, means that the aircraft has departed from the desired
course approximately 1 NM, while the same 5 degrees displacement at 1 mile would represent a distance of approximately 600
feet. Station passage is positively determined when the bearing
pointer moves *through the wing tip position* (90 or 270 degree
indices, no wind condition) as it swings toward the tail.

PROCEDURE:

Correct for bearing pointer drift until station passage but
don't "chase" the needle when it starts moving rapidly to the

side; instead, maintain a constant heading until the pointer moves through the wing tip position. After crossing the station, turn *immediately* to your outbound course and parallel it briefly until the pointer ceases to oscillate then intercept it at about a 30 degree angle (Chapter II, p. 24).

Sample Problems

1. Since there is no To/From indicator window on the face of an ADF dial like there is on the face of a VOR nav head, you cannot readily determine whether the bearing that you are flying will take you to or from the station. True or False? Why?

2. Station passage, although imminent when the bearing pointer moves through the wing tip position, is positively determined when the needle completely reverses and points toward the tail position. True or False?

3. A small lateral displacement from the desired course when flying close to the station, causes a large off course indication during ADF navigation. True or False?

Answers

1. False ... since the bearing pointer (ADF needle) always points to the station, a pilot can tell at a glance whether the station is located in front of his aircraft (ADF needle points toward the nose) or behind it (needle points toward the tail).

2. False.

3. True.

3.   ADF POSITION IDENTIFICATION

PROCEDURE a: *Bearing Determination*

Step 1: Tune the ADF to the proper frequency and aurally identify the beacon.

Step 2: Determine your magnetic bearing "From" the beacon by the formula or by the D.G. visualization method (see Chapter II, p. 27).

> *NOTE:* Your magnetic bearing "From" the beacon is the reciprocal of your magnetic bearing "To" the beacon which is the course that you would have to fly in order to proceed direct to the NDB.

Step 3: Draw your magnetic bearing "From" the beacon (radial) on the chart to describe your "line of position" from the station.

> *NOTE:* Visualize your aircraft's position. If, for instance, you determine that you are south of the beacon (on the 180 degree bearing "From" the station), and you do not know how far south, then either work a time and distance problem (see Chapter V, p. 65) and solve for the distance variable or triangulate your distance by using an intersecting course from another station (see b).

PROCEDURE b: Position Identification by Triangulation

Step 1: Select two NDB stations within signal reception range, and tune both frequencies successively into the ADF receiver.

Step 2: Determine your magnetic bearing "From" each facility (see Chapter II, p. 27) and plot them on the chart. The aircraft is located at the point where these two courses intersect.

> *NOTE:* The aircraft's position may also be determined by tuning the ADF to the compass locator (LOM) of ILS equipped airports along your route and plotting where the magnetic bearings "To" or "From" the beacon intersect the aircraft's flight path.

Sample Problems

1. If your aircraft is on the 152 degree magnetic bearing "From" the Steeple LOM and on the 284 degree magnetic bearing "From" the Belleville LOM (associated with the ILS Rwy 31 approach at Scott AFB) then:

    a. What airport is your aircraft over?
    b. What heading should you turn to in order to proceed direct to Weiss Airport?

2. If your aircraft is eastbound on V-44 and you tune your ADF to the Steeple LOM as a crosscheck of your progress along the airway, then:

    a. What airway are you crossing when your magnetic bearing "To" Steeple is 030 degrees?
    b. What relative bearing (RB) will the "head" of the ADF needle indicate when your aircraft crosses Mounds intersection?

3. If you are located on the 195 degree magnetic bearing "To" the Cahokia NDB and on the 242 degree radial of the Troy VOR then:

    a. What is your aircraft's position?
    b. What magnetic heading would you fly to proceed direct to the St. Louis-Lambert Airport?

Answers

1. a. Your aircraft is over the Bi-State Parks Airport.
    b. You should turn to a heading of 254 degrees.

2. a. Your aircraft will be crossing V-9.
    b. The "head" of your ADF needle will be 42 degrees off the tail of the aircraft to the left and will point to a relative bearing of 222 degrees.

3.   a.   Gateway intersection.
      b.   290 degrees.

C. TRIANGULATION WITH A "DF" STEER

(VOR and ADF)

PROCEDURE:

Step 1: Contact the nearest "DF" (direction finding) facility[1] within radio reception range of the aircraft[2] and request a "DF" Steer to the host airport. The "DF" heading that you receive is your magnetic bearing "To" the airport and its reciprocal is the hypotnetical radial from the facility on which your aircraft is located. Determine this reciprocal course and plot it on the chart as your "line of position" from the airport that represents one leg of the triangle.

NOTE 1: "DF" facilities are specially equipped Flight Service Stations generally located on rural airports that have no tower and are not equipped with Airport Surveillance Radar (ASR).

NOTE 2: VHF radio has "line of sight" range only. You may accurately approximate your distance to the horizon (in nautical miles) by multiplying the square root of your aircraft's altitude times 1.23 (see Appendix B, p. 212).

Step 2: Tune in and aurally identify the nearest VOR station or NDB within radio reception range of the aircraft, and determine on which radial (VOR) or magnetic bearing "From" the station (NDB) you are presently located. Plot this course (second "line of position") on your chart as the second leg of the triangle. Your aircraft is located at the point where these two course lines intersect.*

NOTE: Under certain circumstances (critically low fuel supply, deteriorating weather ahead ... etc.) it might be desirable to plot a new course from this location and proceed direct to the nearest suitable airport. If this is the case and you do not wish to continue receiving "DF" assistance then inform flight service of your intentions and be guided by their advice.

Sample Problems

If the St. Louis FSS (Flight Service Station) has direction finding equipment and acknowledges your request for a practice "DF" steer to the Spirit of St. Louis Airport by giving you a heading of 130 degrees then:

1. What is your aircraft's present position if it is crossing the 035 degree radial of the Foristell VOR and you are advised that the airport is located at twelve o'clock ahead?

2. Having determined your approximate position, what heading should you turn to if you decide to fly direct to the Arrowhead Airport?

Answers

1. Your aircraft is over the Wentzville Airport.

2. A heading of about 110 degrees should take the aircraft to Arrowhead Airport.

CAUTION

The homing and position identification procedures, which are discussed in this chapter, are paradoxically the easiest navigational procedures in the book to understand but among the hardest for some pilots to accomplish. This is true because initially many pilots forget that instrument presentations vary from manufacturer to manufacturer. Pilots familiar with King radio equipment (p.ii), for instance, are used to reading their course information at the *top* of the VOR head, but if they happen to be flying an airplane equipped with older

Narco radios (back cover), reading the top index will give them the reciprocal of the correct course data because the Narco Avionics Company designed their earlier VOR heads with the course information at the *bottom* of the instrument. Remember . . . always read the large numbers and/or the numbers "right side up" because the smaller and/or inverted numbers will always be reciprocals!

$$1 \, dot = 2^{\circ}$$
$$200'/dot/n.mile$$

Chapter II
COURSE INTERCEPTIONS

To insure successful course interception, an intercept heading must be used that results in an angle or rate of intercept sufficient to complete a particular problem. When selecting an intercept heading, the essential factor is the relationship between distance from the station and the number of degrees the aircraft is displaced from course. Each degree or radial is one nautical mile wide at a distance of 60 NM from the station. Course width increases or decreases in proportion to the 60 NM distance. For example, one degree is 2 NM wide at 120 NM and ½ NM wide at 30 NM. In all light general aviation aircraft, navigation receivers with normal course sensitivity have a full scale deflection at 5 dots (10 degrees) and aircraft displacement from course is approximately 200 feet per dot (2 degrees) per nautical mile. This "degree of arc/nautical mile relationship" is relevant not only to course interceptions but also to flying DME arcs (see p. 71).

An intercept angle is the angular difference in degrees between the heading of the aircraft (intercept heading) and the desired course. The minimum acceptable angle of intercept for an *inbound* course interception must be greater than the number of degrees the aircraft is displaced from the desired course and should never exceed 90 degrees (see Note p. 21). The intercept heading may be adjusted within these limits to achieve the most desirable rate of intercept. The normal angle of intercept for an *outbound* course interception immediately after station passage should equal approximately the number of degrees off course, not to exceed 45 degrees . . . 30 degrees is the commonly accepted intercept angle for this type of problem. The rate of intercept, determined by observing the movement of the CDI needle, is a result of intercept angle, groundspeed, inbound or outbound direction of travel and distance from the station. Remember, a one dot needle deflection is *always* equal to a two degree displacement from the course centerline regardless of the aircraft's distance from the station . . . the distance variable only influences an aircraft's miles from the centerline and its rate of intercept to the course!

A.   VOR RADIAL INTERCEPTS

Before you can use the following course interception procedure, you MUST make two important decisions. First, you have to determine what radial that you want to intercept (or if an airway is involved, which radial constitutes the airway) and second, you have to determine whether you want to fly this radial (airway) inbound or outbound.

PROCEDURE

Step 1: Tune the Omni navigation receiver to the proper frequency and aurally identify the VOR station.

Step 2: In order to intercept and fly a given radial in either direction, rotate the OBS knob to set the degrees of your intended course under the index; i.e., to fly *outbound,* set the degrees of the RADIAL under the course index or to fly *inbound,* set the degrees of the RECIPROCAL of the radial under the course index.

Step 3: Confirm that the To/From indicator is consistent with your intentions to fly inbound or outbound[1] i.e., the To/From window should indicate a "To" when you set the reciprocal of the radial (inbound) and it should indicate a "From" when you set the radial (outbound). If the To/From indicator is not consistent with your intentions, the aircraft is on the wrong side of the station, and the intercept is not possible unless you first continue to the other side of the station.[2] Having confirmed that the To/From indicator is consistent with your intentions, proceed to Step 4.

NOTE 1: Do not set the To/From indicator in Step 3; only REFER to it! In addition, remember that the To/From indicator only tells you whether or not the course you have selected *if intercepted and flown* will take the aircraft to or from the station . . . it does not tell you, irrespective of the aircraft's D.G., heading that you are proceeding to or from the station.

NOTE 2: If you still wish to make the intercept even though the To/From indicator reflects that you are on the wrong side of the station, then you must either proceed directly to the station and make the intercept after station passage or use the following procedures:

a. *Inbound:* Fly parallel to the radial you want to intercept and set your OBS to another radial that is 45 degrees from your parallel course. When the CDI needle centers, intercept your inbound course with a 90 degree intercept angle.

b. *Outbound:* Fly parallel to the radial you want to intercept and set your OBS to another radial that is 90 degrees from your parallel course. When the CDI needle centers, intercept your outbound course with a 45 degree intercept angle.

Step 4: If the CDI needle is to the *left,* SUBTRACT an appropriate intercept angle[1] (usually between forty degrees and sixty degrees depending upon the aircraft's distance from the station) from the course set under the index on the omni-bearing dial. If the CDI needle is pointing to the *right,* ADD an appropriate intercept angle to this course. In either case, having predetermined an intercept heading, refer to the D.G. and turn right or left, whichever is the shorter direction, to this heading[2] and double-check that it will, in fact, intercept the desired radial (use the D.G. Visualization Method, p. 48 to verify your intercept heading).

NOTE 1: An intercept angle determined by the following method is always appropriate during VOR course interceptions:

a. *Inbound:* Compute an appropriate intercept angle by doubling the angular difference between the degrees of the course selected in Step 2 above and the degrees of the course indicated under the index on the omni-bearing dial when the CDI needle is centered with a "To" indication. **Example**: To intercept and fly inbound on the 040 degree *radial,* an intercept angle of 60 degrees would be appropriate if the CDI needle centered with a "To" indication on 190 degrees.

b. *Outbound:* Compute an appropriate intercept angle by doubling the angular difference between the degrees of the course selected in Step 2 above and the degrees of the course indicated under the index on the omni-bearing dial when the CDI needle is centered with a "From" indication. **Example**: To intercept and fly outbound on the 040 degree radial, an intercept angle of 60 degrees would be appropriate if the CDI needle centered with a "From" indication on 010 degrees.

NOTE 2: A right or left CDI needle does NOT tell you to turn "right" or "left" to get to your desired course (unless your heading parallels this course; i.e., your CDI needle is directional . . . see Note p. 4), it only tells you whether to *add* (or *subtract*) an appropriate number of degrees (your intercept angle) to (from) the selected course in order to determine your intercept heading.

Step 5: When the CDI needle centers, the intercept is accomplished and you should turn the aircraft to the course set under the index on the omni-bearing dial; that is, the radial which was selected to be flown inbound or outbound in Step 2.*

NOTE: Often, pilots attempting to intercept and fly inbound on a given radial will reach the VOR station before intercepting the radial. This occurs because their intercept angle is insufficient considering the aircraft's proximity to the station. In order to determine ahead of time whether or not an intercept angle (heading) is sufficient to intercept a given radial before reaching the station, use the following procedure:

Rotate the OBS from the course being intercepted to the intercept heading (D.G.) being flown. If the CDI needle reverses, the intercept will occur before the station passage; if not, then station passage will occur first, unless a larger intercept angle is used.

This procedure may best be understood by remembering that the difference between the inbound course to be intercepted and the inbound course indicated under the VOR course index when the CDI needle is centered with a "To" indication, equals the aircraft's minimum intercept angle to the station. A pilot must use a greater or lesser angle to intercept a given course before or after the station because to fly a heading that simply reflects the minimum intercept angle will cause the aircraft to intercept the course over the station. An intercept angle usually twice as large as the minimum angle is considered acceptable for most course interception problems (see Step 4, Note 1 above).

Sample Problems

1. a. What course would you select with the OBS in order to intercept and fly *inbound* on the 100 degree radial (V-4) of the St. Louis VOR?

b. With the appropriate course selected, if the To/From indicator reads "To" and the CDI needle is pegged to the left, then what intercept heading should you turn to if you want to use a 40 degree intercept angle? (Refer to a. above.)

c. Same question as b. above except the To/From indicator reads "From" and CDI needle is to the right.

2. a. What course should you select with the OBS in order to intercept and fly *outbound* on V-12 (082 degree radial of the Foristell VOR)?

b. With the appropriate course selected, (refer to a. above) if the To/From indicator reads "To" and the CDI needle is pegged to the right, then what intercept heading should you turn to if you want to use a 60 degree intercept angle?

c. Same question as b. above, except the To/From indicator reads "From" and the CDI needle is to the left.

3. Asked to intercept and fly inbound on the 030 degree radial of the Foristell VOR by your flight instructor, you dutifully set 030 degrees under the course index which gives you a "To" indication and a left needle. After flying a heading of 345 degrees (you decided to use a 45 degree intercept angle) the needle finally centers and you turn back to 030 degrees only to find out from your instructor that you made a mistake and accomplished the problem incorrectly. What was your mistake?

4. When asked to fly outbound on V-191 (035 degree radial of the Troy VOR), you determine correctly that your aircraft is still south of the VOR. Since you obviously cannot fly outbound on this airway considering your loca-

tion, isn't it perfectly reasonable to go ahead and fly inbound on it by turning directly to an appropriate intercept heading?

5. You are intercepting a given radial (inbound or outbound) at an extreme 60 degree angle. Is it possible to determine exactly when to begin your turn to intercept the radial (without under or overshooting it) or is the timing of the anticipated turn something that experienced pilots always "play by ear"?

Answers

1. a. 280 degrees (the reciprocal of the 100 degree radial).
   b. 240 degrees.
   c. *Intercept is not possible* because the aircraft is on the wrong side of station; i.e., the To/From indicator reads "From" instead of "To"! You must first proceed to the opposite side of the station and then make the intercept.

2. a. 082 degrees (the radial itself).
   b. *Intercept is not possible* because the aircraft is on the wrong side of the station; i.e., the To/From indicator reads "To" instead of "From"! You must first proceed to the opposite side of the station and then make the intercept.
   c. 022 degrees.

3. To intercept and fly inbound on the 030 degree radial you should have set 210 degrees, the reciprocal of the radial. When set, the To/From indicator would read "From" indicating that the aircraft is on the wrong side of the station to make the intercept.

4. When an aircraft is on the wrong side of the station to intercept a particular radial, it makes

no difference in which direction on that radial you intend to fly ... the aircraft must first proceed to the opposite side of the station before the interception (inbound *or* outbound) may be accomplished.

5. Yes! Divide the number of degrees of your intercept angle (60 degrees) by 3 degrees (degrees per second of a standard rate turn) to determine the time (20 seconds) necessary to turn onto the course being intercepted. Time the movement of the CDI needle for 20 seconds (for example) and observe the distance it travels toward center during this time. Keep this distance in mind and when the needle reaches a point of equal distance from the centered position, begin a standard rate turn to intercept the radial and upon rolling out on the course, the needle will be centered.

B. ADF BEARING INTERCEPTS

PROCEDURE 1: The Parallel Method

Step 1: Tune the ADF to the proper frequency and aurally identify the beacon.

Step 2: To intercept and fly *inbound* on a magnetic bearing "To" the station, or to intercept and fly *outbound* on a magnetic bearing "From" the station, PARALLEL THE BEARING. To intercept and fly *inbound* on any specific magnetic bearing "From" the station, PARALLEL THE RECIPROCAL of the bearing.

Step 3: Refer to the HEAD of the ADF needle; if you intend to fly inbound on a magnetic bearing "To" the station and the "head" of the needle indicates that the station is ahead, the intercept is possible ... proceed with Step 4. If you intend to fly outbound and the "head" of the needle indicates the station is behind, the intercept is also possible ... proceed with Step 4. If, however, your intentions to proceed inbound or outbound are not consistent with the needle's indication, the aircraft is on the wrong side of the station to make the intercept* and the intercept cannot be accomplished without first proceeding to the opposite side of the NDB.

NOTE: This may be determined without paralleling the bearing simply by superimposing the ADF needle onto the D.G. and insuring that the "head" or "tail" of the needle points to the same hemisphere or side of the D.G. where the magnetic bearing "To" or "From" the station is located. If the ADF needle indicates that your aircraft is on the wrong side of the station, the intercept is not possible without first flying to the other side of the station. If you desire to make the intercept on the opposite side of the station, then you can either home or track to the station, cross to the other side and then make the intercept or you can alternatively parallel the magnetic bearing "From" the beacon that you wish to fly outbound on (or parallel the reciprocal of the magnetic bearing "To" the station if an inbound bearing is involved) and:

a. *Inbound:* Within 45 degrees of the bearing turn 90 degrees and fly perpendicular to the intercept.

b. *Outbound:* Within 90 degrees of the bearing turn 45 degrees to it for the intercept.

... then fly inbound or outbound, as desired, when the appropriate relative bearing is reflected off the nose of the aircraft by the "head" or "tail" of the ADF needle.

Step 4: Turn toward the HEAD of the ADF needle double the angle it appears off the "nose" (inbound) or "tail" (outbound) indices of the instrument and fly the resultant heading until either the "head" of the needle (inbound) or "tail" of the needle (outbound) reflects the computed intercept angle (90 degrees maxi-

mum) off the NOSE of the aircraft ("zero relative bearing reference" at the top of the ADF
dial).

NOTE: If you are flying an aircraft that is equipped
with an "open face" type D.G. (vertical card), then you
can quickly double-check that you have intercepted a
given magnetic bearing by mentally superimposing the
ADF needle onto the D.G. card and reading the magnetic bearing "To" or "From" the station directly off
the D.G. under the "head" or "tail" of the ADF needle
(see Note p. 27). **Example:** Refer to the instruments
depicted on the back cover and notice that the aircraft
has intercepted the 140 degree magnetic bearing "To"
and/or the 320 degree magnetic bearing "From" the
beacon.

If you are flying an aircraft that is equipped with an
older "closed face" type D.G. (horizontal card) and an
ADF without a rotating azimuth dial (fixed card), then
you **must** either remember your intercept angle or
utilize the above double-check procedure slightly modified as follows: Instead of superimposing the ADF
needle directly onto the D.G., you must first locate the
aircraft's D.G. heading on the fixed ADF card, visualize
this position to be the top of an "open faced" type
D.G. dial, and **then** superimpose the ADF needle just as
above, reading the bearings "To" or "From" the NDB
directly off of the fixed ADF card.

Step 5: When the proper intercept angle is indicated,
turn back to the bearing being intercepted and
the "head" of the ADF needle will come to rest
at 0 degrees or 180 degrees, depending whether
you are inbound or outbound.

PROCEDURE 2: The Direct Turn Method

Step 1: Tune the ADF to the proper frequency and
aurally identify the beacon.

Step 2: Compare the magnetic bearing "To" or "From" the station that the aircraft is actually on, with the magnetic bearing "To" or "From" the station that you are trying to intercept and:*

    a. Confirm that the aircraft is on the proper side of the station to make the bearing interception directly without having to first proceed to the opposite side of the station (see Note p. 25).

    b. Compute an intercept angle (90 degrees maximum) to be ADDED or SUBTRACTED from the *bearing to be intercepted* by doubling the angular difference between the two bearings being compared above (see Note p.20).

    c. Determine whether or not the magnetic bearing "To" or "From" the station to be intercepted is CLOCKWISE or COUNTERCLOCKWISE from the magnetic bearing "To" or "From" the station that the aircraft is presently on.

NOTE: There are two ways to determine the magnetic inbound or outbound bearing that your aircraft is on:

    a. *By Formula:* Your magnetic bearing "To" the station equals your magnetic heading (indicated on the D.G.) plus your relative bearing (indicated on the ADF). Remember that you must subtract 360 degrees from totals over 360 degrees and that your magnetic bearing "From" the station is simply the reciprocal of your magnetic bearing "To" the station (subtract 180 degrees).

    b. *By Visual Reference to the D.G.:* You can easily determine your magnetic bearing "To" or "From" the station by mentally superimposing the ADF needle onto the D.G. card (or onto the rotating azimuth ADF dial set to the aircraft's heading if you are using a "closed face" D.G.) in the same relative position that it appears on the ADF dial, and reading the magnetic bearing "To" or "From" the station that the aircraft is on, directly off the D.G. (azimuth dial) underneath the "head" or "tail" of the superimposed needle.

Step 3:   If the course interception is possible, then after determining the aircraft's direction of travel around the station, apply your intercept angle to the magnetic bearing to be intercepted as follows:

MAGNETIC BEARINGS "FROM" THE STATION:
   Clockwise: "Add" your intercept angle;
   Counterclockwise: "Subtract" your intercept angle;

MAGNETIC BEARINGS "TO" THE STATION:
   Clockwise: "Subtract" your intercept angle;
   Counterclockwise: "Add" your intercept angle;

and turn the aircraft in the shorter direction to this predetermined heading. Confirm that your heading is appropriate by visualizing the intercept on the D.G. (see p. 79), then fly this heading until either the "head" (inbound) or "tail" (outbound) of the needle reflects your *intercept angle* off of the NOSE of the aircraft. Turn to the bearing that you are intercepting and when the "head" of the needle comes to rest at the 0 degree or 180 degree position (depending whether the aircraft is inbound or outbound), notice that the "head" or "tail" of the ADF needle, when superimposed onto the D.G., will verify that the aircraft is on the proper course.

Sample Problems

1.   Refer to the instruments depicted on the back cover of this book and determine (using Procedure 2) what heading you should turn to in order to intercept the:

a. 350 degree bearing "From" the XYZ Locator Outer Marker (station)?

b. 270 degree bearing "To" the station?

c. 120 degree bearing "To" the station?

d. 090 degree bearing "From" the station?

e. 320 degree bearing "From" the station?

2. If your aircraft is on the 120 degree magnetic bearing "To" the Limestone NDB, then what heading should you turn to in order to intercept and fly *inbound* on the:

a. 150 degree bearing "To" Limestone NDB?

b. 120 degree bearing "To" Limestone NDB?

c. 090 degree bearing "To" Limestone NDB?

3. If your aircraft is on the 330 degree bearing "From" Summit LOM, then what heading should you turn to in order to intercept and fly *outbound* on the:

a. 300 degree bearing "From" Summit LOM?

b. 330 degree bearing "From" Summit LOM?

c. 360 degree bearing "From" Summit LOM?

4. Refer to the instruments depicted on the back cover of this book and determine (using Procedure 1) what heading you should turn to in order to intercept the 060 degree bearing "To" the XYZ Locator Outer Marker?

5. Intending to intercept and fly *outbound* on the 225 degree bearing "From" Steeple LOM, you turn the aircraft to parallel this bearing and note that the "head" of the ADF needle is 30 degrees left of the nose:

a. What is your relative bearing?

b. What is your magnetic bearing "To" the station?

c. What heading should you turn to in order

to intercept the 225 degree bearing "From" the station?

6. Intending to intercept and fly *inbound* on the 150 degree bearing "To" the station, you turn the aircraft to parallel this bearing and note that the "head" of the ADF needle is 30 degrees right of the nose:

  a. What is your magnetic bearing "From" the station?
  b. What intercept angle is appropriate here?
  c. What intercept heading should you turn to?
  d. What relative bearing will be indicated when the aircraft intercepts the 150 degree bearing "To" the station?

7. To intercept and fly *inbound* on a magnetic bearing "From" the station, should you parallel the course or its reciprocal?

Answers

1. a. 050 degrees
   b. *Intercept is not possible* because the aircraft is on the wrong side of the station (see Note p. 25).
   c. 160 degrees
   d. *Intercept is not possible* because the aircraft is on the wrong side of the station.
   e. 320 degrees (your aircraft is already on this bearing)

2. a. 090 degrees
   b. 120 degrees
   c. 150 degrees

3. a. 240 degrees
   b. 330 degrees
   c. 060 degrees

4. 150 degrees (90 degrees is the maximum intercept angle)

5.   a.   330 degrees
       b.   195 degrees
       c.   The intercept is not possible because the aircraft is on the wrong side of the station; i.e., the "head" of the ADF points in front of the aircraft instead of behind! You must first proceed to the opposite side of the station and then make the intercept.

6.   a.   360 degree bearing "From" the station
       b.   060 degrees
       c.   210 degrees
       d.   300 degrees

7.   Reciprocal

C.   LOCALIZER INTERCEPTS: ILS "FRONT COURSE" AND "BACK COURSE"

Although the localizer shares the navigation receiver (nav) with the VOR and utilizes many of the same electronic circuits, it should not be exclusively associated with the VOR. As a matter of fact, at airports equipped with a *"Locator* Outer Marker" (outer marker co-located with a low-powered NDB), thinking of the localizer course as an ADF bearing transmitted from the outer marker instead of as a VOR radial emanating from the runway will greatly facilitate a pilot's orientation to the ILS (Instrument Landing System). The ADF enables a pilot to remain oriented both to the beacon (compass locator) itself, and to that particular magnetic bearing "To" the beacon which coincides with the localizer course that runs through the center of the LOM in line with the runway. Every pilot whether receiving radar vectors to the final approach course from Approach Control or proceeding by his own navigation, must stay oriented to the localizer at all times and the ADF is an invaluable tool in helping him monitor his position.

An aircraft's approximate position, north, south, east or west of the localizer course, may also be determined without an ADF by considering in which color sector (blue or yellow) the aircraft is flying, as indicated on the VOR head when the nav is tuned to the localizer frequency. Any time the aircraft is more than 2½ degrees off the centerline of the ILS course (which is 5 degrees wide) the localizer needle will be pegged in either the **blue** (left needle) or **yellow** (right needle) color sector. Not all nav heads are color coded so to remember that the blue sector is on the left side of the instrument, consider how B L U E is spelled . . . BL = Blue Left! Assuming that the runway has one-half of its length painted blue and one-half painted yellow, all a pilot must do to determine from which side of the extended runway centerline he will be turning onto the localizer course is to look at his approach plate for the compass direction of the runway and the relative location of the color sectors. Orientation to the localizer, however accomplished, will enable a pilot to pre-compute the approximate final approach intercept heading that RAPCON (Radar Approach Control) will issue him when he is finally cleared for the approach, and will leave him little to do but wait patiently for the localizer needle to eventually center (see Chapter VIII: p. 93).

Concerning radar vectors to the localizer, specifically, a pilot must ascertain his position relative to the active runway in order to predict how Approach Control will handle his arrival. Aircraft being vectored from a position "downwind" of the active runway will almost always be turned directly onto a localizer intercept heading and the pilot will, generally speaking, have few, if any, orientation problems. Aircraft being vectored from an "upwind" or "crosswind" position will almost always (other traffic, terrain, etc., permitting) be turned parallel to the localizer outbound (downwind leg) before being turned progressively (two or three turns, usually: one or two turns to "base leg" and one to "final") onto a final intercept heading to the localizer. Generally, if the downwind heading parallels the outbound localizer course, the Radar Controller considers the aircraft's lateral spacing from the localizer course satisfactory. If the heading converges with the localizer, either: (1) the aircraft is too far from the final approach course and is being turned in a little closer; or (2) the wind is blowing the aircraft away from a desirable parallel outbound track and the Controller has corrected the outbound heading for wind. If the heading appears to be taking the aircraft farther away from the localizer course, either: (1) the airplane is too close to the localizer for a safe turn to final (without overshooting), (2) the wind is blowing the aircraft too close to the localizer course and the Controller is correcting the airplane's outbound track with the divergent heading, or (3) the Controller is sequencing the aircraft onto the localizer behind other aircraft and is providing additional spacing. Referencing ADF orientation to the ILS approach, if the ADF is tuned to the LOM and the aircraft is approximately paralleling the localizer outbound, the pilot can expect his "base" leg turn (or first of his base leg turns) when the bearing pointer travels about thirty degrees below the wing tip index on the ADF dial. This 90 degree turn (to the heading that appears under the wing tip index on the appropriate side of the D.G.) is intended to put the aircraft on a normal "VFR type" base leg but turns of fewer degrees are not uncommon due to the variables mentioned above. Aircraft being vectored for an ILS approach will never be positioned onto the final approach course, heading straight for the runway. Approach Controllers almost always position an aircraft onto the localizer about two to three miles from the outer marker on an intercept heading within thirty degrees of the inbound course and then clear the aircraft for the approach. A pilot must have his radios already set up for the approach (the degrees of the localizer course should be set under the OBS course index for reference) and be anticipating the localizer needle to center; when it does, he should turn the aircraft inbound onto the localizer course, double-check his prelanding checklist, and wait for the glide slope needle to descend and direct him "down the slide" for another successful ILS approach (see Chapter VIII, p. 100).

> *PROCEDURE 1:* Localizer Intercepts . . . WITH Radar Vectors:
>
> > *Step 1:* Tune the VOR receiver to the localizer frequency, aurally identify the signal, and rotate the OBS knob (reference only) to the inbound course.
> >
> > *Step 2:* Orient yourself to the localizer by analyzing the aircraft's heading in relation to the color sector

in which it is flying and the magnetic orientation of the runway (see p. 42). Visualize
whether the Radar Controller is positioning your
aircraft to parallel the final approach course
outbound for subsequent turns to the inbound
(characteristic of "upwind" and "crosswind"
arrivals) or whether he is positioning it to intercept the inbound directly (characteristic of
"downwind" arrivals). Calculate your approximate base leg and final intercept headings appropriate to the aircraft's position.

Step 3:   Monitor localizer interception with the ADF*
and insure that by the time the Radar Controller turns the aircraft to a heading that could
reasonably be assumed to be your final intercept heading to the localizer that all prelanding
checks are complete.

NOTE: During ILS Back Course approaches, tune the
ADF to the Front Course LOM!

Step 4:   Turn onto the localizer when the needle centers.

PROCEDURE 2: Localizer Intercepts ... WITHOUT Radar
Vectors

Step 1:   Tune the VOR receiver to the localizer frequency, identify the signal, and rotate the OBS
knob (reference only) to the inbound course.

Step 2:   Track to the LOM or localizer on whatever transition radials or bearings are depicted on the
chart or approach plate using the same orientation procedures as above.

Step 3:   Turn onto the localizer when the needle centers
(and track outbound for the procedure turn
after crossing over the outer marker ... see
p. 103).

Sample Problems

1. Your aircraft is on the 210 degree magnetic bearing "From" Alpos LOM at the Alton Civic Memorial Airport and is being radar vectored for the ILS Rwy 29 approach (Appendix E, p. 259):

   a. In what color sector is the aircraft flying?
   b. On what heading do you expect to be cleared for the approach?
   c. Will the localizer needle be to the right or left of the instrument?

2. Your aircraft is in the yellow sector of the ILS Rwy 7 localizer course at the Spirit of St. Louis Airport and is being radar vectored for the approach on a heading of 253 degrees (Appendix E, p. 263):

   a. What relative bearing (Summit LOM) will be indicated on the ADF when you expect Approach Control to issue the "base leg" vector?
   b. What heading will this be approximately?
   c. What final intercept heading do you expect?

3. Your position is southeast ("upwind") of Lambert-St. Louis Airport and Approach Control vectors you northwest across the airport and then west to parallel the BC Rwy 6 localizer outbound (Appendix E, p. 262):

   a. What is your magnetic bearing "To" Steeple LOM as your aircraft crosses the localizer course over Lambert Airport on your northwest bound vector?
   b. If your localizer needle is to the left and you are cleared for the BC Rwy 6 approach, then what color sector is the aircraft flying in?
   c. What final intercept heading to the locali-

zer course do you expect to receive from radar?

Answers

1. a. The aircraft is in the "yellow sector."
    b. You may expect to be cleared for the approach on a heading not to exceed 320 degrees.
    c. The needle will be to the right side of the instrument and will swing to the left approaching the course centerline.

2. a. Approach Control will issue the "base leg" vector when the "head" of the ADF needle travels down to a position approximately 30 degrees below the left wing tip which is a relative bearing of 240 degrees.
    b. The "base leg" heading will be about 160 degrees.
    c. You will be cleared for the approach on a final intercept heading not to exceed about 105 degrees.

3. a. As your aircraft crosses the localizer course over Lambert Airport, your magnetic bearing "To" the station is 059 degrees.
    b. The aircraft is in the "blue sector."
    c. You will be cleared for the approach on a final intercept heading not to exceed about 90 degrees.

Chapter III
MAINTAINING COURSE

To maintain course (track) with a CDI needle (VOR) or bearing pointer (ADF), maintain your heading until the needle or pointer indicates deviation from the desired course. To return to course, use the course intercept procedures presented in Chapter II, avoiding excessive intercept angles. After returning to course, estimate the drift correction required to eliminate further needle or pointer drift and make further corrections from this heading. When close to the station, avoid making large heading changes because course deviation is probably small due to radial (bearing) convergence (see Chapter II, p. 17). Remember, to track means to REINTERCEPT and to CORRECT!

A.   VOR: TRACKING RADIALS

PROCEDURE:

In a crosswind condition, if a constant heading is held on the D.G., the CDI needle may drift off center to the right or left. If it drifts to the right, ADD an appropriate number of degrees (intercept angle) to the heading to recenter the needle. If the CDI needle drifts left, SUBTRACT an appropriate intercept angle.[1] When the needle is recentered again, pick a "base heading" to fly that incorporates a wind correction angle (WCA) sufficient to eliminate further drift and keep the needle centered (see Step 2, p. 43).[2]

NOTE 1: Anytime an aircraft is tracking a radial either inbound or outbound, if the D.G. heading roughly parallels the OBS course then the CDI needle is directional (see Chapter I, p. 4).

NOTE 2: The D.G. heading and OBS course will be different by the amount of this wind correction angle, but the CDI needle will remain centered. The course actually being flown will be indicated on the OBS ... *not* the D.G.! The D.G. reflects the aircraft's compass heading. The WCA must be determined by experimentation, but will always be less than the number of degrees necessary to initially recenter the needle ... usually about fifty percent less!

Sample Problems

1. ATC requests that you proceed *direct* to the St. Louis VOR; how do you do it?

2. Your aircraft is established on V-4 (100 degree radial of the St. Louis VOR) with a heading of 114 degrees:

    a. What is your wind correction angle?
    b. If your actual groundspeed is 150 knots and your true airspeed is 135 knots, then what are the direction and velocity of the winds aloft? (Variation in the St. Louis area is 4 degrees east.)

Answers

1. Center the CDI needle with a "To" indication, and track the indicated course.

2. a. The wind correction angle = + 14 degrees or 14 degrees west.*

b.   The winds aloft at your altitud‿
      degrees at 37 knots.*

NOTE: To compute the winds aloft in flight, simply work a normal wind problem backwards on your E-6B type computer. Instead of setting the wind direction and velocity UP from the grommet with a pencil dot, rotating the compass rose to the true course, and reading the estimated groundspeed under the grommet and WCA left or right of the center track line (under the pencil dot), reverse the procedure. Set your true course (magnetic course of the airway corrected back to "true" by applying the local variation) at the top under the true index, move the slide to position the grommet over the "actual" groundspeed, place a pencil dot over the aircraft's TAS left or right of the center track line by the number of degrees of your WCA (true course ± the D.G. heading corrected back to "true" by applying the local variation), and rotate the compass rose until the pencil dot is directly above the grommet. Read the wind direction at the top of the computer under the true index and the velocity in knots above the grommet (see p. 161).

B.   ADF: TRACKING MAGNETIC BEARINGS

In a crosswind, if an aircraft flies *inbound* to the station without a wind corrected heading to compensate for drift, the "head" of the ADF needle will move DOWN the face of the instrument from the nose position ("zero" degree RB reference) and will point (left or right) in the general direction from which the wind is blowing. If the aircraft flies *outbound* from the station and again does not correct for the effects of the wind, then the "head" of the needle will move UP the face of the instrument from the tail position (180 degree relative bearing) and will again point into the wind.

To correct for crosswind drift, always turn toward the HEAD of the needle, double the angle it appears off the nose or tail position of the ADF card. When the appropriate intercept angle is indicated; i.e., the aircraft is back on course, reduce this angle by about fifty percent to determine your initial wind correction angle and fly this new heading, adjusting it as necessary to maintain the desired course. Tracking with the proper WCA causes the "head" or "tail" of the ADF needle to remain in a constant position right or left of the zero degree nose reference at the top of the ADF dial. This position *always* corresponds exactly to the location on the D.G. where the magnetic bearing "To" or "From" the station may be read directly under the "head" or "tail" of the ADF needle when it is mentally superimposed in the same relative position. **Example**: If the "head" of the ADF needle is 20 degrees left of the nose (on the ADF dial) to track the 225 degree magnetic bearing "To" the station, the number 225 degrees will be 20 degrees left of the nose on the D.G. in the same relative position.

PROCEDURE 1: The Parallel Method:

> *Step 1:*   If the "head" of the ADF needle drifts right or left after paralleling the magnetic bearing "To" or "From" the station, turn right or left toward the "head" of the needle double the angle it appears off the nose or tail of the instrument, to reintercept the course.

> *Step 2:*   When back on course (see Chapter II, p. 26) carry a WCA in the direction of the needle drift (about fifty percent of the intercept angle used in Step 1) to remain on the desired magnetic bearing "To" or "From" the station that the aircraft is tracking.*

PROCEDURE 2: The Direct Turn Method:

Turn directly back onto course (see Chapter II, p. 26) and then carry a WCA in the direction of the needle drift (about fifty percent of the initial intercept angle) to remain on the desired magnetic bearing "To" or "From" the station that the aircraft is tracking.*

*NOTE: Regardless of whether the aircraft is inbound to or outbound from the station, an "insufficient" WCA may be quickly identified by

observing the "head" of the ADF needle move UP the face of the instrument toward the nose position.

Corrective Action: Increase the WCA being used!

Likewise, a WCA which is too great may be identified by observing the "head" of the ADF needle move DOWN the face of the instrument toward the tail position.

Corrective Action: Decrease the WCA being used!

Sample Problems

1. When the "head" of the ADF needle drifts down the face of the ADF card tracking inbound *or* outbound does it mean that your wind correction angle is too great or insufficient? What about when it drifts up the face of the instrument?

2. When the proper wind correction angle has been determined and the aircraft is established on a heading to maintain its track along a given magnetic bearing "To" or "From" the NDB, will the "head" of the ADF needle remain in a constant position or continue to move as the aircraft progresses along its flight path?

3. What magnetic inbound bearing are you on if you are flying a heading of 120 degrees in order to track the 090 degree bearing "To" the station? Are you located north, south, east, or west of the station?

Answers

1. a. Too great
   b. Insufficient

2. Remain in a constant position.

3.   a.   You are on the 090 degree magnetic bearing "To" the station.
     b.   The aircraft is located west of the station.

C.   LOCALIZER TRACKING

To track an ILS localizer, a pilot must REINTERCEPT the published course whenever he drifts off the centerline, and CORRECT his heading with an appropriate wind correction angle in order to prevent further drift. Although localizer intercepts are discussed comprehensively in Chapter II (p. 31), a further explanation of the subject is presented in this section to point out how a pilot who is tracking a localizer may quickly verify by **color sector analysis** whether his reintercept heading to the centerline is suitable . . . even if he momentarily forgets how to fly the needle. The **blue** sector of an ILS Front Course (Back Course) is ALWAYS on the right (left) side of the localizer centerline and the **yellow** sector of an ILS Front Course (Back Course) is ALWAYS on the left (right) side of the centerline. If an aircraft, which is roughly paralleling (within 90 degrees of) the inbound course, drifts to the right of the localizer centerline into the blue sector, the pilot will have to make a correcting turn to the *left* and since the localizer needle is also deflected to the *left* (into the blue side of the VOR display) there is normal needle sensing — the needle indicates both the color sector in which the aircraft is flying and the direction back to the course centerline. Even though the localizer needle ALWAYS indicates the proper color sector where the aircraft is flying, it is not always directional. If, for example, an aircraft is drifting south of the BC Rwy 6 localizer at Lambert Airport (needle moving to the right/yellow side of the VOR) while inbound on the approach, the pilot should correct to the north of the 059 degree course (toward the blue sector) which is a *left* turn and since the localizer needle is to the *right,* there is reverse needle sensing.

PROCEDURE:

Step 1: Determine whether a left or right turn is necessary to reintercept the localizer course by analyzing the aircraft's heading in relation to the color sector in which it is flying and the magnetic orientation of the runway. If the localizer needle is deflected the same way (left or right) as your computed direction of turn, then there is normal needle sensing and correcting turns should be made toward the needle.* If, however, the needle is deflected in the opposite direction, then there is reverse needle sensing and turns should be made away from the needle.

*NOTE: Turning right or left toward the CDI needle in order to recenter it is considered very poor instrument technique during course interceptions (Chapter II) but is acceptable when tracking because in this situation the aircraft's heading virtually parallels its intended course, and the needle is directional. Remember responding to a directional needle is more the exception than the rule!

Step 2: After establishing the aircraft on the localizer* pick a reference heading to fly which incorporates a wind drift correction (WCA). Do not change heading more than five degrees on either side of this "base heading" *unless the wind correction is insufficient.* Having determined that an additional correction is necessary, pick a new base heading and insure that any subsequent corrections remain within this 10 degree bracket.

*NOTE: Don't forget to set the degrees of the localizer course under the course index on the VOR for reference!

Sample Problems

Is there normal or reverse needle sensing in the following problems:

1. Outbound on the Front Course or inbound on the Back Course?

2.   Inbound on the Front Course or outbound on the Back Course?

3.   Tuning in the ILS Front Course of runway 28 at XYZ airport the localizer needle deflects to the right. Assuming that you intend to intercept the localizer at a 30 degree angle, what heading should you turn to?

4.   What heading would you turn to if the localizer needle in question #3 were deflected to the left?

Answers

1.   Reverse sensing . . . turns made AWAY from the localizer needle.

2.   Normal sensing . . . turns made TOWARD the localizer needle.

3.   310 degrees

4.   250 degrees

Chapter IV
INTERSECTION IDENTIFICATION

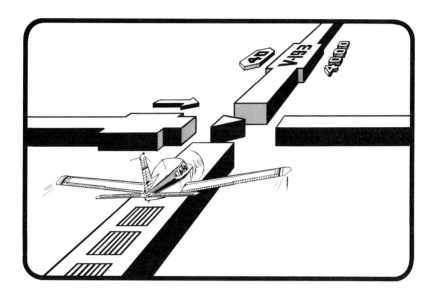

This chapter on intersection identification may be considered an extension of Chapter II on intercepts because there is absolutely no difference between the interception of a given VOR radial (ADF bearing) from an assigned airway course or radar vector than from a pilot's own calculated intercept heading. Instead of having to determine an appropriate heading that the aircraft "must fly" in order to intercept a given course (Chapter II), a pilot will learn in this chapter to determine if a given course is in front of the aircraft or is behind it based upon whether the heading that the aircraft is "already flying" will intersect it. Remember, if you can determine a heading to intercept a particular course, then you can certainly determine whether a particular course will be intersected by the heading you happen to be flying!

Often, pilots, in attempting to comply with their ATC clearance (especially in a non-radar environment), will mistakenly fly away from their assigned airway in the opposite direction because they incorrectly calculated the intercept heading necessary to join the airway. This potentially dangerous error would never occur if pilots would routinely use one of the intersection identification procedures (below) not only to locate intersections but also to "double-check" their calculated headings during all VOR and ADF course interceptions.

In the mountainous western United States, airway intersections frequently identify critical changes in the various enroute IFR altitudes* along route segments where these altitudes reflect the elevation of the surrounding topography. Along V-134, for instance, which extends from 194 nautical miles west of the Denver VOR to the Grand Junction VOR, each one of the nine depicted intersections indicates a different altitude for the MEA or MOCA! A pilot's ability to correctly determine whether an intersection is in front of his aircraft or behind it could well mean the difference between his timely initiation of a climb into smooth stratus skies above . . . or his regrettable failure to climb to a safe altitude and risking a terminal encounter with a rocky cumulo-granite cloud (mountain top) below the published MOCA! Orientation to airway intersections while flying cross-country is extremely important, but remember, the "enroute" phase is only one part of a given flight profile; what about the significance of this orientation during the "arrival phase" of the flight?

Failure to correctly identify a "step down fix" (intersection on the final approach course with an associated lower altitude) during an IFR approach could result in either a missed approach because the pilot failed to descend at the proper point, believing that the intersection is still in front of the aircraft, or an unnecessary accident because the pilot descended too soon, believing that he has already passed the intersection. Remember, a VOR radial or ADF bearing transmitted by an off course station will either cross the aircraft's flight path or it won't. If it will, then it must intersect the course in front of the aircraft . . . or behind it . . . KNOW WHICH!!!

NOTE: Minimum IFR altitudes (MEA, MOCA, MRA and MCA . . . see definitions that follow) are established by the administrator for IFR flight along Federal airways and off-routes in controlled airspace after consideration of obstruction clearance, navigation signal coverage for accurate navigation, and two-way radio communications. Obstruction clearance of 1000 feet above the highest terrain is guaranteed within five miles of the airway in non-mountainous areas and within 2000 feet above the highest terrain in mountainous areas. Pilots who believe that the extra

1000 feet of obstruction clearance separation guaranteed them by the MEA in mountainous areas is a limitation imposed only because of contrary winds aloft or weak radio signal strength should consider the effects of non-standard atmospheric pressure and temperature on their altitude (see Appendix C, p. 225: Pitot-Static Sensing Errors).

Definitions

1. MEA (Minimum Enroute Altitude)

    a. Meets obstruction clearance requirements.
    b. Insures acceptable navigational signal coverage.
    c. Often higher than MOCA.
    d. Sometimes different for opposite directions, due to terrain.

2. MOCA (Minimum Obstruction Clearance Altitude)

    a. Meets obstruction clearance requirements.
    b. Insures acceptable navigational signal *only* within 22 NM of the VOR.
    c. Shown on chart below MEA with asterisk (*).
    d. When no MOCA is shown, the MEA and MOCA are the same.

3. MRA (Minimum Reception Altitude)

    a. Lowest altitude to insure position at a specified intersection.
    b. Designated when MEA is inadequate for radio facilities.

4. MCA (Minimum Crossing Altitude)

    a. Certain radio facilities or intersections must be crossed in specified directions of flight.
    b. Normal climb wouldn't insure adequate obstruction clearance for higher MEA, so a MCA is specified.

A. VOR RADIAL INTERSECTIONS

PROCEDURE 1: The Parallel Method

To determine whether an intersecting VOR radial crosses the aircraft's flight path ahead of or behind the aircraft's present position:

Step 1: Tune the proper frequency of the off course

Omni into the appropriate nav receiver and aurally identify the VOR station.

Step 2: Rotate the OBS knob to set either the RADIAL (you intend to fly *outbound* on the intersecting radial or you simply want to identify the intersection as a position fix) **or** the RECIPROCAL of the radial (you intend to fly *inbound* on the radial) under the course index on the corresponding nav head.

Step 3: Turn the aircraft parallel to the intersecting course (selected above) and confirm that the CDI needle, which is now directional (points to the radial) points toward the aircraft's originally projected flight path (direction of flight before turning to parallel the radial). If it does, then the intersection is still ahead of the aircraft, if it does not, then the intersection is behind.

PROCEDURE 2: The D.G. Visualization Method

Step 1: Tune the proper frequency of the off course Omni into the appropriate nav receiver and aurally identify the VOR station.

Step 2: Rotate the OBS knob to set either the RADIAL (you intend to fly *outbound* on the intersecting radial or you simply want to identify the intersection as a position fix) **or** the RECIPROCAL of the radial (you intend to fly *inbound* on the radial) under the course index on the corresponding nav head.

Step 3: Mentally turn the aircraft parallel to the intersecting course (selected above) by orienting your hand (which represents the nose of the aircraft) to the D.G. as a visual reference. Your hand should be oriented palm down at about a 45 degree angle toward the front right or left side of the cockpit depending upon whether the degrees of the intersecting course happen to be located on the right or left side (hemisphere) of the D.G. when it is bisected down the middle north to south.

Step 4: Determine whether the CDI needle, which is now *directional* relative to your oriented hand (see Note p. 4), is deflected to the right or left side of the VOR head and then refer to the corresponding edge of your hand. If this edge of your hand is closer to the front of the airplane (instrument panel, propeller, etc.) then the intersection is still ahead; however, if this edge of your hand is to the rear of the airplane (your chest, the tail section, etc.) then the intersection is behind.

PROCEDURE 3: The Direct Turn Method

Determine what heading(s) the aircraft would have to fly in order to intercept the radial that defines the intersection. If the aircraft is on an appropriate intercept heading, then the intersection is ahead, but if the aircraft's heading will not intercept the radial then the intersection is behind.

PROCEDURE 4: The Station Location Method

Determine whether the off course station which is generating the intersecting radial is located on the right or left side of the aircraft,[1] then interpret the deflection of the CDI needle as follows: With a "From" indication (in the To/From window) the needle will point toward the station before the intersection, swing away from the station crossing the intersection, and point away from the station after crossing the intersection. With a "To" indication, the needle will point away from the station before the intersection, swing toward the station crossing the intersection and point toward the station after crossing the intersection.[2] KNOW WHERE THE STATION IS! Remembering the needle response with a "To" indication will greatly assist your orientation to the station during DME arcs which are discussed in Chapter VI.

NOTE 1: The determination of whether the station is on the right or left side of the aircraft may be accomplished in several ways:

a. Orient your chart to the direction you are flying and locate the station on the right or left of your projected flight path.

b. Look at your D.G. and decide whether you would have to turn left or right to proceed direct to the station based upon the course indicated under the index when the CDI needle is centered with a "To" reading.

c. Parallel the intersecting radial for directional course (station) guidance.

d. Work the station location method (procedure 4, above) in reverse by considering how the CDI needle swings in relation to the intersection rather than to the station. In other words, solve for the location of the station, given the location of the intersection instead of vice versa. By using any one of the aforementioned intersection identification procedures, determine whether the intersecting course is in front of the aircraft (needle has yet to swing) or behind it (needle has already swung) and then simply analyze whether the needle points toward the station or away from it.

NOTE 2: The station location method is based upon the rule of thumb that anytime the CDI needle is in transition, it ALWAYS swings toward the station with a "To" indication and away from the station with a "From" indication (see Chapter V, p. 62). This rule is only valid, however, when it is used in conjunction with intersection identification or arcing type procedures. During homing, course interception or tracking type procedures the off course station is usually too much in line with the aircraft's projected flight path to give you consistently reliable information about the station's location. The rule will NOT work during any inbound course interception problem where you are using an intercept angle less than the minimum number of degrees necessary to intercept a given radial BEFORE station passage (see Chapter II, p. 21).

Sample Problems

1. If you are flying west on V-44 toward the Foristell VOR and notice that the CDI needle of your second nav receiver (tuned to the St. Louis VOR) is pointing to the right then you should know that:

   a. V-9 is behind your aircraft because the OBS is set to 166 degrees.

   b. V-9 is ahead of your aircraft because the OBS is set to 346 degrees.

   c. V-9 is behind your aircraft because the OBS is set to 346 degrees.

   d. None of the above

2. If you intend to fly *inbound* on a given VOR radial and preset your OBS to the reciprocal of the radial (the To/From indicator reads "To"), will your CDI needle swing "toward" the station or "away" from it as your aircraft actually crosses the intersection?

3. At what point in the standard VOR radial intercept procedure (Chapter II) should you routinely use the intersection identification procedure presented in this chapter to double-check your intercept heading?

4. Intending to fly *outbound* on the 120 degree radial of the XYZ VOR, you rotate the OBS knob to set the radial under the course index:

   a. If your aircraft is flying a heading of 050 degrees, would you orient your hand to the front right side or left side of the cockpit as a visual assist in mentally paralleling the radial?

   b. If the CDI needle is to the "right," is the

radial ahead of your aircraft or behind it as it proceeds on course?

c.   If your airplane is suddenly repositioned on the opposite side of the station and the To/From indicator now reads "To" instead of "From" (the CDI needle remains deflected to the right), will the location of the intersection above reverse itself with respect to the aircraft or will it remain behind as before?

Answers

1.   c.   V-9 is behind your aircraft because the OBS is set to 346 degrees.

2.   Toward the station.

3.   At the end of Step 4 (see p. 20).

4.   a.   You would orient either hand (whichever is more convenient) to the front right side of the cockpit.

   b.   The radial is behind the aircraft. If the CDI needle were to the *left*, then the radial would be in front of the aircraft.

   c.   It will remain behind as before.

B.   ADF BEARING INTERSECTIONS

PROCEDURE 1:   The Parallel Method

To determine whether an intersecting ADF bearing crosses the aircraft's flight path ahead of or behind the aircraft's present position:

Step 1: Tune the proper frequency of the off course beacon (NDB) into the ADF receiver and aurally identify the station.

Step 2: Turn the aircraft parallel to the intersecting course (bearing) and confirm that the "head" of the ADF needle which is now directional and points to the *bearing* (it always points to the beacon), also points toward the aircraft's originally projected flight path (direction of flight before turning to parallel the bearing).* If it does, then the intersection is still ahead of the aircraft; if it does not, then the intersection is behind.

*NOTE: Assuming that the intersection is still ahead of the aircraft, when the aircraft turns back to its original heading, it will in effect be turning toward the "head" of the ADF needle just like during an intercept (see Chapter II, p. 25).

PROCEDURE 2: The D.G. Visualization Method

Superimpose the ADF needle onto the face of the D.G. If the vertical movement of the "head" or "tail" of the ADF needle is in a direction such that the "head" ("tail") of the needle will eventually move down (up) to occupy the same position on the D.G. where the magnetic bearing "To" ("From") the station appears, then the intersection is ahead. If the "head" or "tail" of the needle is already past this position, then the intersection is behind the aircraft.

NOTE: If the "head" or "tail" of the ADF needle points to the opposite side of the D.G. from where the magnetic bearing "To" or "From" the station appears on the D.G., then the aircraft is on the wrong side of the station to make the intercept.

PROCEDURE 3: The Direct Turn Method:

Determine what heading(s) the aircraft would have to fly in order to intercept the magnetic bearing "To" or "From" the beacon that defines the intersection. If the aircraft is on an appropriate intercept heading, then the intersection is ahead, but if the aircraft's heading will not intercept the desired bearing, then the intersection is behind.

Sample Problems

1. You have been cleared for the ILS Rwy 7 approach at the Spirit of St. Louis Airport via the 6NM DME arc (Chapter VI) west of the Foristell VORTAC counterclockwise from V-12. Because your aircraft has only one VOR receiver and you need it to maintain your arc around the VORTAC, you decide to use the ADF to monitor your interception of the localizer:

    a. Would you expect the "head" of the ADF needle to be above or below 073 degrees (when superimposed onto the D.G.) while flying the arc?
    b. What color sector of the localizer is your aircraft flying in?
    c. What will your aircraft's magnetic bearing "To" the Summit LOM be when it finally intercepts the localizer?

2. Does the "head" of the ADF needle *always* move down the face of the instrument and the "tail" of the needle *always* move up?

3. Does the ADF needle move smoothly up and down the face of the instrument as the aircraft turns or is there often a slight lag or jerkiness? Why?

4. If you superimpose the ADF needle onto the D.G., then (see Procedure 2):

    a. Are the various magnetic bearings "To" the station (NDB) that appear above the "head" of the needle as it moves down the face of the ADF dial (D.G.), ahead of the aircraft or behind it?
    b. Are the various magnetic bearings "From" the ADF station that appear above the "tail" of the needle as it moves up the

face of the ADF dial (D.G.), ahead of the aircraft or behind it?

5. Refer to the instruments depicted on the back cover of this book and determine whether the following magnetic courses are ahead of your aircraft or behind it:

a. The 120 degree bearing "To" the station?
b. The 350 degree bearing "From" the station?
c. The 180 degree bearing "To" the station?
d. The 270 degree bearing "From" the station?

Answers

1. a. Above 073 degrees
   b. The yellow sector
   c. The 073 degree magnetic bearing "To" Summit LOM

2. Usually ... the exception would be needle drift associated with tracking a bearing inbound or outbound with an insufficient wind correction angle.

3. There is generally a slight lag and/or jerkiness due to fuselage interference with the antenna when the aircraft is turning.

4. a. Behind
   b. Ahead

5. a. Behind
   b. Ahead
   c. Ahead
   d. Behind

C. DME INTERSECTION IDENTIFICATION

PROCEDURE:

Step 1: Insure that the aircraft is established on the

proper airway or radial (either inbound or outbound) and that the OBS knob has been rotated
to position the correct course under the index
on the VOR head.

Step 2:   Tune the DME and VOR to the same VORTAC
frequency and select the proper mode of operation (distance vs. groundspeed vs. time). If the
distance scale is adjustable to a "Hi" or "Lo"
nautical mile range, then select the appropriate
scale for the distance anticipated.

Step 3:   Monitor the distance scale until reaching the
published (requested) DME intersection identified in nautical miles from the VORTAC.

NOTE: If you are requested to report an intersection
ten miles from the station and your inbound aircraft is
thirteen miles out, the intersection is still three miles
ahead of you and vice versa.

Sample Problems

1.   If you are flying southwest on V-238, and cross
the Troy VORTAC at 1530Z and V-44 at 1538Z
then what is your estimated time to V-9, if:

   a.   Your DME tuned to the St. Louis VOR-
TAC indicates a groundspeed of 95 knots?

   b.   Your DME tuned to the Troy VORTAC
indicates a groundspeed of 120 knots?

2.   Flying inbound to the St. Louis VORTAC on
V-426 at 12,000 feet, if you note that your
DME distance to the station is 40 NM at 1945Z
and 23 NM at 1951Z then:

   a.   What groundspeed do you expect the DME
to indicate?

   b.   What is your estimated time to the St.
Louis VORTAC?

   c.   What distance will the DME indicate as
your aircraft crosses over the station?

3. Inbound on the ILS Rwy 7 localizer at the Spirit of St. Louis Airport (Appendix E, p. 263) you tune your DME to the St. Louis VORTAC and it indicates 22 NM. Is the 220 degree radial of the St. Louis VORTAC ahead of your aircraft or behind it?

Answers

1. a. 6 minutes. The 95 knot readout is unreliable because the aircraft is not established on a course directly to or from the St. Louis VORTAC. In this situation, you must use the computer, plotter and watch to arrive at the correct groundspeed of 120 knots (see p. 74).
    b. 6 minutes
2. a. 170 knots
    b. 8.1 minutes
    c. Two nautical miles . . . the slant range altitude of the aircraft *above* the VORTAC facility.
3. Ahead of your aircraft. The DME distance from the St. Louis VORTAC to the Summit LOM along the 220 degree radial (transition) is indicated on the approach chart as 18.6 NM. Since your distance from the St. Louis VORTAC is 22 NM then the 220 degree radial must still be ahead of your aircraft.

Chapter V
TIME AND DISTANCE

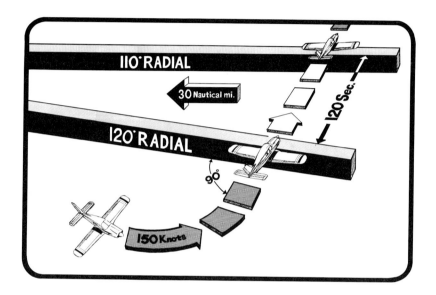

Although the "wing tip" method is the most popular of the VOR and ADF time and distance procedures and is required knowledge for the instrument rating checkride, alternate procedures are also presented in this chapter because they are useful in the actual IFR environment where 90 degree turns off course (characteristic of the wing tip method) are frowned upon by ATC. The wing tip method is more easily accomplished with an open faced type directional gyro (D.G.) than with a closed face D.G. because the former instrument enables the pilot to turn the aircraft and position the indicated VOR course (see procedure below) visually under the closest wing tip without the necessity of having to predetermine a specific heading. Pilots flying older aircraft equipped with a closed face type D.G. should refer directly to Procedure 1b.

A.   VOR

> *PROCEDURE 1a:* The "Wing Tip" Method . . . for use with an *open faced* D.G.:

Step 1: Tune the Omni navigation receiver to the frequency of the VOR that you intend to arc around for the time and/or distance computation, and aurally identify the station (see VOR arcs, p. 191).

Step 2: Rotate the OBS knob to center the CDI needle with a "To" reading and turn the aircraft the shorter direction right or left (refer to the D.G.) to place the indicated course under the NEAREST wing tip. *Begin timing!*

Step 3: Determine whether the aircraft is arcing "clockwise" (course under the right wing tip) or "counterclockwise" (course under the left wing tip) around the station. If arcing "clockwise," then as soon as the timing begins **increase** the OBS course setting by ten degrees;[1] if arcing "counterclockwise," **decrease** the OBS setting by ten degrees and turn the aircraft right or left ten degrees to put the new course under the same wing tip.[2] When the CDI needle centers again, *stop the time!*

NOTE 1: If you increase the OBS setting by ten degrees (indicating that you recognize that the aircraft is arcing "clockwise" around the station) the CDI needle will move left and swing back to the right toward the wing tip that the course is under which points toward the station. If you decrease the OBS setting by ten degrees (indicating that you recognize that the aircraft is arcing "counterclockwise" around the station) the CDI needle will move right and swing back to the left toward the wing tip that the course is under which points again, toward the station. Remember, any time the CDI needle is in transition, it always swings toward the station with a "To" indication in the To/From window (see Chapter IV, p. 49).

NOTE 2: Changing heading 10 degrees to put the new OBS course under the wing tip is optional. If you desire, you can maintain the same heading and simply wait for the CDI needle to recenter. The author strongly recommends the "heading change" technique because it makes the wing tip time and distance procedure almost identical to the DME arcing procedure presented in the next chapter.

Step 4: Determine the TIME to the station by the following formula:*

$$\frac{\text{Minutes to}}{\text{the Station}} = \frac{\text{Elapsed Time (Minutes) x 60}}{\text{Degrees of Bearing Change}}$$

If you wish to determine your time to the station without using the above formula, then remember that: FOR EVERY TEN SECONDS IT TAKES TO FLY THROUGH TEN DEGREES OF BEARING CHANGE, THE AIRCRAFT IS ONE MINUTE FROM THE STATION.

NOTE: Remember this formula by one of the two following ways (assume ten degrees of bearing change):

1. Minutes to the Station = Elapsed Time (Minutes) x 6

2. Minutes to the Station = $\dfrac{\text{Elapsed Time (Seconds)}}{10}$

Determine the DISTANCE to the station by the following formula:*

$$\frac{\text{Distance in Miles}}{\text{to the Station}} = \frac{\text{Groundspeed x Time}}{\text{Degrees of Bearing Change}}$$

NOTE: Remember this formula the following way (assume ten degrees of bearing change):

$$\frac{\text{Distance in Miles}}{\text{to the Station}} = \frac{\text{Groundspeed}}{10} \text{ x Time}$$

When flying cross-country, off airways, these formulas are a convenient way of double-checking aircraft position by utilizing any available radio facility as the aircraft comes abeam of it.

PROCEDURE 1b: The "Wing Tip" Method . . . for use with a *closed face* D.G.:

Step 1: Tune the Omni navigation receiver to the frequency of the VORTAC that you intend to arc around for the time and/or distance computation, and aurally identify the station.

Step 2: Rotate the OBS knob to center the CDI needle with a "To" indication and turn the shorter direction to a heading that is 90 degrees more or less than the indicated course to be placed on the wing tip. If the heading happens to be 90 degrees *less* than the course, then the aircraft is going "clockwise" around the station (station is off right wing tip) and the OBS should be rotated UP ten degrees; if the heading happens to be 90 degrees *more* than the course, the aircraft is going "counterclockwise" around the station (station is off the left wing tip) and the OBS should be rotated BACK ten degrees and, in either case above, the heading should be adjusted ten degrees right or left (clockwise or counterclockwise) as is appropriate depending upon which way the airplane is traveling around the station. Notice that the needle will swing *toward* the station as it swings to center and will, of course, be swinging toward the wing tip where the course could be seen if the airplane were equipped with an open faced D.G. *Begin timing!**

*NOTE: The computation of a heading within 90 degrees of the course indicated on the VOR navigation head is more difficult for some pilots than others and certainly every pilot has his own favorite procedure. Although this deficiency is relatively insignificant during the execution of a wing tip time and distance problem, it becomes critical, as we shall see later when attempting to fly a DME arc with a closed face D.G. where the wing tip course and D.G. heading must continually

change in response to the recentering VOR needle. Simply stated, a pilot has to have some way to quickly double-check his D.G. heading to maintain the ninety degree relationship with the course on his wing tip. The following "Rule of Thumb" will assist pilots in this double-check . . . memorize it!

Rule of Thumb: For ninety degree and one hundred eighty degree relationships, the sum of the first two numbers of any heading will always equal the sum of the first two numbers of either the wing tip headings or its reciprocal heading .

Step 3:   When the needle centers, *stop the time!* Turn the aircraft 90 degrees right or left toward the station (if desired), and apply the above time and distance formulas.

ALTERNATE TIME AND DISTANCE PROCEDURES

PROCEDURE 2a: The "30/40 Degree Method":

Step 1:   Center the CDI needle with a "To" indication and turn to establish the aircraft on the inbound course. Refer to the D.G. and turn the aircraft left or right 30 degrees. *Begin timing!**

*NOTE: The aircraft now has a 30 degree (330 degree) relative bearing (see ADF 30/40 degree method, p. 66).

Step 2:   Holding the aircraft's heading constant, rotate the OBS knob UP or BACK 30 degrees depending upon whether the aircraft is arcing clockwise (left turn in Step 1) or counter-clockwise (right turn in Step 1) around the station. When the needle recenters, *stop the time!**

*NOTE: The aircraft now has a 40 degree (320 degree) relative bearing.

Step 3:   Compute the estimated time to the station as follows:

Time to Station = Elapsed Time X 3

PROCEDURE 2b: The "30/40 Degree Method" . . . during VOR radial intercepts:

Step 1: Turn the aircraft to a heading that will intercept the selected inbound course (reciprocal of the radial you desire to intercept and fly inbound on for your "30/40 degree" time check) at a 40 degree intercept angle (see Chapter II, p. 19). Once established on a heading for this 40 degree intercept, rotate the OBS ten degrees **toward** the heading being flown so as to reduce to thirty degrees the angle between the heading* being flown and the OBS setting. When the needle centers, *begin timing!*

*NOTE: Until the CDI needle becomes sensitive and begins to center, you may, if you desire, increase your intercept angle up to a maximum of ninety degrees to hasten the interception; however, as soon as any needle sensitivity is noted, you must turn back to the heading which you previously determined would give you a forty degree intercept angle to the radial you are intercepting and be ready to *begin your time* when the needle centers.

Step 2: Rotate the OBS back to the original inbound course to be intercepted, holding the same heading as in Step 1 (heading for a forty degree intercept angle) and when the needle recenters, *stop the time!* The aircraft has now intercepted the radial at a forty degree angle and your time to the station may be quickly determined as follows:

Time to the Station* = Elapsed Time X 3

*NOTE: Since for a constant groundspeed, time is proportional to distance in this "30/40 degree method," the formula works for distance as well as for time to the station.

PROCEDURE 3a: The "Double the Angle Off the Nose Method" (Isosceles Triangle):

Step 1: Center the CDI needle with a "To" indication and turn to establish the aircraft on the inbound course. Refer to the D.G. and turn the aircraft left or right 10 degrees. *Begin timing!*

Step 2: Holding the aircraft's heading constant, rotate the OBS knob UP or BACK 10 degrees depending upon whether the aircraft is arcing clockwise (left turn in Step 1) or counterclockwise (right turn in Step 1) around the station. When the needle recenters, *stop the time!*

Step 3: Compute the estimated time to the station as follows: the elapsed time to the intercept (centered needle) equals the time to the station.

PROCEDURE 3b: The "Double the Angle Off the Nose" . . . during VOR Radial Intercepts:

During VOR radial intercepts (Chapter II, p. 20) instead of simply turning to the appropriate intercept angle (determined by doubling the angular difference between the radial the aircraft is on and the radial you want to intercept) and waiting for the intercept to take place, *time the intercept!* Remember . . . the elapsed time to the intercept equals the time to the station!

B.   ADF

PROCEDURE 1: The "Wing Tip" Method:

Step 1: Turn the aircraft the shorter direction to put the "head" of the ADF needle (pointer) ninety degrees right or left of the nose (on either of the two ADF wing tip indices) and *begin timing!*

Step 2: Turn right or left (clockwise or counterclockwise) toward the "head" of the ADF needle to position the pointer 10 degrees ABOVE the appropriate wing tip (relative bearing [RB] 080 degrees for right wing tip or RB 280 degrees for left wing tip) and maintain this new heading until the pointer travels back down to the wing tip position.* *Stop the time!* Compute the "time and distance" to the station using the formulas given above for the VOR wing tip procedure.

NOTE: Changing heading 10 degrees to position the "head" of the ADF needle 10 degrees above the appropriate wing tip is optional. If you desire you can either hold the heading that initially put the ADF needle on the wing tip, and time its downward travel to a position 10 degrees BELOW the wing tip (RB 100 degrees for the right wing tip or RB 260 degrees for the left wing tip) or you can maintain a 90 degree or 270 degree relative bearing to the station and time 10 degrees of heading change instead.

ALTERNATE TIME AND DISTANCE PROCEDURES

PROCEDURE 2a: The "30/40 Degree Method":

Unlike the wing tip method which requires a 90 degree off course deviation to accomplish and has very limited application to IFR flying, the ADF 30/40 degree method is easily adaptable to the IFR environment and is extremely useful during ILS approaches (Chapter VIII, p. 93). So versatile is this procedure, in fact, that you may utilize it with equal success while you are on a radar vector where your heading is strictly controlled or when you are cleared for the "full approach" with headings at your own discretion. You may hold a heading for ten degrees of bearing change or hold a relative bearing for 10 degrees of heading change. Tailor this procedure to suit your own particular needs and let the ADF 30/40 degree method help alleviate your navigational workload.

Step 1: Turn the aircraft the shorter direction to put

the "head" of the ADF needle thirty degrees right or left of the nose (RB 030 degrees for the right side or RB 330 degrees for the left side) and *begin timing!*

Step 2:   Holding the heading* that initially put the "head" of the ADF needle thirty degrees right or left of the nose, wait until the pointer travels down to the position forty degrees right or left of the nose and *stop the time!* Compute the "time" to the station using the same formula given previously for the VOR 30/40 degree method; i.e., Time to the Station = Elapsed Time X 3.

NOTE: You may alternatively elect to *maintain* a 30 or 330 degree relative bearing and time 10 degrees of heading change instead. The net result will be the same . . . at the end of the elapsed time the aircraft will have a 40 degree relative bearing.

PROCEDURE 2b: The "30/40 Degree Method" . . . during ADF Bearing Intercepts:

Step 1:   Turn the aircraft to a heading that will intercept the desired magnetic bearing at a forty degree angle. Maintain this heading and as soon as the "head" of the ADF needle travels down to indicate a thirty degree angle right or left of the nose, *begin timing!*

Step 2:   Holding the same heading as above, wait until the "head" of the needle continues down to a position forty degrees down from the nose on that side and *stop the time!* Compute the time to the station as above using the same formula given for the VOR 30/40 method.

PROCEDURE 3a: "The Double the Angle Off the Nose Method" (Isosceles Triangle):

Step 1:   Turn the aircraft to put the "head" of the ADF

needle on the nose (relative bearing = zero degrees) and then turn left or right ten degrees so that the "head" of the needle will be ten degrees right or left of the nose (RB = 010 degrees if to the right; or 350 degrees if to the left). *Begin timing!*

Step 2:   When the "head" of the ADF needle travels down to a position 20 degrees below the nose, then *stop the time!*

Step 3:   Compute your estimated time to the station as follows: The elapsed time to the intercept (10 degrees of needle travel) equals the time to the station.

PROCEDURE 3b: "The Double the Angle Off the Nose Method" . . . during ADF Bearing Intercepts:

During ADF bearing intercepts (Chapter II, p. 25) instead of simply turning to the appropriate intercept angle (determined by doubling the angular difference between the magnetic bearing "To" or "From" the station that the aircraft is on, and the magnetic bearing "To" or "From" the station that you want to intercept) and waiting for the intercept to take place, *time the intercept!* The elapsed time to the intercept will equal the time from the point of intercept to the station.

Sample Problems

1.   Flying cross-country one night on a heading of 340 degrees, you determine that the To/From indicator is broken on your only VOR. If five minutes ago the CDI needle centered on 250 degrees and now it recenters on 240 degrees, then:

   a.   What should the To/From indicator read if it were working ("To" or "From")?
   b.   What is your time to the station?
   c.   What is your approximate distance from

the station if your groundspeed is 140 knots?

d. When the needle initially centered on 250 degrees, did it eventually swing off center to the right or left side of the instrument?

2. Your aircraft is inbound on the procedure turn to the ILS Rwy 07 approach at Spirit of St. Louis Airport with a heading of 028 degrees:

a. What is your estimated time to the Summit LOM if you have timed one minute between the 30 degree and 40 degree relative bearing indications on the ADF?

b. What is your distance west of the outer marker if your groundspeed is 120 knots?

c. What will be your relative bearing and magnetic bearing "To" the station when you intercept the localizer course?

3. What will your time to the station be if during a VOR or ADF course interception problem, you use an intercept angle computed by the "rule of thumb" double the angle method, and it takes you 10 minutes to intercept the course?

4. While flying a magnetic heading of 130 degrees, the first RB you obtain when tuned to the compass locator at the outer marker is 270 degrees; 2 minutes 20 seconds later the RB changes to 260 degrees. How far are you from the outer marker (in minutes)?

5. What relative bearing is indicated on the ADF depicted on the back cover of this book?

6. What is an Isosceles Triangle?

Answers

1. a. "To"
   b. 30 minutes
   c. 70 NM

d.   Left side

2.   a.   3 minutes
     b.   6 NM
     c.   Relative bearing = 45 degrees
          Magnetic bearing "To" Summit = 073 degrees

3.   10 minutes

4.   14 minutes

5.   080 degrees (see definition on p. 288)

6.   A triangle with two (2) equal sides

IMPORTANT

To calculate your *distance* to the station in all of the "alternate" time and distance procedures presented in this chapter, divide your true airspeed (TAS) or groundspeed by 60 (gives you miles per minute) and multiply this quotient by your computed minutes to the station. This formula can also be used successfully with the VOR and ADF "wing tip" procedures after you have determined your minutes to the station.

The accuracy of the different time and distance procedures is governed by the existing wind, the degree of bearing change, and the preciseness of timing. Although the number of variables involved cause the result to be an approximation, by flying a specific heading and checking the time and bearing closely, you can get a reasonably accurate time/distance computation.

Chapter VI
DME ARCS

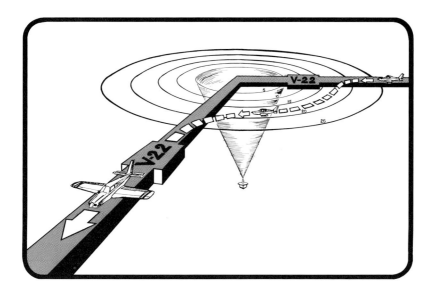

Most light aircraft used by flight schools for IFR training are equipped with dual nav/comms, ADF and transponder, but how many sport a DME (Distance Measuring Equipment)? Very few! The relevance of instruction in the various uses of the DME should not, however, be gauged by the sparse number of DME equipped trainers or by the greater number of "experienced" pilots who consider the radio as a luxury. Usually, it is the cost, not the training value that determines whether a DME will be installed in a given airplane, and the many misconceptions about the DME that even experienced pilots entertain, are fostered almost entirely by their lack of exposure to the radio as an instrument student. A DME arc is *not* an intricate maneuver requiring either the sophistication of a slaved RMI (Radio Magnetic Indicator) or any exceptional powers of orientation to the VORTAC as might be acquired after years of practice; instead, it is a basic "wing tip" time and distance procedure (Chapter V) during which a pilot simply monitors his distance from the station for each arc segment, in lieu of timing the CDI needle.

PROCEDURE:

Step 1: Tune the Omni navigation receiver and DME to the frequency of the VORTAC that the aircraft will be arcing around and determine (from your chart) whether the direction of travel around the station must be clockwise or counterclockwise in order to arrive at the final approach course or enroute airway specified in your clearance.

Step 2: Refer to the DME. When the proper distance from the station has been achieved, rotate the OBS knob to center the CDI needle with a "To" reading in the window, and turn the aircraft to position the indicated course under the right wing tip (D.G. reference) if you intend to arc "clockwise" around the station or left wing tip if you intend to arc "counterclockwise" around the station.*

*NOTE: Unlike the wing tip time and distance procedure where the indicated course may be placed under either (the nearest) wing tip, during DME arcs the direction of travel around the station is critical and *must be predetermined.* You must enter and/or exit your assigned arc according to the instructions issued in your ATC clearance and avoid unauthorized departures from this route of flight which might endanger other IFR aircraft in the area. To fly clockwise (counterclockwise) around the station, turn to a heading that is 90 degrees less than (more than) the course to be positioned under your right (left) wing tip. It is much easier to turn onto an arc by looking at the top of your D.G. for a specific heading than by looking at the wing tip index of your D.G. and waiting for a given heading to appear (see p. 62).

Step 3: If arcing "clockwise," *increase* the OBS course setting (on the VOR) by 10 degrees; if "counterclockwise," then *decrease* the OBS setting by 10 degrees and turn the aircraft right or left 10 degrees to put the new course under the same wing tip. When the CDI needle centers again, rotate the OBS another 10 degrees UP or BACK and continue this operation, turning the aircraft each time until the desired course is intercepted. There is no timing that must be accomplished here, only a continuous check of the indicated DME nautical mile distance.*

*NOTE: If a crosswind is blowing the aircraft to the inside or outside of the arc, then you must carry a wind correction angle into the wind to compensate for this drift. Drift to the "inside" of the circle toward the station is indicated by a steadily *decreasing* DME distance between the VORTAC and the aircraft and is corrected by flying a heading of approximately 20 to 30 degrees toward the outside of the arc and maintaining this correction with each successive heading change. Drift to the "outside" of the circle, away from the station is, of course, indicated by a steadily *increasing* DME distance between the VORTAC and the aircraft and is corrected by flying a heading of approximately 20 to 30 degrees toward the inside of the arc and maintaining this correction with each successive heading change. In either case, this WCA may be monitored easily by comparing the course *on* the appropriate wing tip with the course that normally *should be on* the wing tip (indicated on the VOR), when the aircraft is arcing in calm wind conditions.

Sample Problems

1. The instrument trainer that you are flying does not have a DME installed but your instructor, who is intimately familiar with the local area, tells you that he will give you the simulated DME readouts necessary for you to comply with your practice ATC clearance. If you are flying northeast on V-14 and have been cleared for the LOC (BACK CRS) Rwy 6 approach at the Lambert-St. Louis Airport (p. 262) via the 10 NM

DME arc southwest of the St. Louis VORTAC then:

a. After centering the CDI needle with a "To" indication, under which wing tip would you position the indicated course?

b. What heading would you turn to in order to accomplish the above?

c. Will the CDI needle be swinging toward the station from right to left or away from the station from left to right?

2. After arcing a few minutes, your instructor admits that he is not sure whether or not you are actually 10 nautical miles from the St. Louis VORTAC because the late afternoon haze condition is obscuring his ground references. Recognizing that by timing each successive centering of the CDI needle you can determine your time and distance to the station ("Wing Tip Method" Chapter V) then:

a. What *distance* do you estimate the aircraft to be from the station if it takes one minute for the needle to recenter and your groundspeed is 120 knots?

b. Assuming that your aircraft began its arc exactly 10 nautical miles southwest of the St. Louis VORTAC, does the computed distance above indicate that an easterly wind has drifted you to the *outside* of the arc or that a westerly wind has drifted you to the *inside* of the arc?

c. What is your estimated *time* to the St. Louis VORTAC?

3. Is it the distance function or the groundspeed function of the DME that will only indicate properly when the aircraft is established on a course inbound or outbound from the VORTAC?

4. One evening while you are flying a DME arc in calm wind conditions, your instructor directs you to turn the aircraft 15 degrees toward the INSIDE of the arc. If you hold your heading constant, you would expect to see the indicated DME distance:

   a. Decrease
   b. Decrease then increase
   c. Increase

5. If you are proceeding inbound on the 090 degree radial of the Bemidji VORTAC (see Appendix E, p. 268) and intend to intercept the 16 NM DME arc and fly *clockwise* around the station to the Rwy 31 final approach course (309 degree radial of BJI) then upon reaching the arc (with your OBS set to 270 degrees) you should turn _____ to a heading of _____ and expect to see the CDI needle swing toward the station which is now off your _____ wing tip.

   a. Right, 180 degrees, right
   b. Left, 360 degrees, left
   c. Right, 360 degrees, left
   d. Left, 180 degrees, right

Answers

1. a. Left wing tip
   b. You would initially turn to 152 degrees, but shortly thereafter as the needle begins to swing left of center, you would rotate the OBS knob back 10 degrees, and put 052 degrees under your left wing tip by flying a heading of 142 degrees.
   c. "Toward" the station from right to left

2. a. 12 nautical miles
   b. An easterly wind has drifted your aircraft to the outside of the arc.

c.   Six minutes
3.   The groundspeed function
4.   Decrease then increase
5.   d.   Left, 180 degrees, right.

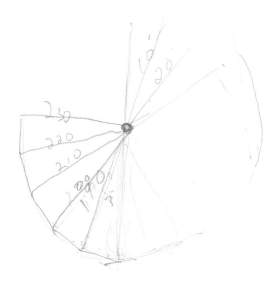

Chapter VII
HOLDING PATTERNS

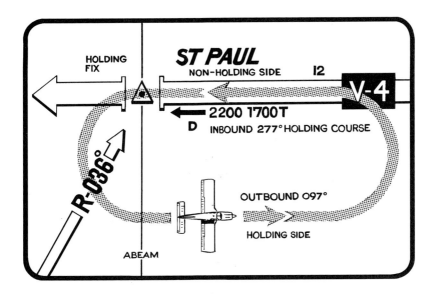

"Holding" is maneuvering an aircraft along a predetermined flight path within prescribed airspace limits with respect to a geographical fix. The fix may be identified visually (without reference to the instruments) as a specified location, or by reference to instruments as a radio facility or intersection of courses. VORs, non-directional beacons, DME distances and airway intersections are used as holding points (Ref: AC 61-27C: *Instrument Flying Handbook,* p. 206). ATC holding clearances include the following general instructions: direction of holding from the fix; radial, course, bearing or airway on which the aircraft is to hold; outbound leg length in miles, if DME is to be used; left turns, if the pattern is non-standard; and the time to expect further clearance or the time to expect approach clearance.

Although any entry into a holding pattern is acceptable as long as the aircraft remains within its "prescribed airspace limits," there are three recommended entries which applicants for the instrument rating are expected to use on their IFR checkride and are urged to use in their subsequent flying: the "teardrop entry"; the "parallel entry"; and the "direct entry." The appropriate pattern entry depends entirely upon the heading of the aircraft when it arrives over the holding fix in relation to the specific course on which the pilot intends to hold. In addition to the two routine procedures presented below that assist pilots to determine which of these pattern entries to use, a special emergency procedure is also included (see p. 84) that helps disoriented pilots to transition smoothly into their assigned hold with complete safety. Expect ATC holding instructions at least five minutes before reaching your clearance limit and upon arrival at the fix, hold in accordance with the procedures outlined in Chapter 4, Section 7 of the *Airman's Information Manual.*

A. HOLDING PATTERNS: "DETERMINING THE ENTRY"

1.   "Sector of Entry Method" (VOR and ADF)

PROCEDURE:

Step 1: Refer to the appropriate chart for the depicted holding pattern or draw (visualize) the "standard" right turn pattern (or "non-standard" left hand turn pattern) onto the holding fix and oriented in the proper direction.

Step 2: Superimpose the three "entry sectors" onto the holding pattern as follows: First, rough-a-line with a pencil (or imagine a line) that runs through the holding fix and extends 70 degrees UP from the holding course into the holding side of the pattern. Second, arc *counterclockwise (clockwise: left turn pattern)* around the holding fix from this line and observe that the 110 degree arc segment (angle) describes the parallel entry sector; the adjoining 70 degree arc segment (angle) describes the teardrop entry sector; and the remaining 180 degree hemisphere describes the direct entry sector.

Step 3: Identify what sector your aircraft is flying in as it approaches the holding fix. This sector determines the appropriate holding pattern entry.

2.   "The 70/110 Degree D.G. Visualization Method" (VOR and ADF)

An instrument pilot cannot look at his D.G. and visualize the entry to a given holding pattern unless he can look at it and visualize the pattern itself. Before considering the specific visualization entry method presented below, first learn how to look at the D.G. and SEE the holding pattern. The 70/110 degree D.G. visualization method assumes that the aircraft is established on a heading proceeding directly toward the holding fix (station or intersection). Since the aircraft has not yet reached the station, it is located somewhere between the bottom and the center of the D.G. proceeding north. *The station is located in the middle of the D.G.* To visualize holding on any radial, locate the radial on the outer edge of the D.G. and draw an imaginary line from that point to the center of the instrument . . . this is the inbound leg of your holding pattern. You may now trace the holding pattern by moving your finger toward the center of the D.G. (station) along this line and making right or left turns upon reaching the station. With the location and direction of the holding pattern now in mind, continue up the D.G. toward the center (from the bottom) and when you reach the station (center) try to visualize the appropriate entry in accordance with the following procedures.

PROCEDURE a: "Standard" Right Hand Turns

> Refer to the aircraft's D.G. and determine specifically where on the face of the instrument the number (degrees) corresponding to the holding radial (VOR) or magnetic bearing "From" the station (ADF) is located.[1] If it is located within 70 degrees *right* of the nose (heading at the top of the instrument), a teardrop entry is required; if it is located within 110 degrees *left* of the nose, then a parallel entry is required;[2] and if it is located anywhere else on the instrument, then a direct entry is required. Should your aircraft be flying a heading that corresponds to the degrees of the assigned radial (the radial is directly off the nose of the aircraft on the opposite side of the station) then a teardrop entry is most appropriate be-

cause the aircraft will be turning into the holding side of the pattern which is more protected airspace.

PROCEDURE b: "Non-standard" Left Hand Turns

The mirror opposite of the above: a teardrop entry is indicated when the holding radial is located within 70 degrees to the *left* of the nose; a parallel entry is indicated when the holding radial is located within 110 degrees to the *right* of the nose; and finally, the direct entry is indicated when the holding radial is located anywhere within the remaining 180 degree hemisphere on the D.G.

NOTE 1: ADF holding instructions are generally issued in terms of a particular magnetic bearing "To" the station (NDB), unlike VOR holding instructions which are issued in terms of a given radial or magnetic bearing "From" the station. To determine the proper holding pattern entry using the 70/110 degree method, refer to your D.G. for the location of the *reciprocal* of this magnetic bearing "To" the station, or as stated above . . . for the location of the appropriate magnetic bearing "From" the station. When determining the proper entry to a holding pattern established at an intersection, treat the intersection like a station and refer to your D.G. for the location of the hypothetical "holding radial" *of the intersection* — not for the location of the actual radial (magnetic bearing) of the distant VOR (NDB) which defines the inbound course to the fix (see Problem 1, p. 88).

NOTE 2: For aircraft equipped with a closed face D.G., do *not* think in terms of degrees "right" or "left" of the nose; instead, think in terms of degrees "more than" or "less than" the aircraft's heading.

B. HOLDING PATTERNS: "FLYING THE ENTRY"

Determining by one of the two methods above that a particular holding pattern entry is appropriate is only half of the problem; you must be able to translate this information into specific headings which will fly your aircraft into the desired pattern and keep it there! Each of the three entry procedures is presented below with the necessary "pilot action" noted, and, in addition, a suggested "emergency entry procedure" is also included as an informal back-up ... just in case!

PROCEDURE 1: Teardrop Entry

    a. **VOR**

After crossing the holding fix, turn the aircraft to a heading thirty degrees *less* than (*more* than: left turn holding pattern) the holding radial[1] and fly this heading outbound for one minute. *While outbound, rotate the OBS to the inbound course* (reciprocal of the holding radial).

At the end of one minute, turn *right* (turn *left:* left turn pattern) to intercept the inbound course.[2] Upon reaching the station, turn *right* (turn *left:* left turn pattern) to fly outbound again and continue around in hold until the Expect Further Clearance (EFC) Time issued by Air Traffic Control (see Appendix F, p. 277)

NOTE 1: For intersection holding patterns where the direction of hold is on the same side of the intersection as the station generating the inbound course (holding radial) you must consider the intersection as the station and fly a heading 30 degrees *less* than (*more* than: left turn pattern) the hypothetical "holding radial" OF THE INTERSECTION not the radial of the distant VOR which defines the inbound course to the intersection.

NOTE 2: Since the CDI needle ALWAYS points *opposite* the direction of the turns in a holding pattern when the aircraft is on the holding side with the OBS set to the inbound course (reciprocal of holding radial), the CDI needle will always be to the *left* (*right:* left turn pattern) during the teardrop entry and the turn to intercept the inbound will always be a *right* turn (*left* turn: right turn pattern) opposite the direction of the needle to a heading of some number of degrees *less* than (*more* than: left turn pattern) the inbound course (see Chapter II, p.19).

b.   *ADF*

After crossing the holding fix, turn the aircraft to a heading 30 degrees *less* than (*more* than: left turn holding pattern) the magnetic bearing "From" the station* that constitutes the "holding radial" and fly this heading outbound for one minute.

At the end of one minute, turn toward the "head" of the ADF needle (*right* turn: right turn pattern; *left* turn: left turn pattern) and track back to the NDB after intercepting the appropriate magnetic bearing "To" the station. Upon reaching the station, turn *right* (turn *left:* left turn pattern) to fly outbound again and continue around in hold until the Expect Further Clearance Time issued by ATC.

*NOTE: ADF holding instructions are usually issued in terms of a particular magnetic bearing "To" the station so you must consider the reciprocal here!

PROCEDURE 2:   Parallel Entry

a.   *VOR*

After crossing the holding fix, turn the aircraft *left* (turn *right*: left turn holding pattern) to parallel the holding radial[1] outbound for one minute. *While outbound, rotate the OBS to the inbound course* (reciprocal of the holding radial).

At the end of one minute, turn *left* again (turn *right* again: left turn pattern) to intercept the inbound course.[2] Upon reaching the station, turn *right* (turn *left:* left turn pattern) to parallel the outbound again and continue around in hold until the Expect Further Clearance time issued by ATC.

NOTE 1: For intersection holding patterns where the direction of hold is on the same side of the intersection as the station generating in inbound course (holding radial) you *must* consider the intersection as the station and turn outbound to parallel the hypothetical "holding radial" OF THE INTERSECTION not the radial of the distant VOR which defines the inbound course to the intersection.

NOTE 2: Since the CDI needle ALWAYS points right or left in the *same* direction as the holding turns when the aircraft is on the non-holding side of the pattern with the OBS set to the inbound course (reciprocal of holding radial), the needle will always be on the *right* (*left*: left turn pattern) during a parallel entry and the turn to intercept the inbound will always be a *left* turn (*right* turn: left turn pattern) opposite the direction of the needle.

b. *ADF*

After crossing the holding fix, turn the aircraft *left* (turn *right*: left turn holding pattern) to parallel the magnetic bearing "From" the station* that constitutes the "holding radial" and fly this heading outbound for one minute.

At the end of one minute, turn toward the "head" of the ADF needle (*left* turn: standard right turn pattern; *right* turn: non-standard left turn pattern) and track back to the NDB after intercepting the appropriate magnetic bearing "To" the station. Upon reaching the station, turn *right* (turn *left*: left turn pattern) to parallel the outbound again and continue around in hold until the Expect Further Clearance Time issued by ATC.

*NOTE: ADF holding instructions are usually issued in terms of a particular magnetic bearing "To" the station so you must consider the reciprocal here!

PROCEDURE 3: Direct Entry

a. *VOR*

After crossing the holding fix, turn the aircraft *right* (turn *left:* left turn holding pattern) to parallel the holding radial outbound for one minute. *While outbound, rotate the OBS to the inbound course* (reciprocal of the holding radial).

At the end of one minute, turn *right* again (*left* again: left turn pattern) to intercept the inbound course. Upon reaching the station, turn *right* (*left*) to parallel the outbound course again and continue in hold until the Expect Further Clearance Time issued by ATC (see Note 1, p. 82).

b.   *ADF*

After crossing the holding fix, turn the aircraft *right* (turn *left*: left turn holding pattern) to parallel the magnetic bearing "From" the station* that constitutes the "holding radial" and fly this heading outbound for one minute.

At the end of one minute, turn toward the "head" of the ADF needle (turn *right*: standard right turn pattern; turn *left*: non-standard left turn pattern) and track back to the NDB after intercepting the appropriate magnetic bearing "To" the station. Upon reaching the station, turn *right* (turn *left*: left turn pattern) to parallel the outbound again and continue around in hold until the Expect Further Clearance Time issued by ATC.

*NOTE: ADF holding instructions are usually issued in terms of a particular magnetic bearing "To" the station so you must consider the reciprocal here!

PROCEDURE 4:   Emergency Entry Procedure:

If you arrive over your assigned holding fix without any idea how to get into your assigned holding pattern (that is, what entry to use), you have to do something and quickly, or else you will violate some other aircraft's airspace and create a hazard both for yourself and for others. The following procedure will enable disorientated pilots to enter any holding pattern with complete safety and should give every pilot an inner sense of confidence that he or she can consistently comply with last minute holding instructions "no matter what!"

a.   *VOR*

Refer to the D.G. and turn the aircraft the shorter direction to parallel the holding radial outbound.[1] Once established on the outbound, start timing for one minute and rotate the OBS to the *inbound* course (reciprocal of holding radial).

At the end of one minute, turn *opposite* the direction of the CDI (localizer[2]) needle and intercept the inbound course.[3] Upon reaching the fix, turn *right* (turn *left*: left turn pattern) to parallel the outbound again and continue around in hold until the Expect Further Clearance Time issued by ATC.

NOTE 1:   A *left* turn to parallel the outbound leg (right turn pattern) or a *right* turn to parallel the outbound leg (left turn pattern) indicates that you are turning your aircraft into the "non-holding side" of the pattern and that you are executing a **parallel** entry. A *right* turn to parallel the outbound leg (right turn pattern) or a *left* turn to parallel the outbound leg (left turn pattern) indicates that you are turning your aircraft into the "holding side" of the pattern and that you are executing either a direct **or** a teardrop entry. To determine which of these latter two entries is being used, consider the magnitude of your *right* turn (*left* turn: left turn pattern). If your turn to parallel the outbound leg is less than 70 degrees then a **teardrop** entry is indicated; however, if your turn is greater than 70 degrees, then a **direct** entry is indicated ... think about it!

NOTE 2:   This procedure may **not** be used to enter a holding pattern on an ILS Back Course localizer unless the second paragraph above is modified as follows: "... turn in the *same* direction that the localizer needle is deflected!"

NOTE 3: If the CDI needle is to the *right,* turn left to an intercept heading which is an appropriate number of degrees *more* (right needle) than the inbound course set. If the CDI needle is to the *left,* then turn right to an intercept heading which is an appropriate number of degrees *less* (left needle) than inbound course set (see Chapter II, p. 19 and Note 2, p. 81).

b.   ADF

Refer to the D.G. and turn the aircraft right or left (whichever is the shorter direction) to parallel the magnetic bearing "From" the station* that constitutes the "holding radial" and fly this heading outbound for one minute.

At the end of one minute, turn toward the "head" of the ADF needle and home back to the NDB. Upon reaching the station, turn *right* (turn *left*: left turn pattern) to parallel the outbound again and continue around until the Expect Further Clearance Time issued by ATC.

*NOTE: ADF holding instructions are usually issued in terms of a particular magnetic bearing "To" the station so you must consider the reciprocal here!

C.   HOLDING PATTERNS: "FLYING THE PATTERN"

Remember the following "Rules of Thumb" and/or comments:

1.   Always slow up to holding pattern speed if necessary . . . the maximum allowable speed for propeller driven aircraft is 175 knots IAS.

2.   With the OBS Set to the inbound course, the CDI needle will "always" point in the OPPOSITE direction of the holding turns when the aircraft is on the holding side of the inbound course. **Example:** An aircraft is on the "holding side" of a standard right turn pattern whenever the CDI needle is to the

left and vice versa ... assuming, of course, that the OBS is properly set to the inbound course! Notice, as an extension of this fact that during *all* holding pattern entries, the turn to intercept the inbound course (after the one minute outbound time has elapsed) will always be made "opposite" the direction of the CDI needle (see emergency entry procedure, p. 84).

3. The "head" of the ADF needle will always point to the SAME SIDE of the instrument (right or left) as the direction of the holding turns when the aircraft is outbound on the holding side. Notice, as an extension of this fact, that during *all* holding pattern entries, the turn to intercept the inbound bearing (after one minute outbound time has elapsed) will *always* be made toward the "head" of the needle.

4. Whenever a wind correction angle is necessary to track in-bound on the holding leg, it must be doubled on the out-bound leg to compensate for the two uncorrected turns at either end of the race track pattern. A crosswind, which is drifting the aircraft (flying outbound) into the *non*holding side, is easily detected by observing: (1) the CDI needle swing *toward* the direction of the holding turns, or (2) the "head" of the ADF needle move *away* from the direction of the holding turns.

5. Always begin the outbound time abeam of the station and proceed outbound for one minute plus or minus whatever seconds must be added or subtracted from this time in order to give the aircraft a one minute inbound leg (below 14,000 feet). Adjust your time for the one minute inbound as follows:

    a. *Tailwind:* Double the error of the inbound and add it to the outbound ... to determine the time of the outbound leg.
        Example: Thirty second inbound = thirty second error; 30 x 2 = 60 seconds added to normal outbound time for a new outbound time of two minutes next time around.
    b. *Headwind:* Halve the error of the inbound and apply it to the outbound ... to determine the time of the out-bound leg.

Example: One and one-half minutes inbound = thirty second error; 30/2 = 15 seconds to be subtracted from the normal one minute outbound time for a new outbound time of forty-five seconds.

6. Remember that for timing ADF holding patterns, station passage is indicated by the first definite move of the bearing pointer 45 degrees to either side of the holding course.

7. Keep the CDI needle swinging during VOR holds . . . don't allow it to remain pegged as the aircraft drifts further off course!

8. DME holding involves the same entry and holding procedures as with the VOR and ADF except that distances in nautical miles are normally used instead of time values. The outbound course of the DME holding pattern is called the outbound leg and its length will always be specified in the clearance. The end of the outbound leg is normally determined by the DME odometer reading.

Example: When the inbound course is toward the navaid and the fix distance is 15 NM and the leg length is 5 NM, the end of the outbound leg is reached when the DME reads 20 NM. When the inbound course of the pattern is away from the navaid and the fix distance is 25 NM and the length of the leg is 10 NM, the end of the outbound leg is reached when the DME reads 15 NM.

Sample Problems

1. Your instructor asks you to hold east of St. Paul Intersection on V-4 with non-standard left hand turns. Quickly you look at your D.G. for the 277 degree radial of the St. Louis VOR (the holding radial) and using the "70/110 degree D.G. visualization method" you determine that a direct entry is the best way to enter the pattern. Unfortunately, your instructor disagrees and points out on his sketch of the holding pattern that from your position on the Foristell VOR 036 degree radial, the parallel entry is the most appropriate. In rebuttal, you

point out to him that the 277 degree radial of the St. Louis VOR is about 120 degrees left of the nose position on the D.G. and is definitely in the direct entry sector, but he is not impressed by your analysis and again emphasizes that the assigned hold requires a parallel entry. Why didn't the "70/110 degree D.G. visualization method" work in this instance?

2.   Does the CDI needle point opposite the direction of the holding turns when the aircraft is on the *non*holding side with the OBS set to the inbound course?

3.   Does a holding pattern always describe a race track pattern over the ground?

4.   Practicing holding patterns one windy afternoon, you time the inbound leg to the station and find that it is only 30 seconds:

   a.   Do you have a headwind or tailwind?
   b.   How much time will you fly outbound next time around?
   c.   While outbound, during left hand turn holds, you notice that your CDI needle is drifting to the left, does this mean you are drifting into the holding or non-holding side of the pattern?

Answers

1.   When determining the entry by using the "70/110 degree method," one must imagine that St. Paul Intersection is a station generating its own radials and look at the D.G. for the location of its hypothetical 097 degree radial, *not* the 277 degree radial of the St. Louis VOR which is its reciprocal. Looking at the D.G. as we proceed toward the intersection on a heading of 036 degrees, 097 degrees is located about 60 degrees right of the nose posi-

tion and confirms the instructor's contention that a parallel entry is required (see p. 77).

2.   No! The CDI needle only points away from the direction of the holding turns when the aircraft is on the *holding* side with the OBS set to the inbound course.

3.   The holding pattern is only a classic race track pattern when the winds are relatively calm. In a strong wind, the pattern looks more like a teardrop!

4.   a.   Tailwind
     b.   Two (2) minutes
     c.   Non-holding side

Chapter VIII
INSTRUMENT APPROACHES

Many enthusiastic instrument students who are anxious to fly VOR and NDB approaches as soon as they begin their training, tend to mentally disassociate these approaches from the various radio navigational procedures that they innately involve (intercepts, tracking, arcs, holds . . . etc.) which must be learned PRIOR to practicing any approaches. Since the navigational procedures associated with the non-precision approaches above are common to the enroute procedures already discussed in Chapters I through VII, this chapter will cover only the ILS (Instrument Landing System), the ASR (Airport Surveillance Radar) and the new ISMLS (Interim Standard Microwave Landing System) approaches specifically. Procedure turns, which do not fall into the spectrum of radio procedures per se (they are timed instrument flight patterns), will also be presented below because they are more closely associated with instrument approaches than with attitude flying discussed in the next chapter. Finally, this chapter will conclude with a few basic "Do's and Don'ts" which pertain to both instrument approaches and to IFR flight in general.

ILS

[FAA INSTRUMENT LANDING SYSTEM]

STANDARD CHARACTERISTICS AND TERMINOLOGY

ILS approach charts should be consulted to obtain variations of individual systems.

VHF LOCALIZER

108.10 to 111.95 MHz. Radiates about 100 watts. Horizontal polarization. Modulation frequencies 90 and 150 Hz. Modulation depth on course 20% for each frequency. Code identification (1020 Hz, 5%) and voice communication (modulated 50%) provided on some channel. At some localizers, where terrain (siting) difficulties are encountered, an additional antenna (slotted waveguide type) provides the necessary course straightness.

UHF GLIDE PATH TRANSMITTER

329.15 to 335.00 MHz. Radiates about 5 watts. Horizontal polarization, modulation frequencies are 90 & 150 Hz, each of which modulates the carrier 40.0% (typical) on path. The glide path is established nominally at an angle of 3 degrees, depending on local terrain.

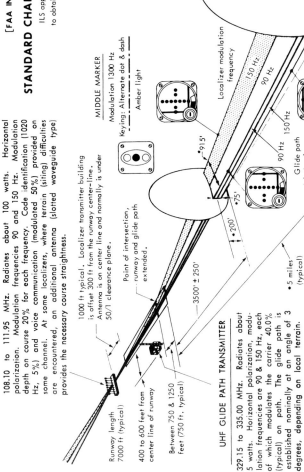

1000 ft typical. Localizer transmitter building is offset 300 ft from the runway center-line. Antenna is on center line and normally is under 50/1 clearance plane.

Point of intersection, runway and glide path extended.

Runway length 7000 ft (typical)

400 to 600 feet from center line of runway

Between 750 & 1250 feet (750 ft. typical)

3500' ± 250'

5 miles (typical)

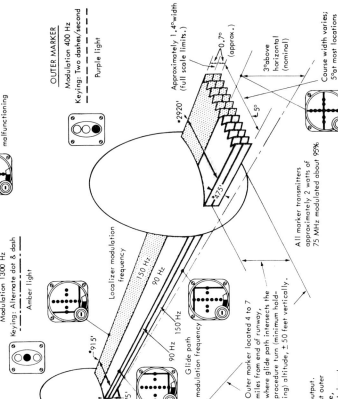

OUTER MARKER

Modulation 400 Hz
Keying: Two dashes/second
Purple light

Flag indicates if facility not on the air or receiver malfunctioning

MIDDLE MARKER

Modulation 1300 Hz
Keying: Alternate dot & dash
Amber light

Localizer modulation frequency

150 Hz
90 Hz

Glide path modulation frequency

90 Hz
150 Hz

Approximately 1.4° width (full scale limits)

0.7° (approx.)

3° above horizontal (nominal)

Course width varies; 5° at most locations (full scale limits)

5°

•2920'

•475'

•915'

•75'

•200'

Outer marker located 4 to 7 miles from end of runway, where glide path intersects the procedure turn (minimum holding) altitude, ± 50 feet vertically.

All marker transmitters approximately 2 watts of 75 MHz modulated about 95%

• Figures marked with asterisk are typical. Actual figures vary with deviations in distances to markers, glide angles and localizer widths.

NOTE:
Compass locators, rated at 25 watts output, 200 to 415 kHz, are installed at most outer and middle markers. A 1020 Hz tone, modulating the carrier about 95 %, is keyed with the first two letters of the ILS identification on the outer locator and the last two letters on the middle locator. At some locators, simultaneous voice transmissions from the control tower are provided, with appropriate reduction in identification percentage.

RATE OF DESCENT CHART
(feet per minute)

Speed (Knots)	Angle			
	2 1/2°	2 3/4°	3°	3°
90	400	440	475	475
110	485	535	585	585
130	575	630	690	690
150	665	730	795	795
160	707	778	849	849

A.   INSTRUMENT LANDING SYSTEM

The Instrument Landing System is a precision approach system that provides course and glide slope guidance to the pilot. It consists of a highly directional localizer (course) and glide slope transmitter with associated marker beacons, compass locators, and at some sites, Distance Measuring Equipment (DME). This ground transmitting equipment, the airborne receiving equipment and the associated runway and lighting aids are covered along with the general principles of ILS operation in Chapter 1, Section 1 of the *Airman's Information Manual.*

1.   **The Front Course Approach (See Chapter II: Localizer Intercepts):**

PROCEDURE

Transition to an ILS is performed by maneuvering the aircraft, as prescribed by published terminal instrument approach procedures (see Appendix: E) or radar vectors, to intercept the localizer course inbound. Analyze the entire approach procedure, landing environment, and missed approach procedure before commencing the approach. Tune the ILS as soon as practicable during the transition. Rotate the OBS (omni-bearing selector) knob to set the degrees of the published localizer Front Course in the course selector window (for reference) prior to attempting localizer interception. Use any available navigational facilities, i.e., ADF, to aid in remaining position-oriented in relation to the localizer course and glide slope localizer point (Chapter II, p. 31).

A localizer course intercept angle of thirty (30) degrees is usually desirable. The localizer needle (LOC) will remain at full scale deflection until the aircraft is within approximately 2½ degrees of the localizer course. If a larger intercept lead point is required, use available magnetic bearing information (ADF) to supplement the LOC needle. Turn to intercept the localizer course when the lead point is reached. Be alert for the first movement of the LOC to avoid overshooting the localizer course. If the LOC indicates full scale deflection during the latter part of the turn, roll out with an intercept angle which will insure course interception prior to the glide slope intercept point.*

*NOTE: When being radar vectored for an ILS approach (pp. 31 and 99) the air traffic controller should provide vectors to position the aircraft on the localizer course at least 2 miles from the Final Approach Fix (FAF) with an intercept angle of not more than 30 degrees and at an altitude not above the glide slope. Repeat all headings, altitudes, and altimeter settings and comply with Controller instructions until he says, CLEARED FOR APPROACH, then fly the approach as depicted.

When the localizer course is intercepted, maintain the published heading corrected for known winds until LOC deflection indicates a need for a heading change. The rate of LOC movement will aid in estimating the magnitude of course correction required. Make heading corrections toward the LOC of sufficient magnitude to stop the LOC displacement and return the aircraft to course. Heading corrections should be reduced as the aircraft continues inbound. Heading changes of approximately 5 degree increments will usually result in more precise control (see Chapter III, p. 43).

Maintain glide slope interception altitude, published or assigned, until reaching the glide slope intercept point. The final approach airspeed and configuration should be established in accordance with the aircraft flight manual. Do not descend below glide slope interception altitude if the LOC indicates full scale deflection.

Prepare to intercept the glide slope as the glide slope indicator (GSI) moves downward from its upper limits. Determine the approximate *rate of descent* required to maintain the glide slope.[1] Slightly before GSI reaches the center position, coordinate *pitch* and *power* control adjustments to establish a rate of descent on the glide slope.[2] Adjust pitch to establish descent rate; adjust power to maintain final approach airspeed (see Scan Patterns chart p. 151: constant **rate** descent). The pitch change required will depend upon aircraft groundspeed and glide slope angle.

NOTE 1: The published rate of descent for any given ILS approach depends upon the final approach speed of the aircraft. This rate of descent may be approximated by multiplying the aircraft's approach speed (knots) by ten (10) and halving the answer. **Example:** The appropriate rate of descent for an aircraft traveling 100 knots is approximately 500 FPM.

NOTE 2: A good approximation of the power setting necessary to maintain a given rate of descent at the approach speed for most higher performance light aircraft is that one inch of MAP (manifold pressure) equals approximately 100 FPM change in the rate of descent if the airspeed is held constant. **Example:** A five inch change in MAP will give a 500 FPM change in the rate of descent. Another close approximation is that the landing gear is equal to a 500 FPM change in altitude if the airspeed is held constant.

Corrections to the glide slope are made by adjusting pitch on the attitude indicator to obtain the desired vertical velocity rate. If the glide slope needle remains off center but stationary after the proper rate of descent is established, then the aircraft is paralleling the glide slope and further slight attitude changes should be initiated to center the needle. Pitch adjustments made in increments of two degrees or less will usually result in more precise glide path control.

Report "Final Approach Fix Inbound" to the controlling agency (tower).

The most common error when flying the ILS is to concentrate on the LOC/GSI and ignore aircraft performance instruments. Coordinated attitude and power corrections are made on the control instruments . . . based upon aircraft (heading/vertical velocity/airspeed) and flight path (LOC/GSI) performance indications.*

NOTE: See Chapter IX, p. 141, for a discussion of the "control and performance" instruments.

The importance of precise aircraft control cannot be overemphasized. The size of the localizer course and glide slope envelope decreases progressively throughout the approach. As the approach progresses, smaller pitch and bank corrections are required for a given LOC/GSI deviation. Lateral distance from the flight path centerline with full scale LOC/GSI displacement can be considerable.

The most critical phase of the approach occurs as the aircraft approaches the published decision height (DH). Maintain a complete instrument cross-check throughout the approach, with increased emphasis on the altimeter during the latter part. Establish a systematic scan for the runway environment prior to reaching DH. If visual reference with the runway environment is established, continue the approach to complete the landing using flight instruments to complement the visual reference.

Perform the missed approach when:
a.   At the decision height, the runway approach threshold, approach lights or other markings identifiable with the approach end of the runway, are not clearly visible.
b.   Directed by ATC
c.   A landing is not accomplished

The ILS approach must be discontinued if the localizer course becomes unreliable or any time full scale deflection of the LOC occurs on final approach (inside the outer marker). If the glide slope warning flag appears, or full scale GSI deflection occurs after intercepting the glide slope, the approach should be flown no lower than the published localizer minimum descent altitude. If localizer minimums are not published, transition may be made to another straight-in approach (if published in conjunction with the ILS approach).

2. **Localizer Only Approach:**

Localizer only approaches are planned for and flown as non-precision approaches.

3. **Back Course Approach:**

Localizer Back Course approaches are non-precision approaches and glide slope information is *usually* not provided (see Appendix E, p. 260). Use the instrument approach techniques applicable to other nonprecision approaches.

4. **Interim Standard Microwave Landing System (ISMLS)**

At the present time there are very few Interim Standard Microwave Landing System approaches in use around the country. One of the first of these approaches to be commissioned is located at Bellaire Michigan (Appendix E, p. 267). It is anticipated in the future that the microwave landing system will become almost as commonplace as the Instrument Landing System (ILS) at major airports around the world.

The ISMLS is designed to provide approach information similar to the ILS for an aircraft on final approach to a runway. The system provides both lateral and vertical guidance which is displayed on a conventional course deviation indicator or approach horizon. Operational performance and coverage areas are also similar to the ILS.

ISMLS operates in the C-band microwave frequency range (about 5000 MHz) so the signal will not be received by unmodified VHF/UHF ILS receivers. Aircraft utilizing ISMLS must be equipped with a C-band receiving antenna in addition to other special equipment mentioned below. The receiving aperture of the C-band antenna limits reception of the signal to an angle of about 50 degrees from the inbound heading. Therefore, an aircraft so equipped will not receive the ISMLS signal until flying a heading within 50 degrees either side of the inbound course. Because of this, ISMLS procedures are designed to preclude use of the ISMLS signal until the aircraft is in position for the final approach. Transition to the ISMLS, holding and procedure turns at the ISMLS facility must be predicated on other navigation aids such as NDB, VOR, etc. *Once established on the approach course inbound, the system can be flown identical to the ILS.* No Back Course is provided.

The Interim Standard Microwave Landing System consists of the following basic components:

a.   C-Band (5000 MHz - 5030 MHz) localizer.
b.   C-Band (5220 - 5250 MHz) glide path.
c.   VHF marker beacons (75 MHz).
d.   A VHF/UHF ILS receiver modified to be capable of receiving the ISMLS signals. This modification requires the addition of:

    1.   C-Band antenna
    2.   Converter unit
    3.   Microwave/ILS Mode Control
    4.   VHF/UHF receiver modification kit.

The identification consists of a three letter Morse Code identifier preceded by the Morse Code for "M" (--). **Example:** "MHOF" the "M" will distinguish this system from ILS which is preceded by the letter "I" (..).

Approaches published in conjunction with the ISMLS will be identified as "MLS Rwy _____ (Interim)." The frequency displayed on the ISMLS approach chart will be a VHF frequency. ISMLS frequencies are tuned by setting the receiver to the listed VHF frequencies. When the ISMLS mode is selected, receivers modified to accept ISMLS signals will not receive the VHF/UHF frequency but a paired LOC/GS C-Band frequency that will be processed by the receiver (see Part 1, Chapter 1 of the *Airman's Information Manual).*

Caution: Aircraft not equipped for ISMLS operation should not attempt to fly ISMLS procedures.

5.   **ILS (MLS) Errors:**

    a.   Failure to understand the fundamentals of ILS ground equipment, particularly the differences in course dimensions. Since the VOR receiver is used on the localizer course, the assumption is sometimes made that interception and tracking techniques are identical when tracking localizer courses and VOR radials. Remember that the CDI sensing is four times sharper and faster on the localizer course.

    b.   Disorientation during transition to the ILS due to poor planning and reliance on one receiver instead of on all available airborne equipment. Use all the assistance you have available; the single receiver you may be relying on may fail you at a busy time.

    c.   Incorrect localizer interception angles. A large interception angle usually results in over-shooting and often disorientation. Turn to the localizer course heading immediately upon the first indication of needle movement, using a small interception angle whenever possible. An ADF receiver is an excellent aid to orientation during an ILS approach.

    d.   Chasing the LOC and glide path needles, especially when the approach is not sufficiently studied before the flight. Flying the proper headings, altitudes, rate of descent, times and power configuration settings is impossible if your mind is on studying the approach plate.

B.   **RADAR APPROACHES**

Radar equipment determines the distance and direction of objects by transmission and return of radio waves. See Appendix B, p. 217 for a further discussion of the principles of radar operation. There are two basic types of radar approaches . . . the "precision" and the "surveillance." The precision approach provides the pilot with precise course, glide slope, and range information. The surveillance approach provides only course and range information and is classified as a non-precision approach. Since the Precision Approach Radar (PAR) equipment has been largely replaced at civilian airports by the

Instrument Landing System (ILS) and is seldom used except at military airfields, the PAR approach is not discussed in this chapter. When radar is approved at certain locations for ATC purposes, it may be used not only for precision and surveillance radar approaches, as applicable, but also may be used in conjunction with instrument approach procedures predicated on other types of radio navigational aids. Radar vectors may be authorized to provide course guidance through segments of an approach procedure to the final approach fix or position. Upon reaching the final approach fix or position, the pilot will either complete his instrument approach in accordance with the published procedure approved for the facility, or will continue a precision or surveillance radar approach to a landing (ref. FAR 91.116f: *Use of radar in instrument approach procedures*).

1. **Transition to Radar Final**:

    PROCEDURE:

    The transition to the final segment of the approach is controlled by surveillance radar equipment. This segment includes all maneuvering up to a point where the aircraft is inbound and approximately 8 NM from touchdown. During the transition to final, the Radar Controller directs heading and altitude changes as required to position the aircraft on final approach (see Chapter II, p. 30). Turns and descents should be initiated immediately after instructed. The radar approach is predicated entirely upon these voice instructions from the approach control Radar Controller. After being advised that vectors will be given to the radar final, repeat all headings, altitudes, and altimeter settings until the Final Controller advises DO NOT ACKNOWLEDGE FURTHER TRANSMISSIONS.

    Lost communications procedures will be issued by the Radar Controller as soon as possible after establishing radar contact and radio communication if weather reports indicate that IFR conditions are likely to be encountered. Lost communications procedures must be understood and remembered . . . written down if necessary!

Weather information issued by the Radar Controller will include altimeter settings, ceiling, and visibility. The Controller is required to issue ceiling and visibility *only* when the ceiling is below 1000 feet or below the highest circling minimum, whichever is greater, or if the visibility is less than three miles.

The Controller will furnish pertinent information on known field conditions which he considers necessary to the safe operation of the aircraft concerned. The pilot should request additional information, as necessary, to make a safe approach.

The pilot will be advised to perform a landing check prior to handoff to the Final Controller. Use available navigational aids to remain position oriented in relation to the landing runway and the glide slope intercept point. The Controller will advise the pilot of the aircraft position at least once before starting final approach.

Start the Before Landing Checklist (landing check), review approach minimums, and tune navigational equipment to comply with lost communication instructions when practical. Determine the final approach airspeed and the approximate initial descent rate required on final approach. Establish the aircraft configuration and airspeed in accordance with the aircraft flight manual. If final approach airspeed and configuration are established prior to turning onto final, avoid using excessive bank angles that could make precise aircraft control difficult.

2. **Surveillance Final Approach:**

PROCEDURE:

When the precision radar equipment is not available, Airport Surveillance Radar (ASR) is used to furnish information required to align the aircraft with the approach runway. Since surveillance radar is not as accurate as precision radar and does not provide elevation data, the landing weather minimums are higher than for precision approaches.

The Controller will inform the pilot of the runway to which the approach will be made, the straight-in MDA, and will issue advance notice of where the descent to MDA will begin. Also all Controllers will provide recommended altitudes each mile on final approach down to the last mile upon request. When the aircraft reaches the descent point, the Controller will advise the aircraft to descend to MDA. In the event a descent restriction exists, the Controller will specify the prescribed restriction altitude. When the aircraft is past the altitude limiting point, the Controller will advise the pilot to continue descent to MDA. A rate of descent that will insure reaching the MDA *prior to the missed approach point* should be used. Fly the aircraft at MDA until arrival at the missed approach point or until establishing visual contact with the runway environment.

The Controller will issue course guidance when required and he will give range information each mile while on final approach. The pilot will be instructed to report the runway in sight. Approach guidance will be discontinued when the runway environment is reported in sight or when the aircraft is at the missed approach point or one mile from the landing threshold, whichever is greater. If the pilot does not report the runway environment in sight, missed approach instructions will be given.

Perform the missed approach when:

a. Communication on final approach is lost for more than 15 seconds.

b. Directed by the Controller.

c. The runway approach threshold, approach lights or other markings identifiable with the approach end of the runway are not clearly visible at the Minimum Descent Altitude (MDA) one (1) mile from the end of the runway.

d.   A landing is not accomplished.

3.   **Gyro Out Approach (Heading Indicator Inoperative):**

PROCEDURE:

If the heading indicator should fail during flight, advise the Radar Controller and request a gyro out approach. The final approach may be either precision or surveillance as previously discussed.

Perform standard rate turns during the transition to final. Perform turns on final by establishing half-standard rate turns. Initiate turns immediately upon hearing the words TURN RIGHT or TURN LEFT. Stop the turn on receipt of the words STOP TURN.

NOTE: Portions of Sections A and B above are excerpts from AF Manual 51-37: *Instrument Flying.*

C.   PROCEDURE TURNS (COURSE REVERSAL TURNS)

Procedure turn is the maneuver prescribed when it is necessary to reverse the direction of an aircraft and establish it on the reciprocal of its original course. Although procedure turns are considered "timed instrument flight patterns," they are used almost exclusively in conjunction with course interceptions during instrument approaches like the procedural track turns discussed on p. 107. There are four types of procedure turns that have evolved over the years: the 45/180 degree (60-second) turn, the 45/225 degree (40-second) turn, the 90/270 degree turn and the 30/210 degree turn. The difficulty of any one of these procedures is relative to its elapsed time from start to finish because the less time a procedure turn requires, the more a pilot has to be ahead of his aircraft and on top of the entire situation.

The 45/180 degree turn is the most frequently used of all of the procedure turns and takes the *maximum time* to execute. It does not incorporate a wind drift correction or align the aircraft directly on the inbound course as does the 45/225 degree turn but it is an easy maneuver for beginners to use and affords pilots a little more flexibility (additional time) in descending to their published final approach altitude. The 45/225 degree turn is a modification of the 45/180 degree turn and requires less time to complete. It involves changes in both the time outbound and the point at which the course will be reintercepted (see below) but it will conclude with a smooth, sweeping standard-rate turn onto the final approach course even if you are off a few seconds in your calculations. The 90/270 degree turn (or 80/260 degree turn if you prefer) is very useful during low-visibility circling approaches and requires no timing. This maneuver will enable you to reverse the direction of your aircraft in the *minimum time* and with the minimum outbound displacement. The final procedure turn is the 30/210 degree teardrop turn. This maneuver is used during all teardrop entries into holding patterns and during those "teardrop type" approaches that specify a 30/210 degree turn. Every teardrop approach incorporates a procedural track turn where the specific courses to be intercepted are clearly indicated on the approach plate but since these courses are seldom exactly 30 degrees apart, the 30/210 degree turn is rarely used for teardrop approaches. Notice that the Rock Sound NDB Rwy 27 approach (Appendix E, p. 261) and the Phoenix VOR Rwy 26L approach (Appendix E, p. 266) are both teardrop type approaches but that neither incorporates a 30/210 degree procedure turn!

Although every procedure turn has its own specific (suggested) application, ANY of them may be used during an instrument approach where the 45/180 degree turn is the depicted procedure and all of them have four things in common: (1) they all have limitations on when they may be used, (2) they all must be accomplished on the specified side of the approach course, (3) they all must be completed within the distance specified in the profile view on the approach plate and finally (4) they all must be executed at or above a specified *minimum* altitude.

1.   **45/180 Degree (60 Second "Barb Type") Turn:**

(Standard course reversal turn used for most instrument approaches.)

PROCEDURE:

Step 1: Established on the outbound course, turn left or right 45 degrees (as depicted) and fly for one minute (using a standard-rate three degree/sec turn).

Step 2: At the end of the elapsed time, turn in the *opposite* direction 180 degrees, roll out, and then time 45 seconds to reintercept the inbound course at a 45 degree angle.

NOTE: "Barb Type" because the U.S. Government approach plates depict this type procedure turn as a pointed barb. A barb indicates the direction or side of the outbound course on which the procedure turn is to be made. Headings are provided for course reversal using the 45/180 degree type procedure turn; however, the point at which the turn may be commenced and the type and rate of turn is left to the discretion of the pilot.

2. **45/225 Degree (40 Second) Turn:**

(Optional course reversal turn generally used for low-visibility circling approaches.)

PROCEDURE:

Step 1: Established on the outbound course, turn left or right 45 degrees (as depicted) and fly for 40 seconds* (using a standard-rate three degree/sec turn).

*NOTE: Depending upon whether your procedure turn is made upwind or downwind of the approach course, add or subtract one second from the 40 second base figure for each degree of crab required on the outbound leg.

Step 2: At the end of the elapsed time, turn in the *opposite* direction 225 degrees and reintercept the inbound course directly (plus or minus your drift correction) without an intercept angle.

3.   **90/270 Degree Turn**

(Optional course reversal turn generally used for low-visibility circling approaches.)

PROCEDURE:

Step 1: Established on the outbound course, turn left or right 90 degrees (as depicted) to the heading that appears under the left or right wing tip on your D.G. (using a standard-rate three degree/sec turn).

Step 2: Upon completion of the 90 degree turn, immediately roll into a 270 degree turn, in the *opposite* direction (to the reciprocal of your original heading that now appears under the same D.G. wing tip reference used in Step 1) and reintercept the inbound course directly without an intercept angle.

4.   **30/210 Degree Teardrop Turn**

(Course reversal turn commonly used in entering holding patterns and required for a few procedural track teardrop approaches.)

PROCEDURE:

Step 1: Established on the outbound course, turn left or right 30 degrees (as depicted) and fly one minute (using a standard-rate three degree/sec turn).

Step 2: At the end of the elapsed time, turn in the *opposite* direction 210 degrees and reintercept the inbound course directly without an intercept angle.

5.   **Limitations on Procedure Turns:**

a. In the case of a radar initial approach to a final approach fix or position, or a timed approach from a holding fix, or where the procedure specifies "NoPT," no pilot may make a procedure turn unless, when he receives his final approach clearance, he so advises ATC and a clearance is received.*

NOTE: If a procedure turn is desired, descent below the procedure turn altitude should not be made since some NoPT altitudes may be lower than the procedure turn altitude.

b. When a teardrop procedure turn is depicted and a course reversal is required, this type turn MUST be executed.

c. When a one minute holding pattern replaces the procedure turn, the standard entry and the holding pattern must be followed except when RADAR VECTORING is provided or when NoPT is shown on the approach course. As in the procedure turn, the descent from the minimum holding pattern altitude to the final approach fix altitude (when lower) may not commence until the aircraft is established on the inbound course.

d. The absence of the procedure turn barb in the Plan View indicates that a procedure turn is not authorized for that procedure.

6. **Procedural Track Turns:**

Unlike the procedure turns above which are timed instrument flight patterns, the procedural track turn is more of a radio navigational pattern utilized during teardrop approaches where a specific flight path is required. Procedural track symbology (Appendix E, pp. 261 and 266) is used to depict the flight path between the IAF (Initial Approach Fix) and the Final Approach Fix (FAF).

PROCEDURE:

Step 1: When over the IAF, turn immediately in the shorter direction to intercept the published outbound track (course). Established on this course, fly outbound for one minute.

Step 2: At the end of the elasped time, turn right or left (as depicted) to intercept the inbound course to the FAF.

*NOTE: Portions of Section C above are excerpts from AC 61-27C: *Instrument Flying Handbook.*

D.   DO'S AND DON'TS

Do:

1.   Use all your navigation radios as much as possible to keep oriented to your position.

2.   Anticipate as much as possible how the Radar Controller intends to position your aircraft for the approach. Once established inbound on the Front Course localizer of an ILS approach, remember that the blue sector IS ALWAYS on the pilot's right and that if the aircraft drifts right into the blue sector, the localizer needle will drift LEFT into the blue color coded side of the nav display.

3.   Plan out your missed approach ahead of time and KNOW the following minimum altitude definitions:

  a.   MDA: "Minimum descent altitude" means the lowest altitude, expressed in feet above mean sea level, to which descent is authorized on final approach, where no electronic glide slope is provided, or during circle-to-land maneuvering in execution of a standard instrument approach procedure.

  b.   DH: "decision height," with respect to the operation of aircraft means the height at which a decision must be made, during an ILS or PAR instrument approach, to either continue the approach or to execute a missed approach. This height is expressed in feet above mean sea level (MSL).

  c.   HAA: "Height above airport" indicates the height of the

MDA above the published airport elevation. HAA is published in conjunction with circling minimums for all types of approaches.

    d. HAT: "Height above touchdown" indicates the height of the DH or MDA above the highest runway elevation in the touchdown zone (first 3,000 feet of runway). HAT is published in conjunction with straight-in minimums.

4. Memorize "IFR Two-Way Radio Communications Failure" procedures (FAR 91.127).

5. Check your destination weather *before* you get there, and never fly when icing is reported. Know your alternate airport minimums.

6. Always set the degrees of the localizer course under the OBS course index *for reference* during an ILS approach.

7. Time EVERY approach! . . . for those approaches where the time is not given in the "time and speed" table below the aerodrome sketch (VOR or ADF procedures where the station is on the airport and is the MAP), then *COMPUTE* the time.*

NOTE: To compute your time from the final approach fix (FAF) to the missed approach point (MAP) when it is not given on the approach plate, set the "seconds index" (SEC), which is #36 on the inner scale of your flight computer, to the aircraft's groundspeed in knots and then read your time in minutes and seconds to the MAP under the published distance (between the FAF and MAP) read on the outside scale. **Example:** At 100 knots groundspeed it takes 2:24 to travel 4 nautical miles from Bethel intersection to the Rock Sound NDB located on the airport (Appendix E, p. 261).

8. Study your approach plates ahead of time and continue to monitor your position even though you are in radar contact and receiving vectors.

9. Confirm that your aircraft is located on the appropriate side of a VOR (ADF) station to intercept a given course *before* turning to an intercept heading!

10. Work out holding pattern entries mathematically when possible, especially at intersections where the courses converge at close to a 70 degree angle because the "sector of entry" method may be improperly interpreted due to the optical illusion created.

Don't:

1. Forget the following seven (7) tips on IFR clearance copying:

     a.   Have clipboard, pencil and blank sheet of paper handy.

     b.   Have pertinent charts available and open to area involved.

     c.   Write as fast as you can and copy your clearance vertically down the page for easier interpretation and analysis.

     d.   Keep writing even if you miss some of it (write what the Controller is currently saying).

     e.   Attempt to remember station designators, write the first three letters of the station as pronounced.

     f.   Stay ahead, learn:

         (1)   Preferential routings
         (2)   Normal departure clearances
         (3)   High density terminal areas

     g.   Ask for repeat if not received, insure complete accurate receipt of all clearances.

2. Take off without your clipboard, paper, pencils, charts, approach plates, computer, plotter . . . etc. organized for quick and easy access. These essential materials SHOULD NOT be placed in the rear seat area where lowering your head and turning around repeatedly could induce severe vertigo (Appendix D).

3. "Waste" your radios by tuning both to the same frequency or by setting up for the approach so far in advance that no useful navigational information is being received.

4. Assume airways are straight and pass through enroute stations

without a possible "dogleg" (see V-14 on the St. Louis area chart).

5. Misinterpret VOR station passage (see Chapter I, p. 5). On many Omni receivers a voice transmission on the communication (comm) frequency will cause To/From fluctuations on the ambiguity meter similar to station passage indications. Read the whole receiver . . . To/From, CDI, and OBS . . . before you make a decision.

6. Forget to either descend on the approach or to tune in a "step down" fix (intersection) necessary to shoot the approach.

7. Fly inbound on a VOR approach with a "From" indication on the VOR head.

8. Forget the mandatory IFR radio calls:

a.	Enter hold	f.	ETA ± 3 Minutes
b.	Leaving hold	g.	TAS ± 10 Knots
c.	Leaving altitude	h.	Equipment malfunction
d.	Final approach fix inbound	i.	Unforecast weather
e.	Missed approach	j.	Reports requested

9. Commence an ILS approach without first listening to the localizer identifier . . . or fly an NDB approach without listening to the Morse Code identifier on the ADF during the entire approach procedure.

10. Forget to set your D.G. *and* altimeter prior to commencing any approach, or to check the accuracy of your altimeter specifically during an ILS approach by confirming that your altitude indicated over the outer marker (when your aircraft is on the glide slope) agrees with the approach chart. **Example:** Your altimeter should read approximately 2,139 feet over the Summit LOM (see Appendix E, p. 263).

11. Confuse a standard no-glide-slope localizer approach with an SDF (Simplified Directional Facility) or an LDA (Localizer Directional Aid) approach. The approach techniques and pro-

cedures used in the performance of an SDF instrument approach are essentially identical to those employed in executing a standard localizer approach except that the SDF course is seldom aligned with the runway and the course may be wider, resulting in less precision. The SDF signal emitted from the transmitter is fixed at either 6 or 12 degrees to provide maximum flyability and optimum course quality. The SDF antenna is normally offset from the runway centerline at an angle of 3 degrees or less; however, it should be noted that inasmuch as the approach course originates at the antenna site, an approach which is continued beyond the runway threshold will lead your aircraft to the SDF offset position rather than along the runway centerline (see Appendix E, p. 265). An LDA final approach course is also similar in utility and accuracy to a localizer but it is not part of a complete ILS and will not be aligned with the runway (see Appendix E, p. 264).

12. Descend below the MDA prior to reaching the Visual Descent Point (VDP). Visual reference of the runway environment prior to reaching the VDP should alert you that you have not yet reached the point from which a normal descent path (approximately 3 degrees) intersects the MDA. Conversely, reaching the VDP prior to acquiring visual reference should alert you to the likelihood of a missed approach. (See Appendix E, p. 268.)

NOTE: A new concept, Visual Descent Point, is being incorporated in selected nonprecision approach procedures. The VDP is a defined point on the final approach course of a nonprecision straight-in approach procedure from which normal descent from the MDA to the runway touchdown point may be commenced, provided required visual reference is established. If a straight-in nonprecision approach procedure incorporates a VDP, it shall be identified by an approved electronic navigational aid. DME will normally be used for VOR and LOC BC approaches. A 75 MHz marker will be used for NDB approaches and where DME cannot be implemented. VDPs will not normally be established for runways served by precision approach aids. VDPs are not a mandatory part of nonprecision approach procedures but are intended to provide additional guidance where they are implemented. A VASI will normally be installed on those runways served by a nonprecision approach that incorporates a VDP.

Chapter IX
ATTITUDE INSTRUMENT FLYING

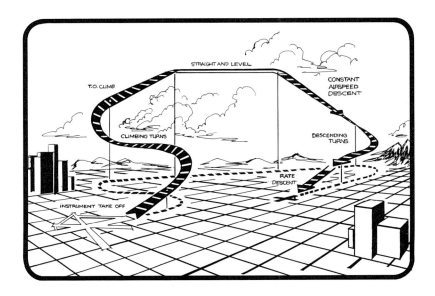

Although learning to fly an aircraft solely by reference to the instruments involves considerable additional training, not all of this instruction covers "advanced" subject matter, and certainly none of this training should ASSUME that a pilot already possesses the skills to fly proficiently in VFR conditions (with a natural horizon) much less in IFR conditions by reference to an artificial horizon.

It is paradoxical that the subject of attitude instrument flying which is so crucial to safe and efficient instrument operations is such an elementary aeronautical subject. The old adage that "familiarity breeds contempt" certainly applies to aircraft control because by the time a pilot begins working on his instrument rating, he generally feels that his airwork is very satisfactory when, in fact, it may be very rusty and undisciplined. Many pilots who are deficient in their basic airwork will become easily overwhelmed and quickly fatigued early in their instrument training, especially if they are paired with a flight instructor who incorrectly ASSUMES that only a brief review of the basic "stick and rudder" fundamentals is sufficient before moving on to the finer points of radio navigation. This situation rarely occurs, however, because most instructors follow an approved* Instrument Flying Course Syllabus like the one presented in Appendix A (p. 173) of this book and structure their lesson plans to conform with the "Instrument Flight Instructor's Lesson Guide" that appears on page 243 of AC 61-27C: *Instrument Flying Handbook.*

Because in flight instruction it is an axiom that to ASSUME anything makes an ASS/ out of both U/ and ME, *IFR Pocket Simulator Procedures* does not assume that the reader has any prerequisite knowledge of attitude instrument flying. A review of the basic instrument flight maneuvers is presented in the first part of this chapter to give readers of different aeronautical experience the necessary background information to understand the "control and performance" concept of attitude flying presented in the last part of the chapter. Learning how to group the flight instruments categorically not only improves a pilot's instrument scan during the execution of these maneuvers, but also minimizes his susceptibility to the false sensory illusions (Appendix D) that they may create in flight.

*NOTE: FAA approved curriculum for flight instruction administered under Part 141 of the Federal regulations.

A.   BASIC INSTRUMENT FLIGHT MANEUVERS

This section is based upon the information in Chapters 3 and 4, of AC 61-27C: *Instrument Flying Handbook,* and Chapter 8, of AF Manual 51-37: *Instrument Flying.*

Understanding the aerodynamic forces affecting aircraft performance will give a pilot a sound basis for predicting how the aircraft will respond to his control. Important as these forces are to the VFR pilot, they must be even more thoroughly understood by the student of instrument flying. An instrument flight, regardless of its length or complexity is simply a series of connected basic instrument maneuvers and failure to consider each portion of the flight as an instrument maneuver often leads to erratic aircraft control. A pilot's knowledge of the aerodynamics of these maneuvers is the key to his interpretation of information shown on the instrument panel. Several basic aerodynamic definitions apply to a discussion of these maneuvers.

1.   **Aerodynamic Forces:**

   a.   *Lift* always acts in a direction perpendicular to the relative wind and to the lateral axis of the aircraft. The fact that lift is referenced to the wing, *not* the earth's surface, is the source of many errors in learning flight control. Lift is not always "up." Its direction relative to the earth's surface changes as you maneuver the aircraft. The magnitude of the force of lift is directly proportional to the density of the air, the area of the wings, and the airspeed. It also depends upon the type of wing and the angle of attack. Lift increases with an increase in angle of attack up to the stalling angle, at which point it decreases with any further increase in angle of attack.* In conventional aircraft, lift is therefore controlled by varying angle of attack (attitude) and thrust.

   *NOTE: Angle of attack is defined as the angle formed between the chord line of the wing and the relative wind. An aircraft in level flight at cruise airspeed forms a small angle of attack. As the airspeed is decreased, the angle of attack will increase if level flight is maintained. At some given angle of attack the wing will stall and this stalling angle will always remain the same for that particular wing, regardless of gross weight, attitude, airspeed or G load. The airspeed at the stall angle of attack varies with the weight supported by the wing. Consider an aircraft in 1-G flight that weighs 2,000 lbs and has a stall speed of 50 knots. The lift required to maintain level 1-G flight is 2,000 lbs. Cruising speed of 150 knots requires a specific angle of attack, slow flight speed of 100 knots requires a greater angle of attack, and finally at stall speed of 50 knots, the wing reaches its critical angle of attack. Place the aircraft into a 4-G maneuver (such as a high G turn), which has the same effect as increasing the gross weight to four times its original value, and the lift required is now 8,000 lbs. To produce the same angle of attack, the airspeed has to be doubled. In other words, the stall angle of attack will be reached at 100

knots (stall speed increases by the square root of the G force; i.e., (50 x $\sqrt{4}$ = 100 knots). See the Note on p. 132!

b.   *Drag* is the total resistance of the air to the movement of the aircraft. Drag acts opposite to the direction of flight of the aircraft and parallel to the relative wind. Induced drag is the result of the same inherent aerodynamic forces that produce lift. Parasite drag is the resistance to airflow caused by inefficient streamlining, skin friction, and projections into the airstream. Total drag is the sum of induced and parasite drag and is affected by airspeed and air density as well as the other factors noted. Changes in drag, whether induced during attitude changes or the result of gear and/or flap extensions, are reflected in performance changes indicated on your flight instruments.

c.   *Thrust* in conventional propeller driven aircraft is the force acting forward with respect to the longitudinal axis of the aircraft. The amount of thrust is determined by the power output of the engine, and for all practical purposes acts parallel to the longitudinal axis. Use of power controls thrust, and therefore lift and performance.

d.   *Weight* is the force of gravity acting on the aircraft and is always downward toward the center of the earth regardless of aircraft attitude and flight path. Both the total weight and its distribution affect aircraft flight characteristics. The relationship of these fundamental factors to aircraft performance in various basic flight attitudes and conditions must be understood if you are to control your aircraft with precision.

2.   **The Four Fundamentals:**

a.   *STRAIGHT AND LEVEL FLIGHT:*

Straight and level flight is a performance term meaning that an aircraft is maintaining a constant indicated altitude, heading and airspeed. Use pitch attitude control to maintain or adjust the altitude. Use bank control to maintain or adjust the heading. Use power control to maintain or adjust the airspeed. In coordinated, unaccelerated straight and level flight, *weight* acts downward toward the center of the earth, *lift* acts perpendicular to the relative wind and is equal and opposite to the weight; *drag* acts parallel to the relative wind; and *thrust* acts forward, parallel to the longitudinal axis, and equal and opposite to drag. In addition, all opposing forces are balanced and as long as the specific flight attitude and thrust are maintained, altitude and heading remain constant. Any variation in these forces requires a different attitude (relationship of the aircraft's longitudinal and lateral axes with the earth's surface) if the aircraft is to maintain level flight.

(1)   *Maintaining a Desired Altitude*

Maintaining a desired altitude requires the ability to maintain a specific pitch attitude and, when necessary, to smoothly and precisely adjust this attitude. This ability is developed through proper use of the attitude indicator and is simplified by good trim techniques. After leveling off at cruise airspeed, adjusting the pitch trim knob on the attitude indicator so that the miniature aircraft is aligned with the horizon bar will aid in observing small pitch changes. Subsequent readjustments may be required because of changes in aircraft gross weight[1] and cruise airspeeds.[2]

NOTE 1: For a given weight and airspeed, a specific angle of attack is required to maintain straight and level flight. To support heavier loads at a given airspeed, the angle of attack must be relatively greater to provide the necessary lift. To overcome the induced drag resulting from the increased angle of attack, more thrust is also needed to maintain the given airspeed.

NOTE 2: At a constant angle of attack, any change in airspeed will vary the lift. At low airspeeds, the angle of attack must be proportionately greater to produce the lift necessary for level flight. The aircraft must therefore be flown in a nose high attitude to maintain level flight at low speeds. At progressively higher airspeeds, the angle of attack necessary to produce sufficient lift for level flight becomes smaller, and the nose of the aircraft is accordingly lowered. Assuming that weight remains constant, any specific airspeed in unaccelerated level flight is associated with a specific thrust and attitude. In other words, if more power is applied than required for level flight, the aircraft will accelerate if held level, or climb if airspeed is held constant.

The small pitch corrections required to maintain a desired altitude are made in fractions of a bar width or in degrees. The pilot should become familiar with the vertical velocity changes which result when specific pitch adjustments are made at various airspeeds and configurations. Thus, he can determine what pitch attitude adjustment is required to produce the desired rate of correction when an altitude deviation is observed.*

NOTE: A technique for predetermining the vertical velocity for a given pitch change depends upon TAS. One degree (normally ½ bar width) of pitch change will result in an approximate vertical velocity that is equivalent to miles per minute times 100. **Example:** At 120 KTAS or 2 NM/min X 100, one degree of pitch change will result in approximately 200 fpm vertical velocity change.

When the pilot makes these pitch adjustments, the altimeter and vertical velocity indications will lag behind changes of pitch attitude on the attitude indicator. This lag should be recognized and accepted as an inherent error in the differential pressure instruments. Because of this error, the pilot must maintain the adjusted pitch attitude on the attitude indicator while waiting for changes on the altimeter and vertical velocity to occur. He must not make a snap decision that the adjusted pitch change is ineffective, and be lured into over-controlling the pitch attitude.

With experience, the pilot can usually estimate the suitability of a pitch adjustment by noting the initial rate of movement of the vertical velocity indicator. For example, assume a pitch adjustment has been made which is expected to result in 200 to 300 feet per minute rate of climb. If the initial rate of movement on the vertical velocity indicator is rapid and obviously will stabilize at a rate greater than desired, the pitch change was too large. Readjust the pitch attitude rather than wait for a stabilized indication on the vertical velocity indicator.

When an aircraft first departs an altitude, an indication often appears on the vertical velocity indicator before one appears on the altimeter. By evaluating this initial rate of movement, the pilot can estimate the amount of pitch change required on the attitude indicator and prevent large altitude deviations. If the estimated pitch change was correct, the vertical velocity will return to zero with a negligible change of altitude on the altimeter.

When a deviation from the desired altitude occurs, exercise good judgment in determining a rate of correction. The correction must not be too large and cause the aircraft to "overshoot" the desired altitude, nor should it be so small that it is unnecessarily prolonged. As a guide, the pitch attitude change on the attitude indicator should produce a rate of vertical velocity approximately twice the size of the altitude deviation. Usually pitch changes are made in fractions (½, 1, 1½, etc.) of bar widths or degrees. For example, if the aircraft is 100 feet off the desired altitude, a 200 feet per minute rate of correction (pitch change of ½ bar width; ref: p. 118) would be a suitable amount. By knowing the present rate of climb or descent and the results to be expected from a pitch change, the pilot can closely estimate how much to change the pitch attitude. Initially, this pitch change is an estimated amount; therefore, the adjusted pitch attitude must be held constant until the rate of correction is observed on the vertical velocity indicator. If it differs from the desired, then further adjustments of the pitch attitude is required.

When approaching the desired altitude, determine a lead point on the altimeter for initiating a level off pitch attitude change. A suitable lead point prevents "overshooting" and permits a smooth transition to level flight. The amount of lead required varies with pilot technique and rate of correction. As a guide, the lead point on the altimeter should be approximately 10 percent of the vertical velocity. For example, if the rate of correction to the desired altitude is 300 feet per minute, initiate the level off approximately 30 feet before reaching the desired altitude.

Devoting too much attention to the vertical velocity indicator can lead to "chasing" its indications and result in erratic pitch control. Although the vertical velocity indicator is an important performance instrument, limitations such as oscillation in rough air, lag, etc., should be thoroughly understood to prevent over-controlling the pitch attitude. For this reason, the pilot must recognize and understand that sufficient reference to the attitude indicator is necessary to insure smooth and precise pitch adjustments for effective altitude control.

(2) *Maintaining a Desired Heading*

Maintaining a desired heading is accomplished by maintaining a zero bank attitude. By observing the heading indicator, the pilot determines if he is maintaining the desired heading. Heading deviations are not normally as "eye-catching" as altitude deviations. Therefore, be aware of this characteristic and develop a habit of cross-checking the heading indicator frequently to prevent significant heading deviations. When a deviation from the desired heading occurs, refer to the attitude indicator and smoothly establish a definite angle of bank which will produce a suitable rate of return. As a guide, the bank attitude change on the attitude indicator should equal the heading deviation in degrees. For example, if the heading deviation is 10 degrees, then 10 degrees of bank on the attitude indicator would produce a suitable rate of correction. This guide is particularly helpful during instrument approaches at relatively slow airspeeds. At higher true airspeeds a larger angle of bank may be required to prevent a prolonged correction. Small bank (and pitch) deviations may occur when a wings level attitude is established on the attitude indicator following a turn or change of airspeed because of gyroscopic precession. Proper bank (and pitch) control requires a pilot to recognize the effects of precession on the aircraft's heading (altitude) and to compensate for them by temporarily establishing a bank (or pitch) attitude other than that ordinarily expected. For example, maintaining straight and level flight on the performance instruments after completing a normal turn, the attitude indicator may depict a slight turn, climb or descent, or a combination of both. The attitude indicator will gradually resume its normal indications as the erection mechanism automatically corrects these errors.

(3) *Establishing and Maintaining Airspeed*

Establishing or maintaining an airspeed is accomplished by referring to the airspeed indicator and adjusting the power or aircraft attitude. A knowledge of the approximate power required to establish a desired airspeed will aid in making power adjustments. After the approximate power setting is established, a cross-check of the airspeed indicator will indicate if subsequent power adjustments are required. The pilot should make it a point to learn and remember the approximate power settings for his aircraft at various airspeeds and configurations used throughout a normal flight.

When an airspeed deviation is observed, a power or pitch adjustment, or a combination of both, may be required to correct back to the desired airspeed. For example, if below the desired altitude with a higher-than-desired airspeed, a proper pitch adjustment may regain both the desired airspeed and altitude. Conversely, a pitch adjustment, if made when at the desired airspeed, will induce the need for a power adjustment.

Changes of airspeed in straight and level flight are accomplished by adjusting the power. To increase the airspeed, advance the power beyond the setting required to maintain the new airspeed. As the airspeed increases, the aircraft gains lift and will have a tendency to climb. Adjust the pitch attitude as required to maintain altitude. When the airspeed approaches the desired indication, reduce the power to an estimated setting that will maintain the new airspeed.

To reduce the airspeed, reduce the power below the setting estimated for maintaining the new desired airspeed. As the airspeed decreases, the aircraft loses lift and will have a tendency to descend. When the airspeed approaches the desired indication, advance the power to an estimated setting that will maintain the new airspeed.*

NOTE: Rotating the aircraft about the lateral pitch axis is accomplished by forward or aft movement of the elevator control to displace the elevators. The use of the elevators varies with changes in power and airspeed. The slip stream striking the elevators in a downward direction creates a negative angle of attack for the elevators and causes them to exert a negative lift. Changes in power and airspeed vary the amount of downwash and the resulting negative lift exerted by the elevators. As power and airspeed increase, slipstream velocity and downwash lift on the elevators increases. At the same time, lift on the wing increases and if the aircraft is trimmed for level flight, an increase in power and airspeed must be accompanied by forward pressure on the controls in order to remain in level flight. A decrease in power and/or airspeed has the opposite effect. The negative lift on the elevators and the lift on the wing decrease, resulting in a nose-low tendency. As power and/or airspeed is reduced, back pressure must be held on the controls to maintain level flight.

b. *CLIMBS AND DESCENTS*

Climbing and descending maneuvers are classified into two general types — constant *airspeed* or constant *rate.* The constant airspeed maneuver is accomplished by maintaining a constant power indication and varying the pitch attitude as required to maintain a specific airspeed. The constant rate maneuver is accomplished by varying both power and pitch as required to maintain constant a specific airspeed and vertical velocity. Either type of climb or descent may be performed while maintaining a constant heading or while turning. These maneuvers should be practiced using airspeeds, configurations, and altitudes corresponding to those which will be used in actual instrument flight.

(1) *Constant Airspeed Climbs and Descents*

Before entering a climb or descent, decide what power setting is to be established and estimate the amount of pitch attitude change (increase in nose attitude) required to maintain the airspeed. Normally, the pitch and power changes are made simultaneously. The power change should be smooth, uninterrupted, and at a rate commensurate with the rate of pitch change.[1] In some aircraft, even though a constant throttle setting is maintained, the power may change with altitude.[2] Therefore, it may be necessary to occasionally cross-check the power indicator(s).

NOTE 1: If the climb is entered without a change in power setting the airspeed gradually diminishes because the thrust required to maintain a given airspeed in level flight is insufficient to maintain the same airspeed in a climb. Due to momentum, the change in airspeed is gradual, varying considerably with differences in aircraft size, weight, total drag, and other factors. As the angle of attack changes, a component of the weight acts in the same direction, and parallel to, the total drag of the aircraft, thereby increasing the total drag of the aircraft and decreasing the airspeed. The reduction in airspeed results in a corresponding decrease in drag until the total drag (including the component of weight acting in the same direction) equals the thrust. On entering a normal descent from straight and level flight without a change in power, a disturbance in balanced forces likewise occurs. As a result of forward pressure on the elevator controls, the angle of attack is reduced and the lift is proportionately reduced. The weight being greater than the lift, the aircraft follows a descending flight path. A component of the weight now acts forward along the flight path parallel to the thrust, causing a gradual increase in airspeed as well as an increase in drag. When the angle of attack stabilizes and the lift/weight and thrust/drag forces again balance, the aircraft descends at a constant airspeed. Therefore, to enter a descent from level flight, maintaining a constant airspeed, you must decrease power to prevent an increase in thrust resulting from the forward alignment of the weight component. In a descent, the component of weight acting forward along the flight path increases as the angle of descent increases and decreases as the angle of descent decreases. The power reduction required to maintain a given airspeed in the descent depends on the rate of descent desired. For example, a high rate of descent at a specific airspeed requires a greater power reduction than does a lower rate of descent. The proper combination of pitch attitudes, airspeeds, vertical velocities, and power settings for climbs and descents must be learned for each individual aircraft. Having learned the principles and techniques for the execution of these maneuvers for one aircraft, you can readily apply them to other aircraft.

NOTE 2: In aircraft with reciprocating type engines, available power (and lift) varies directly with changes in air density, which decreases as either altitude, air temperature or humidity increases. Thus, to maintain a climb (straight and level ... etc.) at a given true airspeed, the power must be greater at higher altitudes and/or outside air temperatures.

While the power is being changed, refer to the attitude indicator and smoothly accomplish the estimated pitch change. Since smooth, slower power applications will also produce pitch changes, only slight control pressures are needed to establish the pitch change. Also, very little trim change is required since the airspeed is constant. With a moderate amount of practice, the pitch and power changes can be properly coordinated so the airspeed will remain within close limits as the climb or descent is entered.[3] Remember, the initial pitch change was an estimated amount to maintain the airspeed constant at the new power setting. The airspeed indicator must be cross-checked to determine the need for subsequent pitch adjustments.

NOTE 3: For all practical purposes, the lift in normal climbs (descents) is the same as in level flight at the same airspeed. Though the flight path has changed, the angle of attack of the wing with respect to the flight path remains the same, as does the lift. There is a momentary change, however, in going from straight and level flight to a climb (descent), a change in lift occurs when back (forward) elevator pressure is applied. Raising (lowering) the nose increases (decreases) the angle of attack and momentarily increases (decreases) the lift. Lift, now greater (less) than weight, causes the aircraft to climb (descend). The flight path is inclined upward (downward), and the angle of attack and lift again stabilize. In a climb (descent) when the airspeed stabilizes at a value lower (higher) than in straight and level flight at the same power setting, the forces are again balanced. Lift is equal in magnitude to the component of weight that is perpendicular to the flight path. During a climb (descent), this perpendicular weight component is only part of the weight, the other component acting to increase (decrease) the total drag. Because the latter component must be balanced by thrust, the pilot must increase (decrease) power to maintain constant airspeed on entering a climb (descent) from level flight, the amount of power depending on the change in angle of attack.

When making a pitch adjustment to correct for an airspeed deviation, the airspeed indicator will not reflect an immediate change. The results of pitch attitude changes can often be determined more quickly by referring to the vertical velocity indicator. For example, while climbing a pilot notes that his airspeed is remaining slightly high and realizes that a small pitch adjustment is required. If the pitch adjustment results in a small increase of vertical velocity, the pilot knows, even though his airspeed may not yet show a change, that his pitch correction was approximately correct.

In a similar manner, the vertical velocity indication will help a pilot note that he has made an inadvertent change in pitch attitude. For example, assume that the desired airspeed and the vertical velocity have been remaining constant, but then, inadvertently, the pitch attitude is allowed to change. The vertical velocity indicator is an excellent aid in maintaining the airspeed constant.

Upon approaching the desired altitude, select a predetermined leveloff lead point on the altimeter. As a guide, use 10 percent of the vertical velocity. Smoothly adjust the power to an approximate setting required for level flight, and simultaneously change the pitch attitude to maintain the desired altitude.

(2) *Rate Climbs and Descents*

Rate climbs and descents are accomplished by maintaining both a desired vertical velocity and airspeed. They are proficiency maneuvers designed to practice the techniques used during ILS and radar precision instrument approaches. Pitch attitude control is used to establish and maintain the desired vertical velocity. Power control is used to maintain the desired airspeed. Proper control techniques require coordinated pitch and power changes and/or adjustments.

Before initiating a rate climb or descent, estimate the amount of pitch change required to produce the desired vertical velocity and the amount of power change required to maintain the airspeed constant.

Enter the climb or descent by simultaneously changing the pitch and power the predetermined amount. Cross-check the performance instruments to determine the resultant changes.

A cross-check of the vertical velocity will indicate the need for the subsequent pitch adjustments. A cross-check of the airspeed will indicate the need for subsequent power adjustments. The rate climb or descent is terminated by using normal leveloff procedures when approaching the desired altitude.

(3) *Pitch and Bank Attitude Control During Climbing and Descending Turns*

Constant airspeed or rate climbs and descents may be performed on a constant heading or while turning. When accomplished on a constant heading, pitch and bank control techniques are essentially the same as discussed under straight and level flight. When accomplished during a turn, a decrease in the vertical component of lift affects pitch control. For example, when entering a turn after a constant airspeed climb or descent has already been established, the pitch attitude will have to be decreased slightly to maintain the airspeed constant. When entering a turn while performing a rate climb or descent, be prepared to raise the nose of the aircraft slightly to maintain the vertical velocity and add power to maintain the airspeed.

c. *TURNS*

An aircraft, like any moving object, requires a sideward force to make it turn. In a normal turn, this force is supplied by banking the aircraft so that lift is exerted inward as well as upward. The force of lift is thus separated into two components at right angles to each other. The lift acting upward and opposing weight is called the *vertical lift component.* The lift acting horizontally and opposing centrifugal force is called the *horizontal lift component.* The horizontal lift component is the sideward force that causes an aircraft to turn. The equal and opposite reaction to this sideward force is centrifugal force. If an aircraft is not banked, no force is provided to make it turn unless the turn is skidded by rudder application. Likewise, if an aircraft is banked, it will turn unless held on a constant heading in a slip. Proper instrument interpretation and aircraft control technique assumes that an aircraft is turned by banking, and that in a banking attitude it should be turning.

Turns are classified into two general types — constant *angle* and constant *rate.* Before entering either type turn, the pilot should decide upon the angle of bank to be used. Factors to consider are true airspeed and the desired rate of turn. A slow turn rate may unnecessarily prolong the turn, whereas a high rate of turn may cause overshooting of the heading and difficulty with pitch control.* To enter a turn, the pilot should refer to the attitude indicator (primary bank) while applying smooth and coordinated control pressures to establish the desired angle of bank. Bank control should then be maintained throughout the turn by reference to either the attitude indicator for a constant angle turn or the turn and slip indicator for a constant rate turn. To roll out of a turn on a desired heading, a lead point must be used. The amount of lead required depends upon the amount of bank used for the turn, the rate the aircraft is turning, and the rate the pilot rolls out. As a guide, a lead point on the heading indicator equal to approximately ½ the angle of bank may be used.

NOTE: The rate of turn at any given airspeed depends upon the horizontal lift component. This sideward force which causes the aircraft to turn varies directly in proportion to bank in a correctly executed turn. Thus, the rate of turn at a given airspeed increases as the angle of bank increases. At 130 knots and approximately 10 degrees of bank, an aircraft completes a 360 degree turn in four minutes; at the same airspeed and approximately 55 degrees of bank, the rate of turn is eight times as great.

(1) *Altitude Control*

The techniques for maintaining a constant altitude during a turn are similar to those used in maintaining straight and level flight. During the initial part of the roll-in, hold the same pitch attitude as was used to maintain altitude with the wings level. As the bank is increased the pilot should anticipate a tendency for the aircraft to lose altitude because of the loss of vertical lift.* Adjust the pitch attitude as necessary by reference to the fuselage dot of the miniature aircraft relative to the horizon bar. After the turn is established, small pitch adjustments may be required to maintain the desired altitude because of pitch errors in the attitude indicator as a result of precession.

When rolling out of a turn, anticipate a tendency for the aircraft to gain altitude. This results from a combination of an increase in the vertical component of lift and a failure to compensate for trim or back pressure used during the turn. Therefore, be aware of these factors, anticipate their effects, and monitor the pitch attitude during the roll-out in the same manner as during the roll-in.

NOTE: Banking an aircraft in a level turn does not by itself produce a change in the *amount* of lift. However, the division of lift into horizontal and vertical components reduces the amount of lift supporting the weight of the aircraft. Consequently, the reduced vertical component results in the loss of altitude unless the total lift is increased by: (1) increasing the angle of attack of the wing, (2) increasing the airspeed, or (3) increasing the angle of attack and airspeed in combination. Assuming a level turn with no change in thrust, you increase the angle of attack by raising the nose until the vertical component of lift is equal to the weight. The greater the angle of bank, the weaker the vertical lift component; and the greater the angle of attack for the lift/weight balance necessary to maintain a level turn.

(2) *Airspeed Control*

The power control techniques for maintaining an airspeed during a turn are similar to those used during straight and level flight. Anticipate a tendency for the aircraft to lose airspeed in a turn. This is caused by induced drag resulting from the increased pitch attitude required to compensate for loss of vertical lift.* The increased drag will require additional power to maintain airspeed during a turn. The additional power required will be less at high true airspeeds than at low true airspeeds. If pilot response to this power change is slow, the airspeed may decrease rapidly to the point where a descent is required to regain the desired airspeeds. Therefore, at low airspeeds, it may be desirable to add an estimated amount of power as the turn is established rather than waiting for the first indication of a loss in airspeed. Accomplish changes of airspeed during a turn as described under straight and level flight.

NOTE: As the pilot raises the nose of the aircraft to increase the lift in a level turn, the drag increases directly in proportion to the increase in angle of attack. The resulting decrease in airspeed is, therefore, proportional to the angle of bank. If a pilot wishes to maintain constant airspeed in a level turn, he must add power in proportion to the angle of bank used.

(3) *Steep Turns*

A steep turn is considered to be a turn in which the angle of bank used is larger than that required for normal instrument flying. For most light aircraft, 20 degrees is the normal angle of bank used because of the ease of control and precision afforded. Entry into a steep turn is accomplished in the same way as for a normal turn. As the bank is increased past normal, greater loss of vertical lift occurs which requires more pitch adjustment. The use of trim in steep turns varies with individual aircraft characteristics and pilot technique. Additional power is required to maintain airspeed as the bank is increased.*

During the steep turn, pitch and power control are maintained in the same way as in a normal turn; however, larger pitch adjustments will be required for a given altitude deviation. Varying the angle of bank during the turn makes pitch control more difficult. Give sufficient attention to the bank (sky) pointer to maintain the bank constant. Precession error in the attitude indicator is more prevalent during steep turns. If altitude loss becomes excessive, reduce the angle of bank as necessary to regain positive pitch control.

When rolling out of a steep turn the pilot should be alert to correct for the more than normal back trim, pitch attitude, and power used during the turn. Roll out at the same rate used in normal turns. The performance instruments must be cross-checked closely during roll-out, since the attitude indicator may have considerable precession error.

NOTE: As the bank steepens, the horizontal lift component increases, centrifugal force increases, and the load factor (ratio of the aerodynamic load on the wing to the total weight of the aircraft) increases. In level flight (in undisturbed air) the load factor is 1; the wings are supporting only the weight of the airplane. In a coordinated level turn with a 60 degree bank, the wings are supporting a load equal to twice the weight of the aircraft (load factor of 2). To provide the lift to balance this load, the angle of attack must be increased. However, if the load factor becomes so great that an increase in angle of attack cannot provide enough lift to support the load, the wing stalls. Since the stalling speed increases directly with the square root of the load factor, you should be aware of the flight conditions during which the load factor can become critical. Steep turns at low airspeed, structural ice accumulation, and vertical gusts in turbulent air can increase the load factor to a critical level.

(4) *Timed turns and use of the Magnetic Compass*

Heading indicator (D.G.) failure may require use of the magnetic compass for heading information. Remember, that this instrument provides reliable information only during straight and level, and unaccelerated flight. Because of this limitation, timed turns are recommended when making heading changes by reference to the magnetic compass.

A timed turn is accomplished by establishing a bank attitude on the attitude indicator which will result in a desired rate of turn as shown by the turn needle (or turn coordinator). The turn needle indicates rate of turn in degrees per second. The rate of turn per needle width depends on whether the instrument is a two-minute or four-minute turn indicator.

The standard rate of turn with a two-minute indicator is 3 degrees per second and a 360 degree turn requires two minutes to complete. The rate of turn with a four-minute indicator is 1½ degrees per second and a 360 degree turn requires four minutes to complete. The maximum rate of turn indication on either instrument is slightly more than 3 degrees per second and is limited by mechanical stops within the gyro assembly.

The heading change is accomplished by *maintaining* the desired rate of turn for a predetermined time.[1] Timing should be started when control pressures are applied to begin the turn. Control pressures should be applied to roll out when the time has elapsed.[2] As an example, assume that a 60 degree heading change is desired using a two-minute turn needle. In this case, 20 seconds should elapse from the time control pressures are applied to enter the turn until control pressures are applied to roll out.

NOTE 1: To maintain a turn at a constant rate, the angle of bank must be varied with changes in airspeed. As airspeed is increased (decreased) in a constant-rate level turn, both the radius of the turn and centrifugal force increase (decrease). This increase (decrease) in centrifugal force must be balanced by an increase (decrease) in the horizontal lift component, which can be accomplished only by increasing (decreasing) the angle of bank. The angle of bank required to sustain a standard rate turn (3 degrees/sec) may be approximated by dividing the aircraft's airspeed by 10 and adding 5. **Example:** a 150 mph aircraft would require a 20 degree bank for a standard rate turn.

NOTE 2: Low Vacuum causes the needle deflections to be less because the slower rotating gyro transmits less precessive force. *High Vacuum* causes the needle deflections to be greater because the faster rotating gyro transmits more precessive force. Remember, if the rotor speed is LESS, the time required for a given 180 or 360 degree standard rate turn will be LESS. If the rotor speed is MORE, the time required will be MORE.

Although timed turns are preferred when using the magnetic compass as a heading reference, an alternate method may be used. Turns to headings can be made by applying control pressures to roll out of a turn when reaching a predetermined "lead" point on the compass. When using the compass in this manner, the aircraft's angle of bank should not exceed 15 degrees in order to minimize magnetic dip error. Learning to fly by the compass is largely a matter of learning how to compensate for this error when turning to specific headings. Magnetic dip consists of two errors: the northerly (southerly) turn error and acceleration (deceleration) error. *Both* of these errors may be remembered and corrected for in-flight by memorizing the word "ANDS"... which has two separate meanings depending upon which error it is applied to:

(a) *Northerly (Southerly) Turn Error* is most apparent on headings of north and south. When the aircraft is banked, the compass card also banks. While the card is in this banked attitude in northern latitudes, the vertical component of the earth's magnetic field causes the north-seeking end of the compass to dip to the low side of the turn, giving the pilot an erroneous turn indication. In a turn from a heading of north, the compass card briefly indicates a turn in the opposite direction before reversing itself to indicate a turn in the proper direction which *lags* the actual turn until the aircraft approaches a heading of east or west. In a turn from a heading of south, the compass card indicates a turn in the proper direction, but the rate of turn indicated *leads* the actual turn until the aircraft approaches a heading of east or west.

To correct for northerly turn error when turning to north or south remember the word ANDS . . . *anticipate* north, *delay* south! To roll out on north from west, for instance, the pilot would anticipate north by the number of degrees of his north latitude, which in St. Louis, Missouri, is approximately 30 degrees and roll out on 330 degrees plus or minus his rollout lead.* To roll out on south, he would delay his rollout until reaching 150 degrees.* Since northerly turn error does not affect the cardinal headings of east and west, a pilot wishing to fly these headings would turn to them directly without any correction.

NOTE: When using the magnetic compass to turn to a heading of north, begin your rollout in advance of north by a number of degrees equal to your latitude plus (+) 50% of your bank angle. **Example**: at 30 degrees north latitude and 15 degrees of bank, start your rollout 37 degrees in advance of north (037 degree or 323 degree heading). When turning to a heading of south, delay your rollout until past south by a number of degrees equal to your latitude minus (−) 50% of your bank. **Example**: at 20 degrees north latitude and 18 degrees of bank, start your rollout 11 degrees past your desired heading of south (191 degree or 169 degree heading).

(b) *Acceleration Error* is also the result of the vertical component of the earth's magnetic field. Because of its pendulous mounting, the compass card tilts during changes of speed. This deflection of the card from the horizontal results in an error which is most apparent on headings of east and west. Remember the word ANDS again . . . *accelerate* north, *decelerate* south! When an aircraft in the northern hemisphere accelerates on a heading of east or west, the compass indicates a turn to the north; when the aircraft decelerates, the compass indicates a turn to the south.

3.   **Coordination of Rudder and Aileron Controls**

Coordination has a very specific meaning as applied to instrument flight techniques. It means using the controls to maintain or establish various conditions of flight with: (1) a minimum disturbance of the forces maintaining equilibrium, or (2) the control action necessary to effect the smoothest changes in equilibrium. A controlled slip or skid,* for example, requires considerable muscular coordination; the resultant slip or skid, however, is not a coordinated maneuver in the aerodynamic sense.

*NOTE: A SKID is caused by using excessive "bottom" rudder in a turn. A skidding turn is characterized by a rate of turn which is too great for the angle of bank. A SLIP is caused by using excessive "top" rudder in a turn. A slipping turn is characterized by a rate of turn which is insufficient for the angle of bank (angle of bank is too great).

Coordination of controls during flight by reference to instruments requires that the ball of the turn-and-slip indicator be kept centered, and that available trim control devices be used whenever a change in flight condition disturbs the existing trim. Development of coordinated control technique depends not only on a pilot's understanding of the foregoing aerodynamic considerations, but on his attention to the characteristics of the particular type of aircraft in which he trained.

Control sensitivites vary considerably in different aircraft and in a given aircraft at various speeds. From experience, a pilot learns that one aircraft is extremely sensitive on rudder control and perhaps noticeably resistant to movement of elevator control; another aircraft has less than normal lateral stability and tends to overbank; another responds to thrust and drag changes unlike other aircraft. His application of control pressures must be adapted to each airplane he flies.

Knowing why the aircraft will respond to his control will accelerate a pilot's progress in acquiring competent instrument flying techniques.

Sample Problems

1. Your aircraft, equipped with a *fixed pitch* propeller, is trimmed for straight and level flight at 100 mph with the power set at 2400 rpm. If you dive the aircraft to 140 mph and then return immediately to straight and level flight without retrimming it for the new increased airspeed, or changing the power, then:

    a. Will the airplane's nose attitude increase or decrease when you release the controls?

    b. What effect will the additional airspeed have (if any) upon the rpm?

2. Your aircraft, equipped with a *constant speed* propeller, is trimmed for straight and level flight at 150 mph with the power set at 2400 rpm. If you climb the aircraft to reduce the speed to 90 mph without changing the power and then return to straight and level flight without retrimming it for its new decreased airspeed then:

    a. Will the nose attitude increase or decrease when you release the controls?

b.   What effect will the reduced airspeed have (if any) upon the rpm?

3.   In question number 2, if you did not retrim the controls after achieving the lower airspeed, but instead held the aircraft straight and level with "muscle power" then:

a.   Would the airspeed remain constant, decrease or increase?

b.   If the airspeed changes, then at what speed do you expect it to restabilize?

c.   If you quickly retrim the aircraft at the lower airspeed without changing the power, then release the controls again, what will happen to the aircraft's pitch attitude?

4.   a.   What is "angle of attack?"

b.   What is a "stall" and how is it caused?

5.   What are the four fundamental instrument flight maneuvers?

6.   If you increase the power while in straight and level flight and hold the airspeed constant, the aircraft will _____; if you decrease the power while holding the airspeed constant, the aircraft will _____.

a.   Descend; climb

b.   Climb; descend

7.   Power plus attitude equals _____, and airspeed plus power equals _____.

a.   Airspeed; rate of climb or descent

b.   Rate of climb or descent; altitude

c.   Altitude; rate of climb

8.   The proper recovery sequence for a high airspeed unusual attitude is _____, _____, _____, and the recovery sequence for a low airspeed unusual attitude is _____, _____, _____.

    a.   Power, pitch, bank/bank, pitch, power
    b.   Bank, power, pitch/pitch, power, bank
    c.   Power, bank, pitch/pitch, bank, power

Answers

    1.   a.   Increase
         b.   The rpm will increase and probably ap-
              proach the "red line" unless the power is
              reduced.

    2.   a.   Decrease
         b.   None . . . the rpm will remain unchanged.

    3.   a.   Increase
         b.   150 mph
         c.   The nose attitude will increase as the air-
              speed increases and attempts to restabilize
              at its former value.

    4.   a.   "Angle of attack" is the acute angle mea-
              sured between the chord line (hypothetical
              line between the leading and trailing edges
              of a wing to measure its width) and the
              relative wind (motion of the air relative to
              the chord line).

         b.   A "stall" is the result of any condition
              that disrupts the smooth flow of air over
              the airfoil to the point where sufficient
              lift is no longer produced by the differ-
              ential pressure. The wing can stall at any
              attitude and at any speed. As the angle of
              attack of the wing is increased, the air
              particles are forced to make sharper and
              sharper changes in direction to follow the
              contour of the wing. With increasing
              angles of attack, disruption of smooth air-
              flow occurs initially at the trailing edge
              and moves forward toward the leading
              edge at higher angles of attack. The wing
              stalls when the progressive increase in tur-

bulence on the top cambered (curved) surface results in a net loss of lift.

5.   Straight and level, climb, descent and turn.*

6.   b.

7.   a.

8.   c.

NOTE: Know the "primary" and "supporting" instruments for these four fundamental maneuvers and for the transitions to them from straight and level flight!

B.   **THE CONTROL AND PERFORMANCE CONCEPT**

1.   "Attitude Instrument Flying" (Chapter 7, AF Manual 51-37: *Instrument Flying*) follows on pages 141 thru 149.

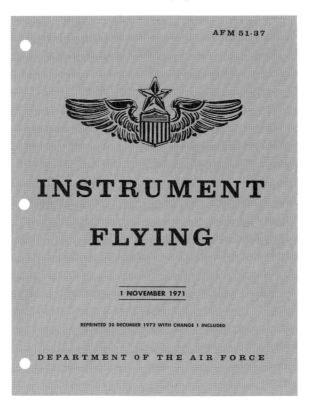

Attitude Instrument Flying

Figure 7-1
Attitude Instrument Flying

Aircraft performance is achieved by controlling the aircraft attitude and power (angle of attack and thrust/drag relationship). Aircraft attitude is the relationship of the longitudinal and lateral axes to the earth's horizon. An aircraft is flown in instrument flight by controlling the attitude and power as necessary to produce the desired performance. This is known as the *Control and Performance Concept* of attitude instrument flying and can be applied to any basic instrument maneuver.

This chapter discusses the procedures and techniques used in the *Control and Performance Concept* of attitude instrument flying. The procedures and techniques for accomplishing specific maneuvers are discussed in Chapter 8.

NOTE FOR HELICOPTER PILOTS: The procedural steps of the Control and Performance Concept apply to helicopters for all instrument maneuvers, however collective (power) controls altitude or rate of altitude change and cyclic (attitude) controls airspeed.

INSTRUMENT CATEGORIES

Instruments can be divided into three general categories.

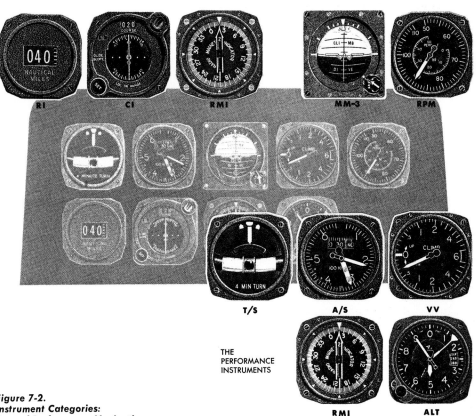

THE
PERFORMANCE
INSTRUMENTS

Figure 7-2.
Instrument Categories:
Control-Performance-Navigation

Control Instruments

Control instruments display attitude and power indications and are
calibrated to permit attitude and power adjustments in definite amounts. The
more common attitude indicators are discussed in Chapter 4. In this manual
the term *power* is used to replace the more technically correct term thrust/
drag relationship. Power is controlled by reference to the power indicator(s).
These vary with aircraft and may include tachometers, exhaust total pressure
gages, exhaust pressure ratio, manifold pressure, etc. For angle of attack
control, see Chapter 6.

Performance Instruments

Performance instruments indicate the aircraft actual performance. Performance is determined by reference to the altimeter, airspeed/Mach indicator, vertical velocity indicator, heading indicator, angle of attack indicator, and turn and slip indicator. These instruments indicate the aircraft performance regardless of whether the pilot is referring to the earth's horizon, the attitude indicator, or both, to control the aircraft attitude.

Navigation Instruments

Navigation instruments indicate the position of the aircraft in relation to a selected navigational facility. This group of instruments includes various types of course indicators, range indicators, glide slope indicators, and bearing pointers. Since this chapter is concerned with basic aircraft control and not with the aircraft position over the ground, navigational instruments are discussed in later chapters.

CONTROL AND PERFORMANCE CONCEPT

Procedural Steps:————————————————————————————

1. **ESTABLISH AN ATTITUDE AND/OR POWER SETTING ON THE CONTROL INSTRUMENT(S) which should result in the desired performance.**

2. **TRIM until control pressures are neutralized.**

3. **CROSSCHECK THE PERFORMANCE INSTRUMENTS to determine if the established attitude and/or power setting are providing the desired performance.**

4. **ADJUST THE ATTITUDE AND POWER SETTING ON THE CONTROL INSTRUMENTS if a correction is necessary.**

Attitude and/or Power Control

Proper control of aircraft attitude is the result of maintaining a constant attitude, knowing when and how much to change the attitude, and smoothly changing the attitude a definite amount. Aircraft attitude control is accomplished by proper use of the attitude indicator. The attitude indicator provides an immediate, direct, and corresponding indication of any change in aircraft pitch or bank attitude. In addition, by means of the attitude indicator, small pitch and bank changes are easily seen and changes can be readily accomplished.

PITCH CONTROL.   Pitch changes are accomplished by changing the "pitch attitude" of the miniature aircraft or fuselage dot definite amounts in relation to the horizon bar. These changes are referred to as bar widths or fractions thereof, or degrees depending upon the type of attitude indicator. A bar width is approximately 2° on most attitude indicators. The amount of deviation from the desired performance will determine the magnitude of the correction necessary.

BANK CONTROL.   Bank changes are accomplished by changing the "bank attitude" or bank pointer(s) definite amounts in relation to the bank scale. Normally, the bank scale is graduated at 0, 10, 20, 30, 60 and 90 degrees and may be located at the top or bottom of the attitude indicator. Normally an angle of bank which approximates the degrees to be turned, not to exceed 30°, is used in instrument flight. TAS and the desired rate of turn are factors to consider.

POWER CONTROL.   Proper power control results from the ability to smoothly establish or maintain desired airspeeds in coordination with attitude control changes. Power changes are accomplished by throttle(s) adjustment and reference to the power indicators. Power indications are not affected by such factors as turbulence, improper trim, or inadvertent control pressures. Therefore, little attention is required to insure that the power indication remains constant, once it is established.

A pilot knows, from experience in an aircraft, approximately how far to move the throttle(s) to change the power a given amount for precise airspeed control. Therefore, he can make power changes primarily by throttle movement, giving a minimum of attention to the power instruments. A knowledge of approximate power settings for various flight conditions will help prevent overcontrolling power.

........TO TRIM

• Apply control pressure
  to maintain desired
  attitude.

• Adjust trim until the
  control pressure is
  relieved.

Figure 7-6.
Trim Technique

Trim Technique

The aircraft is correctly trimmed when it is maintaining a desired attitude with all control pressures neutralized. Proper trim technique is essential for smooth and precise aircraft control during all phases of flight. By relieving all control pressures, the pilot will find that it is much easier to hold a given attitude constant. Also, more attention can be devoted to the navigation instruments and additional cockpit duties.

An aircraft is placed in trim by applying control pressure(s) to establish a desired attitude and then adjusting the trim so that the aircraft will maintain that attitude when the flight controls are released. Trim the aircraft for coordinated flight by centering the ball of the turn and slip indicator. Accomplish this by using rudder trim in the direction the ball is displaced from center. Differential power control on multi-engine aircraft is an additional factor affecting coordinated flight. Use balanced power/thrust, when possible, to aid in maintaining coordinated flight.

Changes in attitude, power, or configuration may require a trim adjustment. Independent use of trim to estabish a change in aircraft attitude invariably leads to erratic aircraft control. Smooth and precise attitude changes are best attained by a combination of control pressures and trim adjustments. The trim controls, correctly used, are aids to smooth aircraft control.

Cross-Check Technique

The control and performance concept of attitude instrument flying requires the pilot to establish an aircraft attitude and/or power setting on the control instruments which should result in the desired aircraft performance. Therefore, the pilot must be able to recognize *when* a change in attitude and/or power is required. By cross-checking the instruments properly, the pilot can determine the magnitude and direction of adjustment required to achieve the desired performance.

Cross-checking is the proper division of attention and interpretation of the flight instruments. Attention must be efficiently divided between the control and performance instruments in a sequence that insures comprehensive coverage of the flight instruments. Looking at each of the instruments at the right time is of no value unless the pilot interprets what he sees. Therefore, *proper division of attention* and *interpretation* are the two essential parts of a cross-check.

Cross-check techniques or the sequence for checking the instruments vary among pilots and throughout various phases of flight. The pilot should

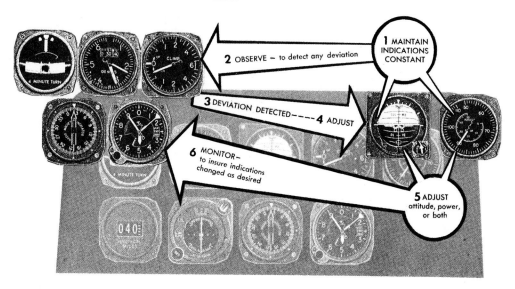

Figure 7-7.
Instrument
Cross-Check
Technique

become familiar with the factors to be considered in dividing his attention properly. He should also know the symptoms which enable him to recognize correct and incorrect cross-check technique.

FACTORS INFLUENCING INSTRUMENT CROSS-CHECKS. A factor influencing cross-check technique is the *characteristic manner in which instruments respond* to changes of attitude and/or power. The control instruments provide direct and immediate indications of attitude and/or power changes. Changes in the indications on the performance instruments will lag slightly behind changes of attitude and/or power. This lag is due to inertia of the aircraft and the operating principles and mechanisms of the performance instruments. Therefore, some lag must be accepted as an inherent factor. This factor will not appreciably affect the tolerances within which the pilot controls the aircraft; however, at times a slight unavoidable delay in knowing the results of attitude and/or power changes will occur.

Lag in the performance instruments should not interfere with maintaining or smoothly changing the attitude and/or power indications. When the attitude and power are properly controlled, the lag factor is negligible and the indications on the performance instruments will stabilize or change smoothly. The pilot must not be lured into making a flight control movement in direct response to the lag in the indications on the performance instruments without first referring to the control instruments. If permitted, such action invariably leads to erratic aircraft control and will cause additional fluctuations and lag in the performance instruments. Sufficient reference to the control instruments will minimize the effect of lag on the performance instruments, nullify the tendency to "chase" performance instrument indications, and result in smooth aircraft control.

Another factor influencing cross-check technique is the *location of the flight instruments.* In some aircraft the flight instruments are scattered over a wide area of the instrument panel. The pilot is unable to bring several instruments into his cross-check at the same time. He must rapidly scan each instrument individually back and forth across the instrument panel. More

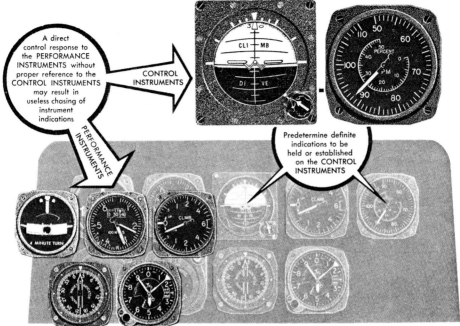

A direct control response to the PERFORMANCE INSTRUMENTS without proper reference to the CONTROL INSTRUMENTS may result in useless chasing of instrument indications

CONTROL INSTRUMENTS

PERFORMANCE INSTRUMENTS

Predetermine definite indications to be held or established on the CONTROL INSTRUMENTS

Figure 7-8.
Factors Influencing
Cross-Check
Techniques

advanced instrument systems such as the flight director and integrated flight instrument systems have reduced the division of attention to a small area. The pilot can see more of the flight instruments with one look. The task of cross-checking the instruments is much easier because the pilot can simultaneously observe the attitude indicator and the proper performance instruments.

An important factor influencing cross-check technique is the *ability of the pilot*. All pilots do not interpret instrument presentations with the same speed. Some pilots are faster than others in understanding and evaluating what they see. One reason for this is that the natural ability of pilots varies. Another reason is that the experience level of pilots differs. The pilot who is experienced and flies regularly will probably interpret his instruments more quickly than the inexperienced pilot who flies only occasionally. The pilot who interprets his instruments quickly and correctly does not have to refer back to them for information as often as the pilot who is slow to interpret. Also, he is able to bring several instruments into his cross-check with one glance, interpreting them simultaneously. Therefore, the speed with which he divides his attention does not have to be as rapid as the pilot with less ability, who must scan the instruments rapidly to stay ahead of the aircraft.

The attitude indicator is the only instrument which the pilot should observe continuously for any appreciable length of time. Approximately 10 seconds may be needed to accomplish an attitude change required for a normal turn. During this 10-second period, the pilot may need to devote his attention almost exclusively to the attitude indicator to insure good attitude control. The attitude indicator is also the instrument that he should observe the greatest number of times. This is shown by the following description of a normal cross-check. A pilot glances from the attitude indicator to a performance instrument; back to the attitude indicator; then a glance at another performance instrument; back to the attitude indicator, and so forth. This cross-check technique can be compared to a wagon wheel. The hub represents the attitude indicator and the spokes represent the performance instruments.

This example of a normal cross-check does not mean that it is the only method of cross-checking. Often a pilot must compare the indications of one performance instrument against another before knowing *when* or *how much* to adjust the attitude and/or power. An effective cross-check technique may require that attention to the attitude indicator be inserted between glances at the performance instruments being compared. Preponderance of attention to the attitude indicator is normal and desirable to keep the fluctuations and lag indications of the performance instruments to a minimum. This technique permits the pilot to read any one performance instrument during a split-second glance and results in smooth and precise aircraft control.

A proper and relative amount of attention must be given to each performance instrument. Pilots seldom fail to observe the one performance instrument whose indication is most important. The reverse is a common error. Pilots often devote so much attention to one performance instrument that the others are omitted from the cross-check. Also, they often fail to cross-check the attitude indicator for proper aircraft control.

CROSS-CHECK ANALYSIS. A correct or incorrect cross-check can be recognized by analyzing certain symptoms of aircraft control. Symptoms of insufficient reference to the control instruments are readily recognizable. If the pilot does not have some definite attitude and power indications in mind that should be maintained or established and the other instruments fluctuate erratically through the desired indications, then the pilot is not referring sufficiently to the control instruments. This is usually accompanied by a lack of precise aircraft control ("chasing" the indications) and a feeling of ineffectiveness and insecurity by the pilot.

Sufficient reference to the attitude indicator can be easily determined. If the pilot has in mind definite pitch and bank attitudes that are to be held constant or changed, he is referring to the attitude indicator sufficiently.

Except for fixation on the power indicators, the problem of too much attention being devoted to the control instruments is rarely encountered. This is normally caused by the pilot's desire to maintain the performance indications within close tolerances. Too much attention to the control instruments can be recognized by the following symptoms. If the pilot has a smooth, positive, and continuous control over the indications of the control instruments but large deviations are observed to occur slowly on the performance instruments, a closer cross-check of the performance instruments is required.

An incorrect cross-check can result in the omission of or insufficient reference to one or more instruments during the scanning process. Pilots are inclined to omit some performance instrument(s) from the cross-check, although other performance instruments and the control instruments are being properly observed. For example, during a climb or descent, a pilot may become so engrossed with pitch attitude control that he fails to observe an error in aircraft heading.

The indications on some instruments are not as "eye-catching" as those on other instruments. For example, a 4-degree heading change is not as "eye-catching" as a 300 to 400 feet-per-minute change on the vertical velocity indicator. Through deliberate effort and proper habit, the pilot must insure that *all* the instruments are included in his cross-check. If this is accomplished, he should observe deviations on the performance instruments in their early stages.

Analysis of the cross-check technique will assist the pilot in recognizing a correct or incorrect cross-check. A correct cross-check results in the continuous interpretation of the flight instruments which enables the pilot to maintain proper aircraft control at all times. Remember, rapidly looking from one instrument to another without interpretation is of no value. Instrument systems and the location of the flight instruments vary. Pilot ability also varies. Therefore, each pilot should develop his own rate and technique of checking the instruments which will insure a continuous and correct interpretation of the flight instruments.

Adjusting Attitude and Power

As previously stated, the control and performance concept of attitude instrument flying requires the adjustment of aircraft attitude and power to achieve the desired performance. A change of aircraft attitude and/or power is required when any indication other than that desired is observed on the performance instruments. However, it is equally important for the pilot to know *what to change* and *how much* pitch, bank, or power change is required.

WHAT TO CHANGE. The pilot knows what to change by understanding which control instrument to adjust to achieve the desired indications on the performance instruments. Pitch attitude control is used primarily to maintain an altitude or to control the rate of climb or descent. Pitch attitude control may be used to maintain airspeed during maneuvers requiring a fixed power setting. Bank attitude control is used to maintain a heading or a desired angle of bank during turns. Power control is used for maintaining or changing the airspeed except for maneuvers using a fixed power setting; for example, full power for a prolonged climb.

HOW MUCH TO CHANGE. How much to adjust the attitude and/or power is, initially, an estimate based on familiarity with the aircraft and the amount the pilot desires to change the indications on the performance instruments. After making a change of attitude and/or power, he should observe the performance instruments to see if the desired change occurred. If not, further adjustment of attitude and/or power is required.

Therefore, instrument flight is a continuous process of:

1. ESTABLISHING AN ATTITUDE AND/OR POWER SETTING ON THE CONTROL INSTRUMENT(S)

2. TRIMMING

3. CROSS-CHECKING

4. ADJUSTING

These procedural steps can be applied to any basic instrument maneuver and should result in more precise attitude instrument flying.

2.   **The "Scan Patterns" Chart (Chapter 5, AC 61-27C:** *Instrument Flying Handbook)*

The "Scan Patterns" Chart that follows identifies the primary and supporting "control and performance" instruments during the different basic flight maneuvers presented in Section A. This chart may at first appear confusing unless one considers that a primary instrument is an "objective" or goal instrument which informs the pilot whether or not a specific pitch, bank or power adjustment IS NECESSARY.* Since the control instruments (artificial horizon and manifold pressure/rpm gage) are adjusted to achieve the desired indications on the performance instruments (altimeter, airspeed, vertical speed, turn and slip and directional gyro), the performance instruments are generally primary . . . they display the aircraft's performance objective! The control instruments, which are calibrated to permit attitude and power adjustments in definite amounts, do not normally display the aircraft's performance objective and are usually considered supporting instruments. The altimeter, for example, (primary pitch in a level turn), will inform a pilot whether he is higher or lower than his assigned altitude (performance objective) during the turn, but the artificial horizon (supporting pitch), which is utilized to correct the nose high or low condition, will *not* inform him when he was corrected back to his proper altitude. The pilot who habitually identifies the performance objectives of each flight maneuver will develop a very effective scan pattern and will be able to efficiently divide his attention among the appropriate instruments as necessary in order to stay "ahead" of his aircraft.

NOTE: It is difficult to assign different functions to each flight control because they are so interrelated; i.e., power and attitude are both capable of changing altitude and airspeed. However, if after cross-checking the instruments and interpreting their indications you determine that an adjustment with the flight controls is necessary then remember that, generally speaking, *power controls* altitude but only *adjusts* airspeed and attitude. Likewise, elevators *control* airspeed but can only *adjust* altitude.

SCAN PATTERNS

	Primary Pitch	Supporting Pitch	Primary Bank	Supporting Bank	Primary Power
Straight and Level Normal Cruise	Altimeter	Airspeed Vert. Speed Art. Horizon	D.G.	Art. Horizon	Airspeed
Climb Entry and Descent Entry	Art. Horizon	Altimeter Airspeed	D.G.	Art. Horizon Turn and Slip	Tach or MP (throttle set)
Stabilized Climb Constant Airspeed	Airspeed	Vertical Speed Art. Horizon	D.G.	Art. Horizon Turn and Slip	Tach or MP (throttle set)
Stabilized Climb Constant Rate	Vert. Speed	Art. Horizon Altimeter	D.G.	Art. Horizon Turn and Slip	Airspeed
Climb Level Off and Descent Level Off	Altimeter	Vert. Speed Art. Horizon	D.G.	Art. Horizon Turn and Slip	Airspeed
Stabilized Descent Constant Airspeed	Airspeed	Vert. Speed Art. Horizon	D.G.	Art. Horizon Turn and Slip	Tach or MP (throttle set)
Stabilized Descent Constant Rate	Vert. Speed	Art. Horizon Altimeter	D.G.	Art. Horizon Turn and Slip	Airspeed
Entry and Roll Out of a Level Turn	Altimeter	Vert. Speed Art. Horizon	Art. Horizon	D.G. Turn and Slip	Airspeed
Turns with a Stated Degree of Rate	Altimeter	Vert. Speed Art. Horizon Airspeed	Turn and Slip	Art. Horizon D.G.	Airspeed
Turns with a Stated Degree of Bank	Altimeter	Vert. Speed Art. Horizon Airspeed	Art. Horizon	Turn and Slip D.G.	Airspeed

Sample Problems

1. During straight and level flight, while attempting to hold constant heading, airspeed and altitude, the instrument which is primary for:

    a.   Pitch is airspeed;
         Bank is heading indicator;
         Power is altimeter.

    b.   Pitch is altimeter;
         Bank is heading indicator;
         Power is airspeed.

    c.   Pitch is attitude indicator;
         Bank is turn indicator;
         Power is airspeed.

    d.   Pitch is airspeed;
         Bank is attitude indicator;
         Power is tachometer or manifold pressure.

2. During a standard rate turn in level flight at a constant airspeed, the instrument that is primary for:

    a.   Pitch is the altimeter;
         Bank is the attitude indicator;
         Power is the airspeed.

    b.   Pitch is the altimeter;
         Bank is the turn indicator;
         Power is the airspeed.

    c.   Pitch is the airspeed indicator;
         Bank is the turn indicator;
         Power is the altimeter.

    d.   Pitch is the airspeed;
         Bank is the attitude indicator;
         Power is the altimeter.

3. During a rate climb in a standard rate turn, the instrument which is primary for:

    a.   Pitch is the airspeed indicator;

        Bank is the turn indicator;
        Pitch is the vertical speed indicator.

b.   Pitch is the attitude indicator;
        Bank is the turn indicator;
        Power is the airspeed indicator.

c.   Pitch is the vertical speed indicator;
        Bank is the turn indicator;
        Power is the airspeed indicator.

d.   Pitch is the vertical speed indicator;
        Bank is the attitude indicator;
        Power is the tachometer or manifold pressure.

4.   The fundamental skills in attitude flying and the sequence in which they are normally used are:

a.   Instrument cross-check;
        Instrument interpretation;
        Proper trim procedures.

b.   Instrument cross-check;
        Proper trim technique;
        Aircraft control.

c.   Instrument interpretation;
        Proper trim procedures;
        Aircraft control.

d.   Instrument cross-check;
        Instrument interpretation;
        Aircraft control.

5.   The "control instruments" are generally primary because they most frequently display the aircraft's performance objective.

a.   True

b.   False

6.   When a pitch error is detected, corrective action should be taken with two distinct changes of attitude: *First* is a change of attitude to

stop the needle movement, *second* is a change of attitude to return to the desired altitude.

a.   True

b.   False

7.   If the airspeed is off the desired value, always check the _____ before deciding that a power change is necessary.

a.   Altimeter

b.   Artificial horizon

c.   Vertical speed

8.   Power control is used when interpretation of the flight instruments indicates a need for a change in *thrust.*

a.   True

b.   False

Answers

1.	b.	5.	b.
2.	b.	6.	a.
3.	c.	7.	a.
4.	d.	8.	a.

Chapter X
INSTRUMENT RECURRENT TRAINING

The Instrument Recurrent Training Schedule (Section A) is arranged to keep an instrument rated pilot current on normal and emergency instrument procedures. This includes both aircraft control procedures and navigation/approach procedures. If the instrument pilot is multi-engine rated, simulated engine failures should be included during appropriate maneuvers.

This schedule assumes that the pilot is reasonably current on the material covered. If not, additional lessons may be necessary. It consists of six (6) lessons, one lesson each month for six (6) months. At the end of the six month period, the schedule is repeated, thus rotating through all the material every six (6) months. Each lesson will consist of approximately thirty (30) minutes ground briefing and one (1) hour and thirty (30) minutes instrument time in either a simulator or an airplane, alternating each lesson. This totals nine (9) hours instrument time each six (6) months, half of this will be in a simulator and half in an airplane.

The Instrument Refresher Quiz (Section B) is included to enable pilots to quickly assess their own operational knowledge of the various flight instruments. If either this quiz, or the oral preflight review of the instruments in the first lesson of the training schedule, indicate that additional familiarization with the flight instruments is necessary, then see Appendix C!

A.   INSTRUMENT RECURRENT TRAINING SCHEDULE

Lesson 1
Simulator   2.0 hours

Pre-Flight   .5 hour

1.   Flight instrument familiarization and review

2.   Attitude flying concepts (full and partial panel)

3.   Scanning procedure

In-Flight   1.5 hours

1.   Attitude control exercise (full and partial panel)
   a.   Level turns (D.G; clock)
   b.   Climbing turns
   c.   Descending turns
   d.   Steep turns
   e.   Slow flight (turns, climbs, descents)
   f.   Stalls
   g.   Unusual attitude recovery (student puts in attitude)

2.   VOR navigation
   a.   Tracking and course changes
   b.   Intercepts
   c.   Time-distance check

3.   ADF navigation
   a.   Tracking and course changes
   b.   Intercepts
   c.   Time-distance checks

Lesson 2
Airplane   2.0 hours

Pre-Flight .5 hour

    1.   Airplane performance and equipment knowledge

    2.   Review of the "V" speeds*

In-Flight   1.5 Hr.

    1.   Attitude control exercises (full and partial panel)

        a.   Level turns (D.G., compass, and clock)
        b.   Climbing turn
        c.   Descending turns
        d.   Steep turns
        e.   Slow flight (turns, climbs, descents)
        f.   Stalls
        g.   Unusual attitude recovery

    2.   VOR navigation

        a.   Tracking and course changes (full and partial panel)
        b.   Intercepts
        c.   Time-distance check

    3.   ADF navigation

        a.   Tracking and course changes
        b.   Intercepts
        c.   Time-distance check

NOTE: AIRCRAFT OPERATIONAL SPEEDS

V_a — design maneuvering speed	_____	kts
V_{fe} — maximum flap extended speed	_____	kts
V_{le} — maximum landing gear extended speed	_____	kts
V_{lo} — maximum landing gear operating speed	_____	kts
V_{ne} — never-exceed speed	_____	kts
V_s — minimum controllable airspeed/stall	_____	kts
V_{so} — power-off stalling speed in landing configuration	_____	kts
V_s^1 — power-off stalling speed in specified configuration	_____	kts
V_x — best angle of climb speed	_____	kts
V_y — best rate of climb speed	_____	kts

Lesson 3
Simulator   2.0 hours

Pre-Flight   .5 hour

   1.   Clearance procedures*

   2.   Holding procedures

   3.   Approach procedures

   4.   Mandatory reports

In-Flight   1.5 hours

   1.   Departure in accordance with simulated ATC clearance

   2.   Holding patterns at VOR and NDB facilities and intersections (full panel and partial panel)

   3.   VOR approach

   4.   NDB approach

> *NOTE:* Longer *simulated* clearances with more courses to inter-
> cept (and altitudes to observe) are good review exercises for instru-
> ment recurrent training. Copy the assigned clearance vertically
> down on your paper for easier in-flight interpretation/revision and
> divide it into its four component parts (clearance limit, route,
> altitude and special instructions) by drawing horizontal lines across
> the column with your pencil. When you analyze the clearance
> prior to take-off, annotate your intended direction of flight on
> each leg of the routing in the left-hand margin (next to the leg) by
> using one of the following abbreviations: IB = inbound, OB = out-
> bound, C = clockwise (for DME arcs) and CC = counterclockwise
> (see p. 110).

Lesson 4
Airplane   2.0 hours

Pre-Flight   .5 hour

  1. Airplane instruments,[1] systems and avionics[2]

  2. Lost communications procedures (FAR 91.127)

  3. Loss of navigational (nav) reception procedures

In-Flight   1.5 hours

  1. Departure in accordance with ATC clearance

  2. Holding patterns at VOR and NDB facilities and inter-sections (with loss of attitude indicator)

  3. VOR approach (with loss of VOR receiver)

  4. VOR-DME approach (with loss of DME receiver)

> *NOTE 1:* For a thorough in-flight review of the flight instruments remember the word SLEDS: **S**imilarity to the natural horizon
> **L**imits of the instrument
> **E**rrors of the instrument
> **D**emonstrate its use
> **S**tudent practice.

> *NOTE 2:* On some radios you can get 720 channels even though there are only five digits showing on the indicator! In 360 channel radios, with five digits in the display, the final digit is always "0" or "5." The frequency 133.72, for instance, is not assigned and cannot be selected by the pilot. However, on a 720 channel radio with display room for five digits, 133.72 can be selected, and when it is, the digit "5" is understood to follow the "2," so that the selected frequency is 133.725. If you can select only frequencies with "0" or "5" on the far right, then you have 360 channels; however, if you can select numbers with "2" or "7" on the right, then you have 720 channels and can assume a "5" to the right of the "2" or "7."

Flight Planning Log

	TC	WCA	TH	Var	MH	Dev.	CH	TO	Rte	VOR IDENT. FREQ.	RADIAL TO	RADIAL FROM	ALT	DISTANCE LEG REMAINING	TIME POINT–POINT CUMULATIVE	TIME TAKEOFF	TAS*	GS
Name:																		
A/C:								DEPARTURE POINT								ETA	EGS	
Date:								CHECK POINT								ATA	AGS	
MP/RPM*																		
TIME of T.O.																		
Time Enroute																		
ET/Dest																		
Weather																		
Fuel																		
GPH																		
Est Total Used (Gal):																		
Plus 45 min. (Gal):																		
Tot Consumption (Gal):																		
Available (Gal)																		
Reserve (Hrs.)								DESTINATION						TOTAL				
Winds Aloft																		
Dir Vel Alt								ALTERNATE										
To:																		
Then: / /								DESTINATION						TOTAL				

Departure Checklist

1. Engine Start Checklist
2. All Radios On
3. Copy ATIS
4. Set Gyros and Altimeter
5. VOT and ADF Test
6. Time Check
7. Clearance Delivery
8. Copy Clearance
9. Ground Control for Taxi
10. Nav Radios Set Up
    No. 1 First Fix
    No. 2 First Intersection
11. X-Ponder Code Set & DME Set
12. Engine Run-Up on Check List
13. Tower Control for Take-Off
14. Note Time on Flight Log
15. Reset Gyro

*EXPLANATION: SELECT DESIRED TAS FROM CRUISE PERFORMANCE CHART IN OWNER'S MANUAL. APPLY ACTUAL OAT AT ALTITUDE AND COMPUTE IAS. ADJUST RPM TO CONFORM. TAS REMAINS CONSTANT.

Lesson 5
Simulator   2.0 hours

Pre-Flight .5 hour

    1.   Flight planning and filing

    2.   Review mandatory reports

    3.   Precision approach procedures

In-Flight 1.5 hours

    1.   Departure in accordance with clearance (with loss of communications)

    2.   VOR-DME approaches (with loss of DME receiver)

    3.   ILS approach

NOTE: Refer to the following diagram to review the terminology used in the Flight Planning Log on p. 160:

$$\text{TC} - \pm\text{VAR} \rightarrow \text{MC} - \pm\text{DEV} \rightarrow \text{CC}$$
$$\downarrow \qquad\qquad \downarrow \qquad\qquad \downarrow$$
$$\pm\text{WCA} \qquad \pm\text{WCA} \qquad \pm\text{WCA}$$
$$\downarrow \qquad\qquad \downarrow \qquad\qquad \downarrow$$
$$\text{TH} - \pm\text{VAR} \rightarrow \text{MH} - \pm\text{DEV} \rightarrow \text{CH}$$

KEY TO NAVIGATIONAL TERMS:

TC   = True Course
WCA = Wind Correction Angle
TH   = True Heading
VAR = Variation
MH   = Magnetic Heading
DEV = Deviation
CH   = Compass Heading
MC   = Magnetic Course
CC   = Compass Course

Lesson 6
Airplane   2.0 hours

Pre-Flight   .5 hour

1. Local clearance procedures
2. Review lost communications procedure
3. Review loss of nav reception procedures
4. Review loss of nav reception procedures

In-Flight   1.5 hours

1. Departure in accordance with local ATC clearance (with loss of heading indicator, and attitude indicator if both are suction or electric)
2. Radar approach (no gyro)
3. NDB approaches (with loss of ADF receiver)
4. ILS approach

The Instrument Recurrent Training Schedule is reprinted with permission of Sawyer School of Aviation in Phoenix, Arizona.

B. REFRESHER QUIZ ON THE FUNDAMENTALS OF FLIGHT INSTRUMENT OPERATION (See Appendix C).

Problems

1. Name the sources of power for the gyro instruments.

2. What is the operating speed range of vacuum gyros?

3. How much suction (inches of mercury is needed to operate the turn indicator, the attitude indicator, and the heading indicator?

4. What is the result of a gyro turning at higher than normal operating speed?

5. Pitot pressure is:

    a.   Ram air pressure

    b.   Ambient air pressure

6. Static pressure is:

    a.   Ram air pressure

    b.   Ambient air pressure

7. Which of the following instruments use pitot pressure (more than one may be correct)?

    a.   Airspeed indicator

    b.   Altimeter

    c.   Vertical speed indicator

    d.   Turn and bank indicator

8. Which of the following instruments use static pressure (more than one may be correct)?

    a.   Airspeed indicator

    b.   Altimeter

    c.   Vertical speed indicator

    d.   Turn and bank indicator

9. Installation error which affects the indications of airspeed and altitude is caused by:

    a.   The location of the pitot tube head; the error gets larger as you increase altitude

    b.   The instrument not being calibrated properly at all altitudes

    c.   Rapid descent or climb; the error gets larger as you decrease altitude

    d.   Inaccurate sensing of static pressure

10. Temporary errors in static pressure sensing may be caused by:

    a.   Configuration changes

    b.   Angle of attack change

    c.   Both

11. Compressibility error, which causes the indicated airspeed on aircraft above 10,000 feet and over 200 knots calibrated airspeed (200 CAS) to read too HIGH, is caused by:

    a. Compression of air in the pitot tube
    b. Sending of erroneous static pressure
    c. Both

12. Generally, the factor that contributes most to the error existing between indicated and calibrated airspeed, is the:

    a. Angle between the pitot tube and the relative wind
    b. Location of the static ports
    c. Effects of compressibility and temperature
    d. Lag error of indicating mechanism

13. If your outside static port should become plugged and you select an alternate static source inside the cockpit, what instrument indications do you get?

14. For aircraft not equipped with a cockpit alternate static source, the pilot in an emergency may restore static pressure to the system by breaking the glass on the face of the:

    a. Airspeed indicator
    b. Vertical speed indicator
    c. Altimeter

15. A decrease in static pressure with pitot pressure remaining constant causes the airspeed indication to:

    a. Increase
    b. Decrease
    c. Remain the same

16. A decrease in pitot pressure with static pressure remaining constant causes the airspeed indication to:

    a. Increase
    b. Decrease
    c. Remain the same

17. An obstruction in the pitot tube would cause pitot pressure to be:

    a. Low
    b. High

18. An obstruction in the pitot tube would cause airspeed indicators to be:

    a. Low
    b. High

19. If the static ports were obstructed by masking tape, polish, etc., as you climbed, the airspeed would read:

    a. Low
    b. High
    c. Accurately

20. If the static ports iced over as you descended, the airspeed would read:

    a. High
    b. Low
    c. Accurately

21. Will increasing the altimeter setting in the "Kollsman window" of the altimeter cause the indicated altitude to increase or to decrease?

22. The setting in the barometric scale is 29.92". You are landing at an airfield where the altimeter setting is 29.57". If you forget to reset the altimeter, you will be:

    a. 350 feet higher than indicated
    b. 350 feet lower than indicated
    c. Altimeter setting has no effect on the indicated altitude

23. The altimeter measures the difference between the static pressure and the barometric scale setting. The altimeter displays this difference in relation to a standard atmosphere. For example, if 29.92" is set

in the barometric scale and 29.92" pressure is supplied to the static system, the altimeter indicates:

   a.   Zero
   b.   Field elevation

24. What determines the amount of acceleration or deceleration error?

   a.   Erection rate
   b.   Time period of acceleration, deceleration
   c.   Both a and b
   d.   None of the above

25. How is acceleration error displayed on the attitude indicator?

   a.   False nose high indication
   b.   False nose low indication
   c.   False bank to the left
   d.   False bank to the right

26. During takeoff, acceleration error would cause:

   a.   An erroneous nose high indication on the attitude indicator
   b.   The pilot to lower the aircraft's pitch attitude, if he maintained a constant pitch on the attitude indicator
   c.   Both a and b
   d.   Neither of the above

27. Which of the following statements are false?

   a.   A high altimeter setting (high surface pressure) means that the aircraft is higher than indicated
   b.   The pressure altimeter reads approximate true altitude if the current setting is maintained
   c.   True altitude may be computed in flight by correcting for flight level temperature

28. What does HALP mean?

29. If the turn needle is properly calibrated, it shows

the correct rate of turn REGARDLESS of the position of the ball (true or false)?

30. If a two-minute 360 degree standard rate turn takes one minute and forty five seconds to complete, is the gyro rotor speed too fast or too slow? Is the needle deflection greater or less?

Answers

1. Vacuum and electric

2. 10,000 to 18,000 rpm

3. 1.9", 4.0", 4.0"

4. It will be more sensitive (see Note p. 134)

5. a. Ram air pressure

6. b. Ambient air pressure

7. a. Airspeed indicator

8. a, b, and c

9. d. Inaccurate sensing of static pressure

10. c. Both

11. a. Compression of air in the pitot tube

12. b. Location of the static ports

13. All instruments show an increase as the static pressure in the aircraft is less

14. b. Vertical speed indicator

15. a. Increase

16. b. Decrease

17. and 18. a. Low. *Note:* A pitot blockage causes the indicated airspeed to decrease with a loss of altitude and to increase with a gain in altitude.

19. a. Low. *Note:* Low because static pressure is trapped at lower altitude and would be higher than actual static pressure

20. a. High. *Note:* High, because static pressure from a higher altitude would be trapped causing static pressure in the case to be low. This would allow diaphragm to expand more than it should, causing airspeed to read high.

21. Increase

22. b. 350 feet lower than indicated

23. a. Zero. *Note:* There is no measurable difference between the static pressure and the pressure selected for comparison by the barometric setting.

24. c. Both a and b

25. a. False nose high indication. Acceleration or deceleration does not affect the attitude display in bank (deceleration would cause a false nose low indication). *Note:* Regardless of the amount of error displayed, the pilot should control the attitude of the aircraft to get the proper performance. Use the attitude picture that gives the desired performance.

26. c. Both a and b

27. All three statements are FALSE

28. High surface altimeter settings with low pressure levels

29. True

30. Rotor speed is LESS and needle deflection is LESS

Appendices

DANIEL PEARLMUTTER

Appendices

Appendix A
INSTRUMENT FLYING COURSE SYLLABUS

The Instrument Flying Course that follows is designed to develop the skills required for conducting IFR flights throughout the Federal Airways system, including operations into and out of high density terminals, in a safe and knowledgeable manner. In order to accomplish this end, a high level of training and exposure has been provided. To meet the course completion standards, the student must demonstrate his proficiency through written and flight tests, and show through appropriate records that he meets the knowledge, skill, and experience requirements necessary to obtain an instrument rating (airplane). The time shown for each lesson is approximate and every lesson will be accomplished except where partial credit has been assigned. When completion standards for a lesson are not met, the lesson (or portions thereof) must be repeated until the appropriate performance level is achieved. Whenever required, the instructor will prescribe a "make-up" lesson to be composed of maneuvers which have been performed at sub-standard or borderline levels.

PHASE I   ATTITUDE INSTRUMENT FLYING, BASIC RADIO NAVIGATION AND SIMPLE CLEARANCES

During this phase the student obtains a thorough knowledge of airplane flight instruments, systems, and basic attitude instrument flying. In addition, he is introduced to precise radio navigation using the VOR, and to simple instrument clearance concepts. The student must demonstrate the ability to safely control and maneuver an airplane solely by reference to the flight instruments and he must also demonstrate a basic understanding of VOR navigation and instrument clearance procedures.

Lesson 1   Dual Simulator 1.3 hours

Objectives

To develop familiarity with flight instrument presentations and with basic principles for precise aircraft control through instrument reference. To develop scanning and cross-check techniques.

1. Simulator layout and familiarization (discussion and demonstration)
2. Artificial horizon familiarization
    A. Adjustment of miniature aircraft (discussion and demonstration)
    B. Acceleration, deceleration and precession errors (discussion)
    C. Useage (discussion and practice)
        1. Pitch
        2. Elevator trimming techniques
        3. Bank
3. Altimeter familiarization
    A. Proper setting technique (discussion and demonstration)
    B. Lag errors (discussion)
    C. Cross-check between altimeter and artificial horizon (discussion and practice)
4. Vertical speed familiarization
    A. Lag discussion and demonstration
    B. Response relationship between VSI and altimeter when changes in pitch are made (discussion and demonstration)
    C. Useage (discussion and demonstration)
        1. As a trend indicator
        2. Problems from "chasing"
        3. Relating rate to changes in the amount of pitch or power
    D. Cross-check between VSI, altimeter, and A/H (discussion and practice)
5. Airspeed indicator familiarization
    A. Relationship of pitch change to airspeed
        1. Constant airspeed related to constant pitch and power

2. Magnitude of airspeed change related to degree of pitch change
   B. Relationship of power, at constant altitude, to airspeed (discussion and demonstration)
   C. Relationship of power to altitude change at constant airspeed
   D. Cross-check between airspeed indicator, A/H, VSI, and altimeter (discussion and practice)
6. Directional gyro familiarization
   A. Setting and checking procedure (discussion)
   B. Precession errors (discussion)
   C. Use as a turn indicator (discussion)
   D. Cross-check between all flight instruments, including directional gyro (discussion and practice)
7. Turn indicator and ball familiarization
   A. Relationship between turn indicator, bank, and airspeed (discussion)
   B. Position of turn indicator in straight and level flight (discussion and practice)
   C. Effects on relationship of bank and turn from having ball out of center (discussion and practice)
   D. Performance of standard rate turns
   E. Add turn indicator and ball to cross-check
8. Instrument scanning and cross-check techniques
   A. Primary instruments (discussion)
   B. Supporting instruments (discussion)
9. Applications (practice in using all flight instruments to develop scanning technique)
   A. Series of 180 degree turns in alternate directions, beginning with 10 degree banks and progressing to 45 degree banks as directed by instructor (practice)
   B. Pattern A (see p. 205)
   C. Pattern B (see p. 206)

Completion Standards
For satisfactory completion of this lesson the student must demon-

strate his ability to maintain constant pitch and bank at angles of bank up to 45 degrees. He must be able to demonstrate precise altitude and airspeed control in straight and level flight, and to perform the Pattern B without excessive deviations in heading, altitude, and bank.

Lesson 2   Dual Flight 1.4 hours

Objectives

To apply the concepts presented in Lesson 1 to actual flight. To develop instrument flying capability while confronted with the various changes in control pressures, accelerations, and turbulence problems which occur while airborne.

1.   Aircraft and equipment familiarization
2.   Flight instrument ground check
      A.   Gyro instrument checks while taxiing
      B.   Altimeter and directional gyro indexing
      C.   Airspeed indicator check on takeoff
3.   Review attitude control techniques
      A.   Bank control
          1.   Attitude (full) panel
          2.   Emergency (partial) panel
      B.   Pitch control
          1.   Attitude panel
          2.   Emergency panel
4.   Review altitude control at constant power
      A.   Attitude panel
      B.   Emergency panel
5.   Review altitude control at constant airspeed
      A.   Attitude panel
      B.   Emergency panel
6.   Review airspeed control
      A.   Maintaining constant altitude
      B.   In climbs and descents
          1.   Attitude panel
          2.   Emergency panel
7.   Applications
      A.   Pattern flying (attitude panel)

        1.   Pattern A
        2.   Pattern B
    B.   Steep turns
        1.   Attitude panel (at 30 degree bank)
        2.   Emergency panel (at 1.5 Std. rate)

8.   Unusual attitude recoveries (approach to climbing stalls and spirals)
    A.   Attitude panel
    B.   Emergency panel

Completion Standards

For satisfactory completion of this lesson the student must, in actual flight, demonstrate ability to maintain constant pitch and bank at angles of bank up to 45 degrees. He must demonstrate precise altitude and airspeed control in straight flight and must be able to perform the Pattern B without excessive deviations in heading, altitude, and bank.

Lesson 3   Dual Simulator 1.3 hours

Objectives

To improve control and scanning capabilities. To develop VOR navigational ability, including tracking and course interception.

1.   Review scanning techniques (discussion and practice)
2.   Review altitude control (discussion and practice)
    A.   Constant power, both attitude and emergency panel
    B.   Constant airspeed, both attitude and emergency panel
3.   Emergency panel exercise
    A.   Standard rate turns at constant altitude (90, 180, and 360 degree turns)
4.   Precision pattern flying. Practice Pattern C (see p. 207)
5.   Tune and index radios. Aurally identify VOR station (discussion and practice)
6.   D.G. visualization of VOR radial interception and tracking (discussion)
7.   VOR course tracking (discussion and practice)
    A.   Inbound

      B.   Outbound
      C.   "Close-in" tracking techniques (inbound to the station, station passage, and outbound on the new course)
      D.   Stair-step navigation route (alternating inbound and outbound course interceptions using two VOR stations)
8.   Radial interceptions (discussion and practice)
      A.   Changing radial within 20 degrees (inbound and outbound)

Completion Standards

For satisfactory completion of this lesson the student must be able to hold headings within 10 degrees, altitudes within 100 feet, and airspeed within 10K. He must be able to set his course selector correctly for the course he wishes to track and to track the desired course without excessive weaving. He must demonstrate a good understanding of radial interception procedures and be able to perform simple interceptions correctly and efficiently.

Lesson 4   **Dual Flight 1.4 hours**

Objectives

To further improve control of the airplane through instrument reference and scanning techniques, to develop proficiency in VOR navigation while airborne.

1.   Check flight instruments and radios for proper operation and accuracy. Index and tune
2.   Precision flying: Pattern C
3.   Emergency panel exercise
      A.   Standard rate turns at constant altitude (90 and 180 degree turns)
      B.   Standard rate turns with climbs and descents
4.   Steep turns
      A.   Attitude panel: 45 degree bank (180 degree turns)
      B.   Emergency panel:
            1.   Double standard rate
            2.   Recovery from spirals
5.   VOR course tracking

      A.   Review of basic tracking techniques
      B.   Review "close-in" tracking techniques
      C.   Review crossing VOR and proceeding outbound on new course
6.   Stair-step navigation route (two stations)
7.   Radial shifts of 10 – 15 degrees (one station)

Completion Standards

The proficiency level for this lesson requires heading accuracy within 10 degrees, altitudes within 100 feet, and airspeed within 10K. Also required are correct setting of the course selector, tracking which is essentially accurate, the ability to follow a route involving the intersection of courses from two VOR stations and the efficient performance of radial shifts (simple intercepts).

Lesson 5   Dual Simulator 1.3 hours

Objectives

To refine aircraft control and scanning ability. To improve VOR navigation and to teach orientation techniques.

1.   Precision flying
      A.   Pattern D (see p. 208) attitude panel
      B.   Pattern B (emergency panel) with timed turns
2.   Tune and index radios
3.   VOR course tracking in strong crosswind (practice)
4.   Radial intercepts from unknown positions (discussion and practice)
      A.   Outbound
      B.   Inbound
5.   Cross bearing fix techniques (VOR) discussion and practice
      A.   Plotting
      B.   While tracking on a radial
      C.   With unknown position
6.   Time-distance checks (discussion and practice)

Completion Standards

Before progressing from the elements of this lesson the student must be able to fly the Pattern D without incurring repeated deviations greater than 10 degrees in heading and 10K in airspeed. In addition, his rate of turn must be constant and his timing accurate within 10 seconds. Headings flown for radial intercepts must be consistently correct and he must display a basic understanding of time-distance checks and cross-bearing fix techniques.

Lesson 6   Dual Flight 1.4 hours

Objectives

To further improve aircraft control by instrument reference. To practice the VOR navigation techniques initiated in the previous (simulator) lesson in actual flight. In addition, to give practice at making compass turns.

1. Check flight instruments and radios (for proper operation and accuracy). Index and tune
2. Precision flying
   A. Pattern D attitude panel
   B. Pattern B emergency panel with timed turns
3. Steep turns
   A. Attitude panel: 45 degree bank, 180 degree turns
   B. Emergency panel: double standard rate
4. Unusual attitude recoveries (demonstrate and practice)
   A. Attitude panel (includes stall recoveries and spirals)
   B. Emergency panel (climbing turns and spirals)
5. Radial intercepts from unknown positions
   A. Inbound
   B. Outbound
6. Cross-bearing fixes from unknown positions
7. Time-distance checks
8. Stair-step navigation route
9. Compass turns

Completion Standards

While performing the patterns, including the Pattern D smooth handling of the aircraft should be displayed. Heading must be kept substantially within 10 degrees while altitude limits are 100 feet. Correct navigation procedures must be used. Basic ability to recover from unusual attitudes and to perform compass turns must be displayed.

Lesson 7   Dual Simulator 1.3 hours

Objectives

To further improve aircraft control proficiency. To master the basic elements of holding patterns and to introduce "clearance" concepts.

1. Precision flying (practice)
   - A. Attitude panel, Pattern E (see p. 209)
   - B. Emergency panel, Pattern C with timed turns
2. Tune and index radios
3. D.G. visualization of the various holding pattern entries (discussion)
4. Holding patterns over a VOR using direct entries (discussion and practice)
   - A. With calm wind conditions
   - B. With crosswind conditions
5. Holding on a DME fix (discussion and practice)
6. Holding at a VOR intersection (discussion and practice)
7. Receiving and executing simple clearances (discussion and practice)
   - A. Clearance format
   - B. Clearance interpretation
   - C. Clearance execution
8. Use of ATC communications (discussion)

Completion Standards

To progress from this lesson the student must demonstrate ability to perform the more complicated Pattern E smoothly and with the same tolerances as for previous patterns. Relatively precise performance of holding patterns should be demonstrated prior to completion, plus a basic understanding of clearances.

Lesson 8   Dual Flight 1.4 hours

Objectives

To perform a complicated flight pattern in a relatively precise manner and to further improve emergency panel proficiency. To increase the student's ability to perform holding patterns and to develop his familiarity with IFR clearances.

1. Check flight instruments and radios. Index and tune

2. Simulated IFR departure, executing simple clearance (discussion and practice)
3. Precision flying
    A. Attitude panel: Pattern E
    B. Emergency panel: Pattern B with compass turns
4. Time-distance check
5. Radial intercepts
6. Holding at a VOR
    A. Direct entries
    B. Teardrop entries
    C. Parallel entries
7. Emergency panel exercise
    A. Slow flight at 1.2 x VSO (½ flap)
    B. Stalls with low power
8. Radial tracking while flying on emergency panel (carry out simple clearance)

Completion Standards
Demonstration of basic understanding of an IFR clearance. Ability to fly a correct holding pattern, once established in that pattern. Performance of Pattern E with headings maintained within 5 degrees and altitude within 50 feet. Radial intercepts correctly performed.

Lesson 9   Phase I Test   Dual Flight 1.0 hour

Objectives
This check is for the purpose of insuring that the student has mastered control of the aircraft to the degree required for progressing to Phase II where training will be concentrated to a much greater degree on radio navigation exercises. In order to make satisfactory progress in Phase II it is important for aircraft control to have been previously mastered to the point where great concentration is not required in merely maintaining precise heading, altitude and airspeed control. In order to insure that the above will occur, a high degree of proficiency in aircraft control must be demonstrated during this flight.

For this check the student will be required to demonstrate the following:

1. Check flight instruments for proper operation and indexing
2. Basic aircraft control; precision pattern flying
    A. Attitude panel: Pattern E
    B. Emergency panel: Pattern C with timed turns
3. Recovery from unusual attitudes; emergency panel
    A. Approach to a stall
    B. High speed spiral
4. Steep turns
    A. Attitude panel: 360 degree turns in each direction with a 45 degree bank
    B. Emergency panel: one minute turn each direction at double the standard rate
5. Compass turns
    A. Turns to specified magnetic headings

Acceptable Performance

1. Equipment check
    Between engine start-up and takeoff the student will be expected to check the functioning of all flight instruments. Knowledge of which instruments to check and how to perform the checks is required.
2. Basic aircraft control
    Smooth and accurate control of the airplane throughout with only infrequent deviation from the following standards:
    A. Attitude panel: Altitude during level segments; ± 50 feet. Airspeed; ± 5K
    Heading: within 5 degrees
    Climbs and descents: within 100 FPM of target figure
    B. Emergency panel: Altitude during level segments;
    ± 75 feet. Airspeed; within 5K
    Heading on completion of turns: within 15 degrees per 360 degree turn
    Climbs and descents; within 10 seconds of estimated time
3. Recovery from unusual attitudes using emergency panel

prompt, smooth and accurate recovery. Any loss of, or error in, control which makes it necessary for the check pilot to take over will be disqualifying.

4. Steep turns
    A. Attitude panel; smooth control with accurate turn rate and airspeed positioning. Altitude ± 150 feet
5. Compass turns
    Accurate turn rate control. Recovery within 15 degrees of designated heading.

PHASE II   INSTRUMENT APPROACHES, ADVANCED RADIO NAVIGATION AND COMPLEX CLEARANCES

During this phase, the student will develop a high level of skill in the performance of instrument approaches and will gain proficiency in the interpretation of, and compliance with, more complex instrument clearances. This training will involve the use of VOR, ADF, DME, and ILS navigation procedures. The student must demonstrate the ability to accurately perform all normal types of instrument approaches and he must also demonstrate a high degree of ability in the handling of all communications required for actual instrument flight. A high level of instrument proficiency must be developed in preparation for advancement to the instrument cross-country phase of the course.

Lesson 10   Dual Simulator 1.3 hours

Objectives

To improve proficiency in performance of holding patterns and to develop an understanding of holding pattern entries. To develop IFR clearance comprehension and to provide training in ATC communications.

1. Use of ATC communication (discussion)
2. Tune and index radios
3. Execution of IFR clearance (discussion and practice)
4. Review D.G. visualization of the various entries into right and left turn holding patterns (discussion)

5. Holding over a VOR (discussion and practice)
   A. Direct entries
   B. Teardrop entries
   C. Parallel entries
   D. Strong winds
6. Holding over an intersection (discussion and practice)
   A. Direct entries
   B. Teardrop entries
   C. Parallel entries
7. Time-distance check (practice)
8. Radial interceptions (practice)
9. Reception and execution of clearance while in flight (practice)

Completion Standards
Accurate interpretation and execution of a simple clearance. Good progress in working out holding pattern entries and in making correct responses to high wind situations. Correct procedure for time-distance checks and radial interceptions.

Lesson 11   Dual Flight 1.4 hours

Objectives
Continued progress in performance of IFR clearance work and holding patterns as well as in accuracy and smoothness of aircraft control.
1. Check flight instruments and radios. Index and tune
2. Execute simulated IFR clearance (discussion and practice)
3. Use of ATC communications
4. Holding over an intersection (practice)
   A. With various entries
5. Precision flying on emergency panel (practice)
   A. Pattern D using compass turns
   B. Stall and spiral recoveries
6. Steep turns
   A. Attitude panel; 45 degree bank (120 and 180 degree turns)
7. Orientation exercise (practice)
   A. Two station fix

        B.   Time-distance check
        C.   Radial intercept
  8.   Holding over a VOR (practice)
        A.   With various entries
  9.   Execute simulated IFR clearance for return to vicinity of airport

Completion Standards
Indications of progress in interpretation and execution of IFR clearance. Relatively accurate holding pattern entries. Precise execution of the holding pattern itself. Smooth performance of Pattern D using emergency panel, plus basic understanding of compass turn procedure.

Lesson 12   Dual Simulator 1.3 hours

Objectives
To introduce the instrument approach concept and to develop basic ability to perform the VOR based instrument approach.

  1.   ATC communication (discussion)
  2.   Tune and index radios
  3.   Execute simulated IFR clearance to an airport via a VOR which will be used for an approach (discussion and practice)
  4.   Holding pattern work over the VOR (practice)
  5.   Procedure turns (discussion and practice)
        A.   45/180 degree (60 second) turn
        B.   45/225 degree (40 second) turn
        C.   90/270 degree turn
        D.   Procedural track turn
  6.   Perform visual "run-through" of a VOR approach and missed approach procedure
  7.   Execution of full VOR instrument approaches incorporating teardrop procedure turns (discussion and practice)
  8.   "Straight-in" VOR approach using radar vectors to find approach course (discussion and practice)

Completion Standards
Display a substantial understanding of the VOR approach, plus the

ability to fly the complete approach with only minor coaching. Correct holding pattern entry.

Lesson 13   Dual Flight 1.4 hours

Objectives

To advance the student's familiarity with the VOR instrument approach.

1. Check flight instruments and radios. Index and tune
2. Execute simulated IFR clearance to a VOR which may be used for practice instrument approaches
3. Perform radial intercepts and time-distance check enroute
4. Perform practice VOR approaches at destination VOR with at least one missed approach procedure
5. Practice holding pattern entries
6. Perform holding using emergency panel instruments, including compass turns
7. Steep turns
   - A. Attitude panel
   - B. Emergency panel
8. Return to airport in conformance with a clearance, using emergency panel.

Completion Standards

Demonstration of ability to perform the majority of the functions and operations required in performing a standard VOR based instrument approach. Continued progress of precise control of the airplane using emergency panel as well as attitude panel.

Lesson 14   Dual Simulator 1.3 hours

Objectives

To further refine the standard instrument approach technique. To initiate training in the use of the automatic direction finder (ADF) as a navigational device.

1. Tune and index radios (demonstrate how to tune and identify a low frequency radio beacon on the ADF receiver)

2. Intensify ATC communications
3. Execute simulated IFR clearance which involves an immediate VOR instrument approach upon arrival at destination (discussion and practice)
4. Perform a series of VOR instrument approaches using various approach procedures
5. D.G. visualization of ADF bearing interception and tracking
6. Compute magnetic bearings "To" and "From" a radio beacon and perform ADF tracking on selected inbound and outbound bearings (discussion and practice)

Completion Standards

For successful completion of this lesson the student must demonstrate performance of VOR instrument approaches without coaching from the instructor. Also demonstrated must be his proper correction for course deviations while tracking inbound and outbound on assigned magnetic bearings of a radio beacon.

Lesson 15   Dual Flight 1.4 hours

Objectives

To reach relatively high level competence in performance of VOR instrument approaches and to improve proficiency in simple ADF tracking. In addition, to refine the techniques for recovery from unusual attitudes.

1. Check flight instruments and radios. Index and tune
2. Execute simulated IFR clearance with at least one leg to be navigated by ADF tracking and with an immediate VOR instrument approach at the destination
3. Perform a series of VOR approaches using various approach procedures
4. Track to, and then from a non-directional beacon on assigned inbound and outbound bearings
5. Recoveries from stalls and steep turns (AP)*
6. Steep turns (45 degree) (AP)*
7. Recoveries from unusual attitudes with emergency panel instruments (both approaches to stalls and spirals)

Completion Standards

Ability to perform instrument approaches without committing substantial errors. Demonstration of correct ADF tracking procedures,
both toward and away from a non-directional transmitter. Correct
and efficient recoveries from unusual attitudes using emergency
panel instruments.
*AP: Attitude Panel

Lesson 16   Dual Simulator 1.3 hours

Objectives

To refine ADF tracking technique and to introduce ADF course
(bearing) intercepts from assigned headings and unknown positions.
To acquaint the student with the "straight-in" type of VOR approach, which incorporates vectors to the final approach course.

1.   Tune and index radios
2.   Make maximum use of ATC communications
3.   Track to, and then from a non-directional beacon (NDB)
     on assigned inbound and outbound bearings with large
     course changes over the station
4.   Intercept specific magnetic bearings "To" and magnetic
     bearings "From" a NDB while on assigned headings
5.   Intercept specific magnetic bearings "To" and "From" a
     NDB while tracking on VOR courses
6.   Intercept specific magnetic bearings "To" and "From" a
     NDB from unknown positions
7.   Perform holding practice over a non-directional transmitter
8.   Perform "straight-in" VOR approaches involving vectors to
     the final approach course

Completion Standards

Substantially correct performance of ADF tracking and intercept
procedures. Demonstrate progress in performing the "straight-in"
VOR approach.

Lesson 17   Dual Flight 1.4 hours

Objectives

To continue progress in ADF tracking and intercept capability in the airborne environment. To accelerate practice at working with ATC while performing instrument procedures.

1. Check flight instruments and radios. Index and tune
2. Make use of all opportunities for actual ATC communications
3. Track to, and then from a non-directional transmitter on assigned inbound and outbound bearings with large course changes over the station
4. Intercept specific magnetic bearings "To" and magnetic bearings "From" a NDB while on assigned headings
5. Intercept specific magnetic bearings "To" and "From" a NDB while tracking on VOR courses
6. Intercept specific magnetic bearings "To" and "From" a NDB from unknown positions
7. Perform holding practice over a non-directional transmitter
8. Perform "straight-in" VOR approaches to the airport

Completion Standards
Continued progress in ADF tracking and intercepts, also progress in "straight-in" VOR approaches.

Lesson 18   Dual Simulator 1.3 hours

Objectives
To continue to develop proficiency in ADF navigation, including introduction of the NDB based instrument approach. To produce additional experience in performing "straight-in" approaches. To initiate training in performing a DME arc.

1. Tune and index radios
2. Execute simulated IFR clearance involving interception of an ADF leg and a holding assignment over a non-directional beacon
3. Practice at making varied holding pattern entries
4. Execute ADF approaches, both "full" approaches and "straight-in" approaches, including at least one which involves vectors to final
5. Perform ADF time-distance check
6. Review VOR approaches, including the "straight-in"

approach
7. Review VOR time-distance check, then progress to performance of the DME arc

Completion Standards
Display of a high degree of proficiency in ADF navigation. Good progress in performing the ADF approach. Accurate performance of VOR approaches. Basic understanding of DME arc tracking.

Lesson 19   Dual Flight 1.4 hours

Objectives
To refine ADF navigation, including holding patterns and approaches while in actual flight. To achieve a high level of proficiency in VOR approaches and to develop proficiency in flying an arc on the VOR.
1. Check flight instruments and radios. Index and tune
2. Continue to intensify use of ATC communications
3. Execute simulated IFR clearance involving an ADF leg and a holding assignment over a NDB
4. Execute ADF approaches, both "full approaches" and "straight-in" approaches
5. Perform ADF time-distance check
6. Perform VOR time-distance check and VOR arc practice
7. On emergency panel, perform stalls with lower power settings (no flap)
8. Unusual attitude recoveries, emergency panel
9. VOR approach to the airport

Completion Standards
Demonstrated evidence that continued drill on VOR approaches and ADF navigation is not necessary

Lesson 20   Dual Simulator 1.3 hours

Objectives
To introduce the ILS approach and to continue progress in ADF approaches and DME arcs.
1. Tune and index radios
2. Execute simulated IFR clearance involving a course to and

> a holding assignment over the outer compass locater
> 3. Perform localizer approaches
> 4. Perform ILS approaches from holding positions at the outer marker, using a complete procedure turn, and using a "straight-in" vector from Approach Control
> 5. Perform ADF approaches
> 6. Perform DME arc exercises
> 7. Use ATC communications as much as practicable

Completion Standards
Basic grasp of ILS and localizer approaches. High level of proficiency in ADF approaches. Good progress in conduct of DME arc procedures.

Lesson 21   Dual Flight 1.4 hours

Objectives
To review basic aircraft control in instrument flight and to refine the ADF approach and performance of the time-distance check (VOR arc maneuver) while airborne.

1. Check flight instruments and radios. Index and tune
2. Execute simulated IFR clearance to an intersection. Include holding at the intersection
3. Perform steep turns (both attitude panel and emergency panel)
4. Perform Pattern E (attitude panel)
5. Perform Pattern C (emergency panel and timed turning)
6. Perform VOR and ADF time-distance checks
7. Execute ADF arrival and approach
8. ATC communications

Completion Standards
Correct and accurate procedures throughout.

Lesson 22   Dual Simulator 1.3 hours

Objectives
To substantially master the ILS approach and to develop proficiency in performing ILS Back Course localizer approaches.

1. Tune and index radios
2. Execute simulated IFR clearance incorporating a holding assignment and terminating in an ILS approach
3. Perform practice ILS approaches using various initial approach procedures (i.e., procedure turn, from holding pattern, straight-in on VOR and ADF courses to localizer or LOM, radar vectors to final, from DME arc
4. Missed approaches
5. Introduce more complex clearances and ATC procedures

Completion Standards
Performance of an ILS approach without coaching from the instructor and without excessive deviations in course, glide path, and altitude.

Lesson 23   Dual Flight 1.4 hours

Objectives
To gain proficiency in the interpretation of more complicated clearances and in the copying and execution of clearances received while airborne. In addition, to develop proficiency in flying ILS and localizer approaches.

1. Check flight instruments and radios. Index and tune
2. Interpretation and execution of a relatively complicated clearance. This clearance should include various types of courses (VOR, ADF, ILS) with at least two short legs
3. Enroute clearance amendments or changes and holding problems
4. Front and Back Course ILS approaches with at least one missed approach procedure
5. Attitude panel exercise; steep turns
6. Emergency panel
   A. Steep turns
   B. Stalls with 20 degrees of flap and a high power setting
   C. Unusual attitude recoveries

Completion Standards
Accurate execution of the clearance and clearance amendments.

Correct holding entries and precise holding patterns. Accurate execution of ILS approaches.

Lesson 24   Dual Simulator 1.3 hours

Objectives

To bring all radio navigation procedures thus far introduced to a high level of proficiency.

1. Tune and index radios
2. Interpretation and execution of clearances which involve the use of all the types of facilities and all of the procedures thus far practiced. The clearances are to include area departures (SIDs), area arrivals and Profile Descent Procedures (STARs), holding problems, enroute amended clearances, VOR, ADF, and ILS courses, as well as DME arcs.
3. Time-distance checks
4. Fix orientation
5. Execute instrument approaches
    A. VOR
    B. ADF
    C. ILS
    D. Localizer
    E. Back Course localizer

Completion Standards

Performance of all maneuvers and procedures must be on a level equal to that required in the Instrument Pilot Flight Test Guide.

Lesson 25   Dual Flight 1.4 hour

Objectives

To review in actual flight all radio navigation procedures thus far introduced in order to bring them to the high level of proficiency required for advancement to instrument cross-country work, (Phase III).

1. Check flight instruments and radios. Index and tune
2. Interpret and execute an instrument clearance involving at least four courses (including an ADF course) and an area

departure
3. Perform holding pattern entries and at least one complete holding pattern
4. Perform time-distance check and fix orientation
5. Execute instrument approaches
    A. VOR
    B. ADF
    C. ILS

Completion Standards
Performance of all maneuvers and procedures must be on a level equal to that required in the Instrument Pilot Flight Test Guide.

Lesson 26   Phase II Test   Dual Flight 1.5 hours

Objectives
This progress check is for the purpose of insuring that the student has reached the level of proficiency necessary for advancing to the instrument cross-country phase of the course.

For this check, the student will be required to demonstrate the following:
1. Check flight instruments and radios. Index and tune
    A. Demonstrate checking flight instruments and radio equipment for proper functioning and accuracy
    B. Tune and index radios and instruments, as appropriate, for the forthcoming departure
2. Copying and interpreting an IFR clearance
3. Performance of an area departure in accordance with a clearance
4. Performance of a holding pattern entry
5. Performance of a radial intercept
6. Performance of an area arrival and instrument approach
7. Two additional instrument approaches, so that in all an ILS (or Back Course localizer) plus a VOR and an ADF approach are accomplished

Acceptable Performance
1. Performance of an accurate VOT check of VOR receivers.

Correct tuning and indexing of all navigational equipment after receiving the clearance. Correct checks while taxiing, including the functioning of directional gyro and artificial horizon.

2. Clearance copying and interpretation will be evaluated on the basis of accuracy and efficiency.

3. Performance of navigational exercises will be evaluated for accuracy of track, identification of courses, and operation of the navigational equipment. Altitude maintenance for cruising operations must be substantially held within 100 feet.

4. Holding pattern entries must be efficient and the pattern must be performed in the assigned position with proper corrections for the effects of wind.

5. The accurate performance of instrument approaches down to authorized minimums. Errors no greater than 100 feet below prescribed altitudes during initial approach and no descent below minimums after passing the final fix will be acceptable for required performance.

6. A high degree of knowledge of ATC procedures must be demonstrated. Performance of radio communications will be evaluated on the basis of the use of correct radio phraseology, selection of the appropriate frequencies, accuracy and clarity of transmissions, and the timing of communications.

7. Evaluation of the missed approach will be based on accuracy of the procedure, timing of the decision to execute a missed approach, and the appropriateness of communications.

PHASE III INSTRUMENT CROSS-COUNTRY PROCEDURES

During this phase the student will develop a thorough understanding of instrument cross-country procedures. He will gain experience in the performance of the instrument pilot operations in a complex, higher performance airplane, and in performing instrument operations within a high density terminal environment containing multiple terminal airports. The student must demonstrate the ability to plan and safely conduct cross-country flights under instrument flight rules both enroute and within a high density terminal area. He must demonstrate that he can correctly handle the communications and procedures involved.

Lesson 27 Dual Flight 1.4 hours

Objectives

To furnish experience in performing the instrument maneuvers and procedures in a complex, higher performance airplane. This lesson should be preceded by a thorough briefing on the airplane and it's equipment.

1. Check flight instruments and radios. Index and tune
2. Instrument flight familiarization, attitude panel
   A. Normal climb
   B. Level cruise, normal speed
   C. Steep turns
   D. Slow cruise
   E. Slow speed descents
   F. Normal cruise speed
   G. Stalls with and without flap
3. Familiarization, emergency panel instruments
   A. Straight and level
   B. Standard rate turns
   C. Steep turns
   D. Climbs
   E. Slow speed descents
   F. Cruise speed descents
   G. Stalls with and without flap
   H. Unusual attitude recoveries
4. Pattern flying, attitude panel
   A. Pattern D
   B. Pattern E
5. Area arrival and ILS approach
6. Missed approach

Completion Standards

Substantial grasp of controlling the airplane during an instrument flight.

Lesson 28   Dual Flight 1.4 hours

Objectives

To develop proficiency in performing instrument navigation procedures in a higher performance airplane.

  1. Check flight instruments and radios. Index and tune
  2. Execute an instrument clearance involving an area de-
      parture (SID if available), amended clearance problem, and
      a holding assignment
  3. Simulated emergencies (not on IFR flight plans)
      A. Gyro instruments failure (incorporate with a
          navigation exercise)   .
      B. Communications radio failure
      C. Navigation radio failure
  4. Perform area arrival and Runway Profile Descent Proce-
      dure (STAR if available), terminating in instrument ap-
      proaches (DME arcs incorporated where practical)
  5. Missed approaches
  6. Communications with Approach Control

Completion Standards

All maneuvers performed to the same standards required in the
Phase II progress check.

Lesson 29   Dual Flight X-C 1.8 hours

Objectives

To develop proficiency in planning and executing IFR cross-country
flights.

  1. Plan an IFR flight and develop written flight logs
  2. Obtain a weather briefing and check facilities status
  3. Make out and file an instrument flight plan for the flight in
      each direction
  4. Check flight instruments and radios. Index and tune
  5. Perform the IFR flights which have been planned including
      an instrument approach at each destination. The entire
      flight will be accomplished in conformance with an ATC
      clearance and normal ATC communications

Completion Standards
Demonstration of good progress in the performance of IFR cross-country flights.

Lesson 30   Dual X-C flight 1.8 hours

Objectives
To continue building instrument cross-country experience and proficiency in preparation for the advanced instrument navigation work which is to follow.
1.   Plan an IFR flight and develop written flight logs
2.   Obtain a weather briefing and check facilities status
3.   Make out and file an instrument flight plan for the flight in each direction
4.   Check flight instruments and radios. Index and tune
5.   Perform the IFR flights which have been planned, including an instrument approach at each destination. The entire flight will be accomplished in accordance with an ATC clearance and normal ATC communication.

Completion Standards
Demonstration of sufficient proficiency in instrument cross-country flying that the maximum value will be gained from the advanced cross-country series.

Lesson 31   Dual X-C Flight 12.0 hours

Objectives
To develop the student's level of proficiency and experience in operating an airplane on instruments under instrument flight rules in a high density terminal environment to an acceptable stage. Whenever practicable the student will, in this phase, operate the airplane in actual instrument conditions. During this lesson the commercial course student will receive night cross-country flight instruction over a route of at least 100 miles distance between takeoff and landing.

Context
1.   Plan advanced X-C flights to high density terminal areas

and work up log planning sheets
2.   Obtain a weather briefing and check facilities status
3.   Make out and file flight plans for all routes, except where tower to tower clearances are available.
4.   Check flight instruments and radios. Index and tune
5.   Perform the IFR flights which have been planned. (The instructor may, if he deems it advisable, modify the routing and/or terminals used.) All segments will be accomplished in conformance with ATC clearances, using normal ATC communications.

Completion Standards

Prior to the termination of this trip the student will be expected to demonstrate the ability to plan, file for, and conduct an IFR flight (including copying and interpreting clearances) with a high level of accuracy and without assistance from the instructor.

In conducting the flight, he must be able to properly check, set and tune all equipment, perform the departure, enroute, and arrival phases, including an instrument approach, in a knowledgeable and correct manner. Accuracy of course and altitude holding must be at a level compatible with the instrument flight test standards.

The student will have received instrument cross-country flight training which meets the requirements of FAR 61.65(c)(4).

Lesson 32   Dual Flight 1.5 hours

Objectives

To correct any deficiencies which may exist in the student's proficiency. To ascertain that he has reached the graduation level.

1.   Check flight instruments and radios. Index and tune
2.   Review all areas and polish or correct all maneuvers and procedures for which such work is required.

Completion Standards

All maneuvers and procedures performed at final progress check standards or better.

Lesson 33   Phase III Test   Dual Flight 1.5 hours

Objectives

This progress check is for the purpose of insuring that the student has reached advanced phase standards for instrument flight performance.

For this check the student must demonstrate the following:

1.   Check flight instruments and radios. Index and tune
2.   Radio Navigation
     A.   Receive and interpret a clearance involving at least four courses, one of which is an ADF course
     B.   Execute the above clearance
     C.   Execute a holding pattern entry and fly a holding pattern
     D.   Perform an orientation by fix or time-distance, check method (exclude DME and radar)
     E.   Perform radial intercepts
     F.   Demonstrate tracking of a DME arc
     G.   Execute an area arrival and an instrument approach
     H.   Missed approach
     I.   Two additional approaches (include ILS [or BC LOC] ADF, and VOR)
     J.   ATC communications throughout the exercise
     K.   Navigational radio malfunctions
3.   Aircraft control
     A.   Attitude instruments
          1.   Straight and level (may be incorporated in Par 2 exercise)
          2.   Climbs and descents (may be incorporated in Par 2 exercise)
          3.   Maneuvering at approach speed (may be incorporated in Par 2 exercise)
          4.   Steep turns (360 degrees each direction with 45 degrees of bank)
     B.   Emergency panel instruments
          1.   Pattern C (with timed turns)

2. Steep turns (approximately double standard rate)
3. Compass turns (may be incorporated in Par 2 exercise)
4. Stall recoveries
5. Recoveries from unusual attitudes

Acceptable Performance
Performance of all maneuvers and procedures must be on a level at least equal to that required in the Instrument Pilot Flight Test Guide. In addition, the student must demonstrate knowledge of the static system check required by FAR 91.170 and determine that the airplane used for the flight check has the required log book entry.

PHASE IV   INSTRUMENT REVIEW

During this phase the student will review and practice all instrument procedures required in order to enhance his capability to successfully pass the graduation test. The student must demonstrate the high level of understanding and ability in instrument flight which will assure the meeting of graduation flight test standards.

Lesson 34   Dual Flight 1.5 hours

Objectives
This lesson is designed to afford the student and instructor the opportunity for a general review of instrument flying techniques and procedures. The review should include, but is not limited to, the following areas:
1. Instrument pre-takeoff cockpit checks
2. Copying, readback, and execution of an actual, or simulated, IFR clearance
3. VOR and ADF radial/bearing interception and tracking
4. Holding pattern entry and execution
5. Instrument approach(es)
6. All areas identified in lesson 33 (phase test) as requiring increased proficiency

7. Any IFR procedure identified by instructor or student for which practice is required to enhance the student's instrument flying proficiency

Completion Standards

This lesson is complete when instructor determines that student is performing the instrument manuevers and procedures at a skill level which assures his capability of meeting the graduation flight test performance standards under test conditions.

Lesson 35 Graduation Test Dual Flight 1.5 hours

Objectives

In this graduation test, the Chief Instructor or his assistant will determine that the student can meet the performance levels for the Instrument Pilot rating.

1. Graduation Test

The Chief Instructor or his assistant will administer this test in accordance with the guidelines prescribed in the current FAA Instrument Pilot Flight Test Guide.

The test will be preceded by a discussion of objectives and procedures and followed by a post flight review.

Completion Standards

The student will meet the acceptable performance guidelines of the Instrument Pilot Flight Test Guide and qualify for the Instrument Rating.

INSTRUMENT RATING FLIGHT TEST 1.5 Hours

LESSON/FLIGHT TIME OUTLINE

Instrument Pilot Certification Course*

Instruction Hours	Instrument			Complex Aircraft
	Simulator	Aircraft	X-C	
59.3	15.6	43.7	15.6	24.4

* Reprinted with permission of Sawyer School of Aviation in Phoenix, Arizona.

NEW PART 61 FLIGHT REQUIREMENTS

Instrument Rating Airplane

Total Flight Time:	200 hours
Pilot-in-Command:	100 hours
Includes cross-country in category (airplane)	50 hours
Total Instrument Time:	40 hours
May include ground trainer instruction	20 hours
Instrument Flight Instruction:	15 hours
Includes at least 5 hours in an airplane	
Instrument Approaches:	VOR, ADF, ILS
ADF and ILS may be given in a ground trainer	

Cross-Country: One trip of at least 250 nautical miles on Federal airways (or as routed by ATC) including VOR, ADF, and ILS approaches at different airports.

Pattern A

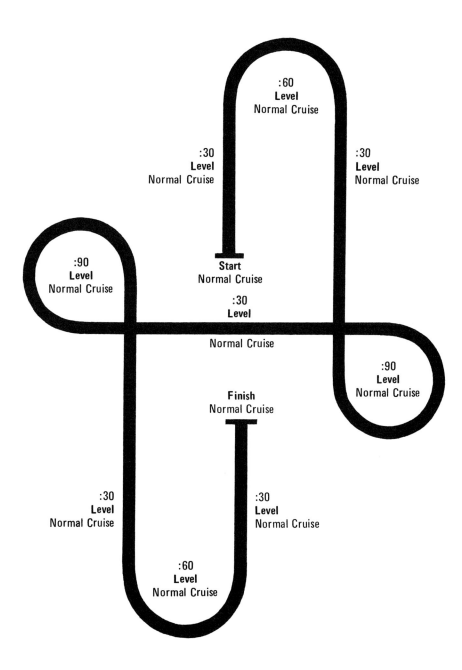

:60
Level
Normal Cruise

:30
Level
Normal Cruise

:30
Level
Normal Cruise

:90
Level
Normal Cruise

Start
Normal Cruise

:30
Level

Normal Cruise

:90
Level
Normal Cruise

Finish
Normal Cruise

:30
Level
Normal Cruise

:30
Level
Normal Cruise

:60
Level
Normal Cruise

Pattern B

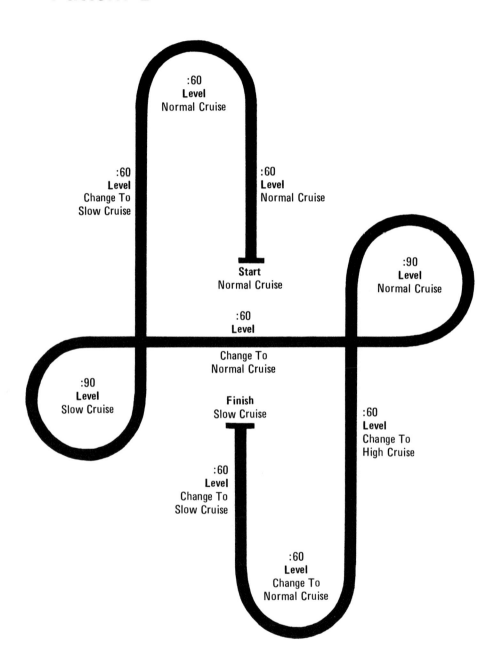

:60
Level
Normal Cruise

:60
Level
Change To
Slow Cruise

:60
Level
Normal Cruise

:90
Level
Normal Cruise

Start
Normal Cruise

:60
Level

Change To
Normal Cruise

:90
Level
Slow Cruise

Finish
Slow Cruise

:60
Level
Change To
High Cruise

:60
Level
Change To
Slow Cruise

:60
Level
Change To
Normal Cruise

Pattern C

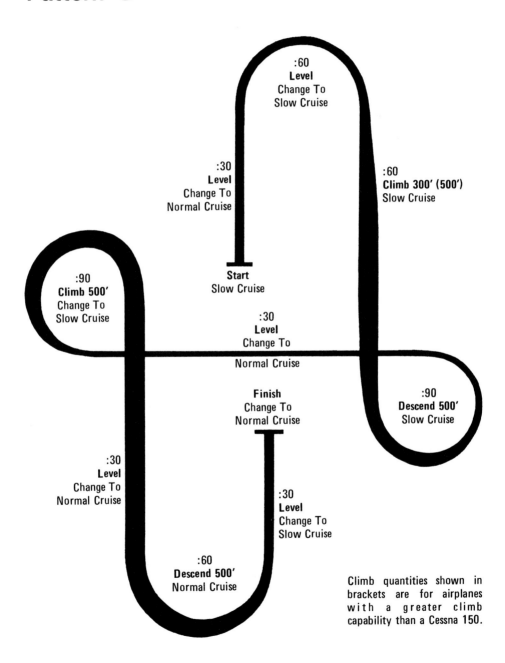

:60
Level
Change To
Slow Cruise

:30
Level
Change To
Normal Cruise

:60
Climb 300' (500')
Slow Cruise

:90
Climb 500'
Change To
Slow Cruise

Start
Slow Cruise

:30
Level
Change To
Normal Cruise

:90
Descend 500'
Slow Cruise

Finish
Change To
Normal Cruise

:30
Level
Change To
Normal Cruise

:30
Level
Change To
Slow Cruise

:60
Descend 500'
Normal Cruise

Climb quantities shown in
brackets are for airplanes
with a greater climb
capability than a Cessna 150.

Pattern D

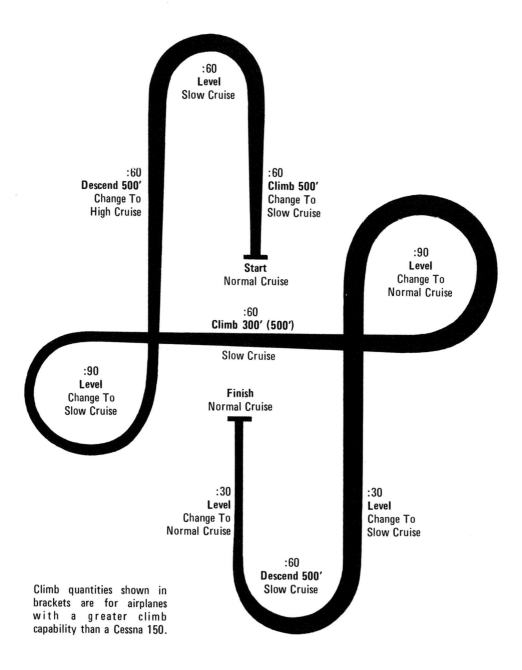

:60
Level
Slow Cruise

:60
Descend 500'
Change To
High Cruise

:60
Climb 500'
Change To
Slow Cruise

:90
Level
Change To
Normal Cruise

Start
Normal Cruise

:60
Climb 300' (500')

Slow Cruise

:90
Level
Change To
Slow Cruise

Finish
Normal Cruise

:30
Level
Change To
Normal Cruise

:30
Level
Change To
Slow Cruise

:60
Descend 500'
Slow Cruise

Climb quantities shown in
brackets are for airplanes
with a greater climb
capability than a Cessna 150.

Pattern E

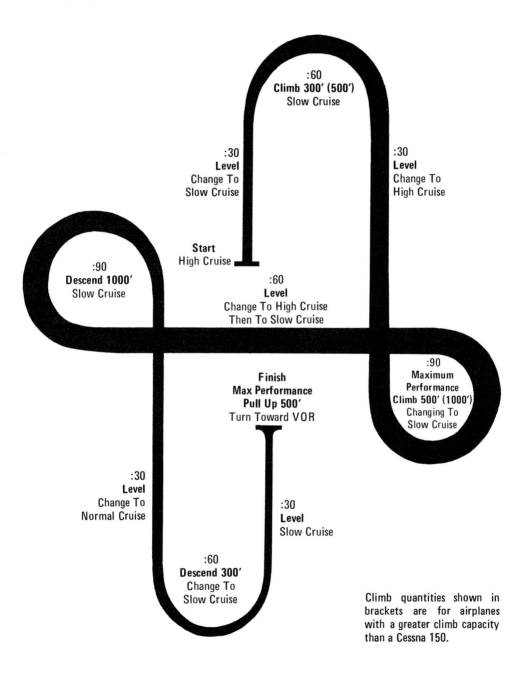

:60
Climb 300' (500')
Slow Cruise

:30
Level
Change To
Slow Cruise

:30
Level
Change To
High Cruise

Start
High Cruise

:90
Descend 1000'
Slow Cruise

:60
Level
Change To High Cruise
Then To Slow Cruise

:90
**Maximum
Performance
Climb 500' (1000')**
Changing To
Slow Cruise

**Finish
Max Performance
Pull Up 500'**
Turn Toward VOR

:30
Level
Change To
Normal Cruise

:30
Level
Slow Cruise

:60
Descend 300'
Change To
Slow Cruise

Climb quantities shown in brackets are for airplanes with a greater climb capacity than a Cessna 150.

Appendix B
FUNDAMENTALS OF RADIO OPERATION

I. BASIC RADIO THEORY AND FREQUENCY UTILIZATION

    A.   **Wave**: A pulse of energy which travels through a medium by means of vibrations from particle to particle.

        1. *Amplitude:* The linear distance between a wave's highest or lowest fluctuation measured from its midpoint.

        2. *Wave Length:* The linear distance of a cycle and the determining factor in the length of an antenna.

        3. *Frequency:* The number of cycles completed in one unit of time.

        4. *Audio Frequency:* 15 to 20,000 CPS superimposed on the radio carrier wave.

        5. *Modulation:* Amplitude and frequency modification of the wave.

        6. *Current:* The flow of electrons through a conductor. Direct current (DC) flows only in one direction. Alternating current (AC) flows in one direction during a given time interval, then in the opposite direction for the same interval, reversing continuously.

    B.   **Radio Waves**: Waves produced by sending a high-frequency alternating current through a conductor (antenna). The frequency of the wave radiated by the antenna is equal to the frequency, or number of cycles per second, of the alternating current. Notice that since radio wave cycles per unit of time involve very high numbers, radio frequencies are expressed in kilo hertz (thousands of cycles per second). Thus a frequency of 1,000 Hz equals 1 kHz and 1,000 kHz equals 1 MHz. The velocity of the radiated wave is 186,000 miles per second.

1. *Radio Wave Propagation:*

    a. *Low Frequency* (L/F) radio waves (30-300 kHz) and medium frequency radio waves (300-3000 kHz) radiate from an antenna in all directions. The "ground wave" travels along the earth's surface until its energy is dissipated (attenuates). The "sky wave" travels upward into space and is reflected back to earth by the ionosphere permitting reception of signals at varying distances from the transmitter. The distance between the transmitting antenna and the point where the sky wave first returns to the ground is called the "skip distance" and the distance between the point where the ground wave can no longer be received and the point where the sky wave returns to the ground is called the "skip zone."

    b. *High Frequency* (H/F) radio waves (3000 kHz - 30 MHz) attenuate so quickly along the ground that the ground wave is of little use except at very short distances. The sky wave must be utilized and since it reflects back and forth from sky to earth, it may be used over very long distances.

    c. *Very High Frequency* (VHF) radio waves (30-300 MHz) and *Ultra High Frequency* (UHF) radio waves (300-3000 MHz) have practically no ground wave propagation and ordinarily have no reflection from the ionosphere. They are "line of sight"* transactions only and are limited by the position of the receiver in relation to the transmitter.

        *NOTE: "Line of sight" distance in nautical miles may be accurately approximated by multiplying the square root of the aircraft's altitude by 1.23 (see Chapter I, p. 14).

2. *Static Disturbance to Reception:* Only low frequency airborne equipment is susceptible to static disturbance. Signals in the higher frequency bands are static free but may be susceptible to "frequency interference" instead, caused by the operation of an FM radio in close prox-

imity to an aircraft's navigational receivers. Whether the source of the static originates away from the aircraft in lightning discharges or from electrostatic discharges from the aircraft's own surfaces (precipitation static) it distorts the radio wave and interferes with normal reception of both communications and navigation signals.

C.   Radio Frequency Utilization

1.   *Low/Medium Frequencies:*

200-415 and 510-535 kHz: Transmitting frequencies of L/MF radio ranges, aeronautical and marine radio beacons, and ILS compass locators.

535-1605 kHz: Radio broadcasting stations (AM) that are extensively used for aircraft homing.

500 kHz: International distress frequency for ships and aircraft over the seas.

2.   *Very High Frequencies:*

VHF frequencies that are not specified below as transmitting or guarding frequencies are normally used for both purposes (see Note p. 159).

a.   *Navigation Aids:*

75 MHz: Transmitting frequencies of fan markers, Z markers and ILS markers.
108.0 MHz: Used for VOR test facilities.
108.1-111.9 MHz: ILS localizers with or without voice. Operated on odd tenths.
108.2-111.8 MHz: Transmitting frequencies of terminal VORs. Operated on even tenths (nav and voice). Also used for VOR test facilities (VOT).
112.0-117.9 MHz: Transmitting frequencies of VORs (nav and voice).

b.   *Voice Communications:*

118.0-121.4 MHz: Air Traffic Control
121.5 MHz: Emergency Frequency, ELT signals

121.6-121.9 MHz: Airport Ground Control (ELT test on 121.6)

121.95 MHz: Flight Schools

121.975 MHz: Private Aircraft Advisory (FSS)

122.0 MHz: FSS "Flight Watch" Weather Advisory

122.1 MHz: FSS receive only with VOR or FSS Simplex

122.2 MHz: FSS Common Enroute Simplex

122.7 MHz: Unicom, uncontrolled airports

122.75 MHz: Air-to-Air Communications and Private Unicom

122.8 MHz: Unicom, uncontrolled airports

122.85 MHz: Multicom

122.9 MHz: Multicom (agricultural, ranching, forest fire fighting, parachute jumping and air-to-air communications)

122.950 MHz: Unicom, controlled airports

123.0 MHz: Unicom, uncontrolled airports

123.1 MHz: Search and Rescue, temporary control towers

123.15-123.575 MHz: Flight Test

123.3 & 123.5 MHz: Flight Schools

123.6-123.65 MHz: FSS or Air Traffic Control

123.675-128.8 MHz: Air Traffic Control

126.2 MHz: Military facilities guard for civil aircraft

128.825-132.0 MHz: Aeronautical Enroute (airlines)

132.05-135.95 MHz: Air Traffic Control

II. OPERATING PRINCIPLES OF THE NAVIGATION RADIOS

The information in this Appendix is based upon Chapter 7, AC 61-27C: *Instrument Flying Handbook;* Chapters 11 and 13, AFM 51-37: *Instrument Flying;* and Chapter 1 of the *Airman's Information Manual.*

A. VOR

The VHF omnidirectional range (VOR) is a radio facility used extensively for departure, enroute and arrival operations. Distance measuring equipment (DME) may be installed with a VOR facility. Since VOR transmitting equipment is in the VHF band, the signals are free of atmospheric disturbances. VOR reception is limited to line of sight, and the usable range varies according to the altitude of the aircraft and the class of the station being received. Normal usable altitude and range limitations for various classes of VOR stations, based on interference-free signal reception, are specified in Chapter 1, Section 1 of the *Airman's Information Manual.*

The transmission principal of the VOR is based on creating a phase difference between two signals. One of these signals, the REFERENCE PHASE, is omnidirectional and radiates from the station in a circular pattern. The phase of this signal is constant through 360 degrees. The other signal, the VARIABLE PHASE, rotates uniformly at 1800 rpm and its phase changes one degree for each degree change in azimuth around the VOR. Magnetic north is used as the baseline for electronically measuring the phase relationship between the reference and variable phase signals. At magnetic north, the signals are exactly in phase; however, a phase difference exists at any other point around the station. This phase difference is measured electronically by the aircraft receiver and displayed on the navigation instrument as a magnetic course (bearing) "To" or "From" the station. The VOR provides an infinite number of courses which radiate from the station like spokes from the hub of a wheel and are known as radials. It is possible to fly any one of these radials *inbound* to or *outbound* from a VOR. Radials are identified by their magnetic bearing "From" the station. An aircraft on the 210 degree radial is physically located southwest of the station. Flying to the station on this radial, the aircraft's magnetic course would be 030 degrees.

B.   ADF

The automatic direction finder (ADF) is a navigational radio *in the aircraft* which indicates the aircraft's relative bearing to any non-directional beacon (NDB) *on the ground* within its frequency and sensitivity range. The "radio compass" is used extensively for arrival operations but also may be used as an auxiliary receiver for the reception of range signals, weather broadcasts and other broadcast information.

The operation of an ADF depends chiefly upon the characteristics of a loop antenna. A loop-receiving antenna gives maximum reception when the plane of the loop is parallel to, or in line with, the direction of wave travel. As the loop is rotated from this position, volume gradually decreases and reaches a minimum when the plane of the loop is perpendicular to the direction of wave travel. This position of the loop called the null position rather than the maximum (parallel) position is used for direction finding; that is, a bearing is obtained when the plane of the loop is perpendicular to the line on which the radio waves are traveling when they strike the loop. With the loop rotated to a null position, the radio station being received is on a line perpendicular to the plane of the loop. However, the direction of the radio station from the aircraft may be either one or two directions 180 degrees apart. The inability of the loop antenna to determine which of the two possible directions is correct is called the 180 degree ambiguity of the loop. This 180 ambiguity is eliminated with a non-directional or sensing antenna which is used in conjunction with the loop antenna to generate a combination of signals that energize a phasing system which rotates the loop. The bearing pointer is electronically synchronized and turns with the loop, indicating the magnetic bearing "To" the station when the loop has stopped in the null position.

The newer ADF radios use a "fixed loop" antenna that is generally smaller and more trouble-free than the older rotating loop type. The antenna is permanently mounted in one direction on the outside of the aircraft and because it has no moving parts there is no possibility of moisture getting into the mechanism and corroding it. The principle of operation for both systems is the same, but the fixed loop utilizes sophisticated electronic circuitry to eliminate the bulky rotating antenna. The fixed loop system actually has a rotating loop, but it is located inside the aircraft, and is inside the indicating instrument. Since it is inside and protected, it is much more reliable.

C. DME

Distance is determined with distance measuring equipment by measuring the elapsed time between transmission of interrogating pulses of the airborne radio and reception of corresponding reply pulses from the ground VORTAC station. The aircraft transmitter starts the process by sending out the distance interrogation pulse signals. Receipt of these signals by the ground station receiver triggers its transmitter which sends out the distance reply pulse signals. These pulses require about 12 microseconds round-trip travel time per nautical mile of distance from the station. The distance scale displays distance to the VORTAC in nautical miles.

Since a large number of aircraft could be interrogating the same station, the airborne radio must sort out only the pulses which are replies to its own interrogations. Interrogation pulses are transmitted on an irregular, random basis by the airborne set which then "searches" for replies synchronized to its own interrogations. If signals are interrupted, a memory circuit maintains the indication on the distance scale for approximately 10 seconds to prevent the search operation from recurring. The searching process starts automatically whenever the airborne radio is tuned to a new station or when there is a major interruption in the VORTAC signal. Depending upon the aircraft's actual distance from the station at the time, the searching process may require up to 22 seconds.

D. RADAR

The basic principle of *Ra*dio *D*etection *a*nd *R*anging equipment (radar) may be stated in a single word . . . reflection. An echo is a simple demonstration of the reflection of sound waves. A radiated noise strikes a reflecting surface and is returned to its source. The time lag between the original sound and its echo is directly proportional to the distance the sound must travel. This same principle applies in the use of radio waves. The frequency band used contains very short radio waves of ultra-high or super-high frequency which travel, essentially, in a straight line and are easily reflected from objects in their path. Longer radio waves are not as easily reflected; they continue around obstacles and tend to follow the curvature of the earth.

A very short radio wave is produced and transmitted in a certain direction in the form of a short pulse lasting from one-half to several microseconds (millionths of a second). When this pulse strikes a reflecting surface, some of the reflected waves return to the point of origin where the energy is picked up by a receiver. Multiplying the time interval by the velocity of the radio waves and dividing the product by two gives the distance to the reflecting object.

The best means of presenting the return of the "echo" is by use of cathode-ray tubes, commonly called scopes. With this type presentation, the object (aircraft) reflecting the radio wave appears as a "pip" on a scope. The Radar Controller determines the position of the aircraft through scope interpretation.

III. SELF-STUDY METHOD OF MORSE CODE

The following is presented as a SELF-STUDY method of morse code. The recommended method is to learn the first group before proceeding to the second group and etc.

Group I

1. These four letters have all dots, study the code for:

E	I	S	H
(•)	(• •)	(• • •)	(• • • •)

Group II

2. These three letters have all dashes, study the code for:

T	M	O
(−)	(− −)	(− − −)

Group III

3. These three letters have dots followed by one dash, study the
    code for:

    A   **U**   **V**
    (• −)   (• • −)   (• • • −)

Group IV

4. These three letters have a dash followed by dots, study the
    code for:

    N   **D**   **B**
    (− •)   (− • •)   (− • • •)

Group V

5. These two letters have a dot followed by dashes, study the
    code for:

    W   **J**
    (• − −)   (• − − −)

Group VI

6. These three letters have alternate dots and dashes, study the
    code for:

    K   **C**   **R**
    (− • −)   (− • − •)   (• − •)

Group VII

7. These two letters have the same dots and dashes only back-
    wards, study the code for:

    L   **F**
    (• − • •)   (• • − •)

Group VIII

8. These two letters have dots and dashes backward, study the code for:

P	X
(• – – •)	(– • • –)

Group IX

9. These two letters have one dot and dashes in reverse order, study the code for:

Y	Q
(– • – –)	(– – • –)

Group X

10. These two letters have two dashes followed by dots, study the code for:

G	Z
(– – •)	(– – • •)

Group XI

11. Numbers all have five dots and/or dashes, study the code for:

1	2	3	4	5
(• – – – –)	(• • – – –)	(• • • – –)	(• • • • –)	(• • • • •)

6	7	8	9	0
(– • • • •)	(– – • • •)	(– – – • •)	(– – – – •)	(– – – – –)

RADIOTELEGRAPH CODE AND PHONETIC ALPHABET
INTERNATIONAL (ICAO)

Letter	Word	Code
A	ALFA	• —
B	BRAVO	— • • •
C	CHARLIE	— • — •
D	DELTA	— • •
E	ECHO	•
F	FOXTROT	• • — •
G	GOLF	— — •
H	HOTEL	• • • •
I	INDIA	• •
J	JULIETT	• — — —
K	KILO	— • —
L	LIMA	• — • •
M	MIKE	— —
N	NOVEMBER	— •
O	OSCAR	— — —
P	PAPA	• — — •
Q	QUEBEC	— — • —
R	ROMEO	• — •
S	SIERRA	• • •
T	TANGO	—
U	UNIFORM	• • —
V	VICTOR	• • • —
W	WHISKEY	• — —
X	XRAY	— • • —
Y	YANKEE	— • — —
Z	ZULU	— — • •
0	ZE-RO	— — — — —
1	WUN	• — — — —
2	TOO	• • — — —
3	TREE	• • • — —
4	FOW-er	• • • • —
5	FIFE	• • • • •
6	SIX	— • • • •
7	SEV-en	— — • • •
8	AIT	— — — • •
9	NIN-er	— — — — •

Appendix C
FUNDAMENTALS OF FLIGHT INSTRUMENT OPERATION

The information in this Appendix is based upon Chapter 4, AC 61-27C: *Instrument Flying Handbook;* Exam-O-Grams 10, 18, and 24; and Advisory Circulars AC 60-6 and 90-14a.

Aircraft instruments differ from other types of measuring instruments in that they must operate in a very unfavorable environment for accuracy and reliability. For example, in the design of pressure-sensing indicators, it is simple to measure the effect of pressure to the required degree of accuracy. The real challenge, however, is to produce an instrument that will not also respond to temperature changes from -60°F to 160°F and acceleration forces varying from -1 to +5 times that of gravity. Aircraft instruments are selective solutions to a very special set of problems. Unlike Chapter 7 of AF Manual 51-37: *Instrument Flying* (see Chapter IX, p. 141) which divides the instruments according to their control, performance or navigation function in attitude instrument flying, this appendix categorizes the instruments by their principles of operation. Except for the magnetic compass which is a completely self-contained instrument that operates independently of the aircraft electrical or pressure sensing systems, the flight instruments may be categorized as either differential pressure or gyroscopic instruments. The fact that an instrument is driven by electricity or suction DOES NOT influence the general category it falls into. For example, the turn and bank indicator is a gyroscopic instrument regardless of the fact that it may be electrically powered! An IFR pilot must know the capabilities and limitations of his instruments in order to interpret them properly. This appendix covers the various differential pressure and gyroscopic flight instruments and discusses both their operation and inherent errors.

I.   PITOT-STATIC INSTRUMENTS

   A.   Pitot-Static System:

      1.   *Pitot System:* The pitot system is designed to supply ram or impact pressure to the airspeed indicator. The system consists of a pitot tube and the lines used to supply this pressure. The pitot tube is normally located parallel to the longitudinal axis or thrust line of the aircraft in an area of minimum airstream disturbance. The preferred location is the nose section of the fuselage but other locations include the leading edge of the wing, the wing tip or even the vertical stabilizer. An electrical heating element is used in most pitot tubes to prevent the formation of ice.

      2.   *Static System:* The static system is designed to supply the ambient (still) air pressure surrounding the aircraft to the speed, altitude, and vertical velocity indicators. To minimize sensing errors, the static ports used to supply this pressure are located in an area that has the least disturbed air flow. Most aircraft have the static ports mounted on both sides of the fuselage so an average pressure is sensed during turning or yawing maneuvers. The static ports may or may not be heated, but they should always be checked that they are free of obstructions prior to flight. Pay particular attention to this area after the aircraft has been washed or polished; check the area to insure that tape, polish residue, or trapped water do not obstruct the static ports. Distorting the holes or surrounding skin area a few thousandths of an inch can cause pressure sensing errors.

      3.   *Alternate Static System:* An alternate static system is provided in some aircraft in the event the normal system becomes obstructed by ice or otherwise fails. The alternate static ports are usually located at a point within the airframe that is not susceptible to icing conditions. There is usually a pressure difference between the alternate and normal systems, and when the pilot switches to the alter-

nate system, the indications of airspeed and altitude will normally change. The amount of and direction of this error normally is not available in the performance charts, so the pilot should familiarize himself with the differences in cruise, letdown, and especially the approach configurations.

B. **Pitot and Static Sensing Errors:**

1. *Compressibility Error:* Both the pitot and the static systems have inherent characteristics that affect the pressures supplied to the instruments. One characteristic that affects pitot pressure is called compressibility error. The magnitude of this error is the same for all aircraft flying at the same equivalent airspeed and density altitude. The error is caused by air being compressed in the pitot inlet which results in a higher than actual airspeed reading in the cockpit. It is negligible below 10,000 feet and 200 knots CAS (calibrated air speed).

2. *Installation Error:* Installation or position error is caused by static ports supplying erroneous static pressure to the instruments. The slip stream airflow causes disturbances at the static ports, introducing an error in atmospheric pressure measurement which varies with type of aircraft, airspeed and configuration. When the static ports are flush-mounted on the fuselage, the pressure sensed is usually lower than actual static pressure because of the venturi effect of the fuselage. The amount and direction of this error is determined by flight test and is found in the performance section of the aircraft flight manual. Since this is a static pressure sensing error, it affects the indications of airspeed and altitude; it DOES NOT appreciably affect the vertical speed indications. The vertical speed indicator will initially show this pressure change, then stabilize with the proper indication.

3. *Reversal Error:* Reversal error is caused by a momentary static pressure change when the aircraft pitch attitude is changed. **Example:** when an aircraft is rotated for take-

off, the instruments may indicate a temporary descent, loss of altitude and airspeed, due to a momentary higher pressure being sensed by the system. The effects of this error can be minimized by smooth pitch changes.

C. **Pitot-Static Instruments:**

1. ***Pressure Altimeter:***

   a. *Principle of Operation:* The pressure altimeter operates through the response of trapped air within the instrument to changes in atmospheric pressure. The air is trapped within the elastic metal wafers which expand or contract as atmospheric pressure changes. This expansion or contraction rotates the pointers that are connected through a shaft and gearing linkage. For each pressure level, the aneroid assumes a definite size and causes the hands to indicate height above whatever pressure level is set into the Kollsman window.

   b. *Barometric Setting Feature:* Because surface pressures are always changing, a means of changing the altimeter reference is necessary. A barometric set knob is provided to change the reference shown on the barometric scale and is designed to change the altimeter indication approximately 10 feet for each .01" Hg change on the scale. This approximates the rate of pressure change found in the first 10,000 feet of atmosphere; i.e., 1" Hg for each 1,000 feet. Increasing the barometric setting will cause the altitude indication to INCREASE, while decreasing the value on the barometric scale will cause the altitude indication to DECREASE. The majority of altimeters have mechanical stops at or just beyond the barometric scale limits (28.10 to 31.00).

   c. *Types of Altitude:*

      (1) Altitude: The vertical distance of a level, a point, or an object considered as a point, measured from a given surface.

(2) Absolute Altitude: The altitude above the terrain directly below the aircraft.

(3) Pressure Altitude: The altitude above the standard datum plane. Altitude read on altimeter when "Kollsman" window is set to 29.92 Hg (inches of mercury).[1]

(4) Density Altitude: Pressure altitude corrected for temperature. Pressure and density altitudes are the same when conditions are standard. As the temperature rises above standard, the density of the air decreases, hence an increase in density altitude.

(5) Indicated Altitude: MSL (mean sea level) altitude read on altimeter when "Kollsman" window is set to local barometric pressure.[2]

NOTE 1: You can convert your indicated altitude to pressure altitude without resetting the altimeter to 29.92 by considering the current altimeter setting. Suppose your altimeter registers 5000 feet (field elevation) and the current setting is 30.42 inches of mercury. Your pressure altitude is 4500 feet and is arrived at as follows: The pressure corrected to sea level is 30.42 inches, but to get pressure altitude the setting should be based on 29.92 inches. This shows that the actual pressure of 30.42 is HIGHER than standard, therefore the pressure altitude is LESS (higher pressures at lower altitudes). Using a figure of 1 inch per thousand feet you see that the pressure difference is 0.50 inches of mercury or 500 feet. The pressure altitude is 5000 minus 500 = 4500 feet. This will be as close as you can read an altitude conversion chart anyway. If your altimeter setting were 29.42 your pressure altitude would be 500 feet higher (29.92 - 29.42 = 0.50 inch = 500 feet) or 5,500 feet.

NOTE 2: There are only three (3) variables which determine the altitude indicated on pressure altimeter:

　　1. The *atmospheric pressure* which the instrument is measuring.

2. The *mechanical displacement of the indicator needles* — the altimeter setting.

3. *Instrument error,* which is largely an unknown but may be expected to be within plus or minus three percent of the reading.

Aside from possible instrument error, it is easy to anticipate the effects of the other two variables by asking for *two* specific items of information during your preflight weather briefing at the Flight Service Station (FSS). For example, consider a flight out of XYZ airport over high terrain. Since you want to determine if you will be higher or lower than indicated over the mountains and by what amount, you have the following discussion with the weather forecaster:

Pilot: I intend to file for 11,000 feet. What is the height of the constant pressure level closest to my planned altitude?

Forecaster: According to the latest soundings and forecasts, the 700 millibar level (10,000 feet) is at 9,580 feet or about 420 feet below normal.

Pilot: Well, that will put me 420 feet lower than indicated to begin with. What are the altimeter settings through this area?

Forecaster: Altimeter settings are averaging around 30.60 inches. What effect does that have?

Pilot: Because a HIGH setting increases the altimeter scale indications, my aircraft will really be flying lower than its altimeter indicates. In this case, it will be . . .

Current set	30.60
Normal set	− 29.92

.68 x 1000 = 680 ft.

Forecaster: How high will you actually be?

Pilot: Add the two effects . . .

Flight-level pressure low	420 feet
Altimeter setting high	+ 680 feet

1,100 feet

I will actually be 1,100 feet below my indicated altitude. You have some goodsized hills around here so I'll file for 13,000 instead — just to be on the safe side.

HIGH surface altimeter settings combined with low pressure levels (HALP) at your flight altitude can cause the altimeter to indicate more than 2000 feet in error. If you are one who relies upon the current altimeter setting when flying at minimum altitudes, you had better think again!

(6) Calibrated Altitude: Indicated altitude corrected for installation error.

(7) True Altitude: Calibrated altitude corrected for non-standard atmospheric conditions. Actual height above mean sea level.

d. *Altimeter Errors:*

(1) Scale Error: Scale error is caused by the aneroids not assuming the precise size designed for a particular pressure difference. This error is irregular throughout the range of the instrument; i.e., it might be -30 feet at 1,000 feet and +50 feet at 10,000 feet. Scale error may be observed in the following manner:

(a) Set the current reported altimeter setting on the altimeter setting scale.

(b) Altimeter should now read field elevation if you are located on the same reference level used to establish the altimeter setting.

(c) Note the variation between the known field elevation and the altimeter indication. If this variation is in the order of plus or minus 75 feet, the accuracy of the altimeter is questionable and the problem should be referred to an appropriately rated repair station for evaluation and possible correction.

(2) Friction Error: Friction error is caused by friction in moving parts of mechanical altimeters and causes lags in instrument indications.

Usually, natural vibrations will resolve friction error in reciprocating engine aircraft.

(3) Mechanical Error: Mechanical error is caused by misalignment or slippage in the gears/ linkage connecting the aneroids to the pointers or in the shaft of the barometric set knob. This error is checked by the altimeter setting procedure.

(4) Hysteresis Error: This error is a lag in the altitude indications caused by the elastic properties of the materials used in the aneroids. It occurs after an aircraft has maintained a constant altitude for a period of time and then makes a large, rapid altitude change. It takes a period of time for the aneroids to "catch up" to the new pressure environment, hence, a lag in indications.

2. *Airspeed Indicator:*

   a. *Principle of Operation:* Speed measurement for purposes of aircraft performance is accomplished by comparing PITOT (ram) pressure to STATIC (ambient) pressure. The difference between these two pressures is DYNAMIC pressure. The dynamic pressure and angle of attack on the wing determine the amount of lift generated; i.e., aircraft performance. These two pressures are compared in the airspeed indicator by supplying pitot pressure to a flexible metallic diaphragm and static pressure to the airtight chamber which surrounds the diaphragm. The expansion or contraction of the diaphragm is linked mechanically by gears and levers to the airspeed pointer. Expansion of the diaphragm (increase in airspeed) is caused either by increasing pitot pressure while static pressure remains constant, or by decreasing static pressure while pitot pressure remains constant. Diaphragm contraction (decrease in airspeed) is caused either by lowering pitot pressure while the static pressure remains constant or by increasing static pressure while pitot pressure remains constant. The airspeed dial may show indicated airspeed, true airspeed, or a combination of these values calibrated in miles per hour or knots.

b. *Types of Airspeed:*

(1) Indicated Airspeed (IAS): The uncorrected airspeed read on the face of a standard airspeed indicator.

(2) Calibrated Airspeed (CAS): Indicated airspeed corrected for installation (position) and instrument error. Airspeed limitations, such as those found on the color-coded face of the airspeed indicator are calibrated airspeeds.* A pilot should refer to the "Airspeed Calibration Chart" included in the aircraft flight manual to allow for possible airspeed errors.

NOTE: See Chapter X, p. 157 for a partial listing of the airspeed limitations that are expressed as "V" speeds. Not all of these operational speeds are color-coded on the airspeed indicator.

(3) Equivalent Airspeed (EAS): Calibrated airspeed corrected for compressibility error. Equivalent airspeed is equal to calibrated airspeed in a standard atmosphere at sea level.

(4) True Airspeed (TAS): Equivalent airspeed corrected for air-density variation from the standard value of sea level. True airspeed increases about 2 percent per thousand feet of altitude.

(5) Groundspeed (GS): True airspeed corrected for wind. This speed may be determined by reference to a DME readout or by computation on the "wind side" of any standard flight computer.

    c. *Airspeed Errors:*

      (1) Density Error: Density error is introduced by changes in altitude and temperature for which the instrument does not automatically compensate. The standard airspeed indicator cannot adjust for variations from sea-level standard atmosphere conditions. See types of airspeed above.

      (2) Installation (Position) Error: See B.: Pitot Static Errors, p. 225.

      (3) Compressibility Error: See B.: Pitot Static Errors, p. 225.

3. *Vertical Speed Indicator:*

    a. *Principle of Operation:* The vertical speed indicator (also called vertical-velocity or rate-of-climb indicator) uses "rate of change of static pressure" for measuring vertical rate. The rate of change of static pressure is obtained by furnishing static pressure directly to a thin metallic diaphragm and through a calibrated orifice to an air-tight case surrounding the diaphragm. As the aircraft climbs, the static pressure in the case is momentarily "trapped" by the calibrated orifice and the static pressure in the diaphragm is allowed to decrease immediately. This decrease causes the diaphragm to contract and through a mechanical linkage, the pointer indicates a climb. When the pressures are equalized in level flight, the needle reads zero. In a descent, the opposite is true. Case static pressure is momentarily "trapped" at the lower static pressure while the diaphragm expands because of the higher static pressure furnished and this expansion causes the pointer to indicate a descent. Because of this "delay" or "lag" caused by the calibrated orifice, it requires up to 9 seconds for the indications to stabilize. However, immediate trend information is available. Many of the "instantaneous" types of indicators use either a pitch gyro signal or an accelerometer signal for the initial indication and then stabilize the indication with barometric information.

b. *Limitations:* Limitations in the use of the vertical-speed indicator are due to the calibrated leak. Sudden or abrupt changes in aircraft attitude cause erroneous instrument readings as the airflow fluctuates over the static ports. Both rough control technique and turbulent air result in unreliable needle indications. When used properly, the instrument provides reliable information to establish and maintain level flight and rate climbs or descents.

II. GYROSCOPIC INSTRUMENTS

A. Gyroscope Construction

1. *The Mounting:* A gyroscope is a spinning mass or wheel, mounted so that only one point — its center of gravity — is in a fixed position, the wheel being free to turn in any direction around this point. The two mountings used in flight instrument gyroscopes are the *universal mounting* which allows the spin axis to turn and tilt, and the *restricted mounting* which allows the spin axis only to tilt.

A gyroscope that has three or more gimbals is universally mounted. Most universally mounted gyros have four gimbals. The instrument case, and therefore the aircraft itself, acts as one of the gimbals for flight instruments. A gyro that has two gimbals is a restricted gyro. This gyro is allowed to tilt, but not to turn.

In the attitude indicator, which uses the universal mounting, the horizon bar is gyro-controlled to remain parallel to the natural horizon and changes in position of the aircraft are shown pictorially. In the turn indicator, the restricted (semirigid) mounting is used to provide controlled precision of the rotor, and the precessing force exerted on the gyro by the turning aircraft causes the needle to indicate a turn.

A gyro may be mounted with the spin axis either parallel or perpendicular to the earth's surface. Horizontal gyros have the spin axis parallel to the earth's surface; vertical gyros have the spin axis perpendicular to the surface of the earth.

2. *Rotor Inertia:* Gyroscopic inertia depends upon several design factors:

    a. *Weight:* For a given size, a heavier mass is more resistant to disturbing forces than a lighter mass.

    b. *Angular Velocity:* The higher the rotational speed, the greater the rigidity, or resistance to deflection.

    c. *Radius at which the Weight is Concentrated:* Maximum effect is obtained from a mass when its principal weight is concentrated near the rim rotating at high speed.

    d. *Bearing Friction:* Any friction applies a deflecting force to a gyro. Minimum bearing friction keeps deflecting forces at a minimum.

B. **Power Requirements**

The directional gyro and the artificial horizon are both vacuum driven instruments. The gyroscope or the rotor in each instrument is driven by air. The engine-driven vacuum pump evacuates air from the case of the instrument which allows a flow of air to enter the instrument. This occurs through either a central air filter, or through a small filter contained directly within the instrument. This inward flow of air is directed by a nozzle directly onto the buckets of the gyro rotor. This, in turn, causes the rotor to rotate a speed of between 10,000 to 18,000 rpm, depending on instrument design.

NOTE: Electrically operated gyros, such as the J-8 type attitude indicator, are driven by 115-volt, 400-cycle alternating current and turn at 21,000 rpm.

To give the pilot an indication that the engine-driven pump is evacuating the instrument case and allowing this flow of air, the suction gauge is attached to the case of the instrument. For proper operation, the suction gauge reading can be as low as 3.5 and as high as 5.0 inches of mercury, with 4.0 of the desired suction. Limits for adjustment of the vacuum are 3.75 and 4.25, or as specified in your aircraft operating handbook.

Unfortunately, the suction gauge indication is nothing more than a relative reading. As the central filter or the internal filter of the instrument becomes clogged, the suction gauge reads higher. In many cases, this causes the pilot to inform a mechanic that the suction is excessively high. In turn, the mechanic re-adjusts the regular valve, cutting down the suction which results in still less air being driven against the buckets of the rotor and, of course, the rotor turning at still a slower speed. Do not have regulator reset without first changing the filter!

C. **Principles of Gyroscope Operation**

In present day aircraft, gyroscopes are used in turn and bank indicators, attitude systems, and heading systems. The turn and bank gyroscope has a restricted mounting and uses the gyroscopic property of *real precession* for its operation. Attitude systems and heading systems use two gyroscopic properties. Attitude systems use *rigidity in space* to establish a reference plane and real precession (erection device) to orient the gyro spin axis vertical to the earth's surface. Heading systems use rigidity in space to establish a reference plane and real precession to keep the gyro spin axis horizontal to the earth's surface. See the following explanation of these two important gyroscopic principals:

1. **Rigidity in Space:** Rigidity in space is a basic principle used in all flight instruments containing a universally mounted gyroscope. When the rotor of such a gyroscope

is spinning rapidly, the spin axis will maintain its orientation in space regardless of any movement of the gyroscope base.

2. *Precision:* To serve as an attitude or heading reference, the gyroscope spin axis must remain aligned with relation to the earth's surface. Any movement (real or apparent) of the spin axis is called precession.

    a. *Apparent Precession:* As the earth rotates or as a gyro is flown from one position on the earth to another, the spin axis remains fixed in space. However, to an observer on the surface of the earth, the spin axis appears to change its orientation in space. Either the earth's rotation (earth rate precession) or transportation of the gyro from one geographical fix to another (earth transport precession) may cause apparent precession. To control this apparent drift, as well as random drift caused by the friction of bearings or any small amount of unbalance, the instrument is provided with an erecting mechanism which maintains the spin axis in the required position. The erecting mechanism applies a force to the rotor whenever drift occurs. The force or precession returns the spin axis to its normal position, maintaining an accurate reference.

    b. *Real Precession:* Real precession is movement of the gyro spin axis from its original alignment in space. Although a gyro rotor which is spinning resists any force which attempts to change the direction of its spin axis, it does move in response to such a force or pressure. The movement is not a direct one, in response to the force applied, but rather it is a resultant removement. The axis of the rotor is displaced, not in the direction of the force applied but at 90 degrees to the applied force in the direction of rotation and the rotor will move in such a way as to tend to cause the direction of rotation of the rotor to assume the direction of the torque resulting from the applied force.

D. **Gyroscopic Instruments**

1. *Attitude Indicator (Artificial Horizon):*

    a. *Principle of Operation:* The rotor, mounted within a sealed housing, spins in a horizontal plane about the vertical axis. The housing pivots about the lateral axis on a gimbal, which in turn is free to pivot around the longitudinal axis. The instrument case is the third gimbal necessary for universal mounting.

      The horizon bar is linked to the gyro by a lever, attached to a pivot on the rear of the gimbal frame and connected to the gyro housing by a guide pin. While the gyro rotates in a fixed plane, the miniature aircraft is super-imposed on the horizon line in straight-and-level flight. As the aircraft climbs, dives, or banks, the instrument case rotates on the gimbals while the bank index and horizon bar remain rigid. Thus, the instrument reflects any movement of the aircraft around the pitch and roll axes.

    b. *Limitations:* The limits of the instrument refer to the maximum rotation of the gimbals beyond which the gyro will tumble. The older type vacuum-driven attitude indicators have bank limits of approximately 100 to 110 degrees, and pitch limits of 60 to 70 degrees. The limits of the newer indicators exceed those given above. The gyro rotor is self-erecting and will process bank to the horizontal plane at a rate of approximately 8 degrees per minute. This self erection is accomplished by the imbalance in exhaust air which occurs when the rotor precesses from the proper plane of rotation. This unequal exhaust air precesses the gyro back to an erect position where the exhaust air from all ports is equal again.

    c. *Attitude Indicator Errors:*

      (1) Manufacturing and Maintenance Induced: Low vacuum, clogged filters, poorly balanced com-

ponents, improperly adjusted valves and
vacuum pump malfunction. These errors may
be minimized by proper installation and inspec-
tion.

(2) Induced During Normal Operation of the Instrument:

(a) Skid error — A skidding turn moves the
pendulous vanes out of their vertical position precessing the gyro toward the inside
of the turn. After return to straight and
level flight, the miniature aircraft shows a
bank in the direction opposite the skid.
The maximum error is 3 to 4 degrees.
When the skidding stops, the erecting
mechanism soon returns the rotor to its
normal plane of rotation.

(b) Turn error — During a normal coordinated
turn, movement of the pendulous vanes
by centrifugal force causes the gyro to
precess toward the inside of the turn. The
error is greatest in a steep turn. After roll-
ing-out at the end of a 180 degree turn,
the miniature aircraft shows a slight climb
and a banked attitude opposite the direction of the turn. This precession error is
quickly corrected by the erecting mechanism. The precession induced by a second 180 degree turn cancels the error of
the first.

(c) Acceleration error — When the aircraft
accelerates, the pendulous vanes of the
erecting mechanism are moved out of
position resulting in a precession of the
gyro. The horizon bar moves down and
the instrument indicates a climb.

(d) Deceleration error — Deceleration causes
the erecting mechanism to react in such a

manner that the horizon bar moves up, indicating a descent.

(e) Haphazard error — This error is caused by a defective erecting mechanism or low suction. There is a loss of rigidity and the reaction of the instrument is unpredictable.

2. *The Heading Indicator (Directional Gyro)*

a. *Principles of Operation:* The operation of the heading indicator depends upon the principle of rigidity in space of a universally mounted gyroscope. The rotor turns in a vertical plane, and fixed at right angles to this plane (to the vertical gimbal) is a circular compass card. Since the rotor remains rigid in space, the points on the card hold the same position in space relative to the vertical plane. As the instrument case revolves about the vertical gimbal, the card provides clear and accurate heading references.

b. *Limitations:* The design of the vacuum-driven directional gyro imposes limitations on rotation about the gimbals preventing operation of the instrument in abnormal flight attitudes. Beyond the normal operating limits of 55 degrees of pitch and bank . . . when the horizontal gimbal touches the stop, the precessional force causes the card to spin rapidly.

c. *Heading Indicator Errors:*

(1) Precession: Caused mainly by bearing friction.

(2) Failure to Apply Magnetic Deviations: Caused by failure to apply deviation from the compass correction card to the course data set into the directional gyro from the magnetic compass.*

(3) Failure to maintain straight and level flight while setting the directional gyro to the magnetic compass.*

NOTE: The heading indicator commonly used in light aircraft is the relatively simply directional gyro which has no direction-seeking properties and must be set to headings shown on the magnetic compass. Knowledge of the magnetic compass is thus essential to proper use of the directional gyro (see p. 242).

3.   *Turn and Bank Indicator*

The turn and bank indicator, also referred to as the "needle and ball" and "turn and slip" indicator is composed of a turn needle and the inclinometer. The principal functions of the turn and bank indicator are to provide an alternate source of bank control and to indicate a need for yaw trim.

a.   *Turn Needle:* See Chapter IX, p. 132: "Timed Turns and use of the Magnetic Compass."

b.   *Inclinometer:* The inclinometer is used to indicate coordinated flight. The forces acting on the ball are *gravity* and *centrifugal force.* During a coordinated turn these forces are in balance and the ball will remain centered. When the forces acting on the ball become unbalanced the ball moves away from center, indicating uncoordinated flight — a skid or slip.

In a skid, the rate of turn is too great for the angle of bank and the excessive centrifugal force causes the ball to move to the outside of the turn. Correcting to coordinated flight requires increasing the angle of bank or decreasing the rate of turn, or a combination of both.

In a slip, the rate of turn is too slow for the angle of bank, and the lack of centrifugal force causes the ball to move to the inside of the turn. Correcting to coordinated flight requires decreasing the angle of bank or increasing the rate of turn, or a combination of both.

c. *Principles of Operation:* The gyro in the turn and bank indicator has a horizontal spin axis with a restricted mounting and is only free to tilt. The tilting of the gyro is displayed to the pilot as a deflection of the turn needle in the proper direction. The needle actually tilts opposite the direction that the aircraft is turning, but the linkage between the gyro assembly and the turn needle called the "reversing mechanism" causes the needle to indicate properly!

d. *Turn and Bank Indicator Errors:*

(1) High or Low Vacuum: See Chapter IX, p. 134. "Timed Turns and Use of the Magnetic Compass."

(2) Inaccurate Calibration: This causes the turn rate to be greater or less than the normal 3 degree per second and causes timed turns to be inaccurate.

(4) Turn Coordinator: Recent years have seen the development of a new type turn indicator, referred to as a "turn coordinator" or "pictorial turn indicator." This instrument, which is generally electric, displays a movement of the aircraft on the roll axis that is proportional to the roll of the gyro in such a manner that it senses aircraft movement about the yaw and roll axes and pictorially displays the resultant motion as described above. The instrument which is better dampened than the conventional turn and bank indicator, provides a more stable turn indication and still retains the conventional inclinometer (ball).

E. **Operating Tips:**

1. Allow ample time after starting the engine, for the gyro rotors to come up to speed. (Five minutes)

2. If the take-off is to be an instrument take-off, do not

taxi from run-up position with a 90 degree turn into the runway at a fast speed, for immediate take-off. This will cause precession to both the directional gyro and the artificial horizon. It will take approximately one minute before instruments will give accurate indications.

3.   Remember to check and reset the directional gyro at least once every fifteen minutes and especially just prior to procedure turns on an instrument approach.

4.   *Never Forget:* The artificial horizon will show slight errors and turns should be stopped and level flight attitude checked against the directional gyro as well as the needle and ball.

III. MAGNETIC COMPASS:

A. Magnetic Compass Construction:

A magnetic compass is a self-contained instrument which operates independently of the aircraft's electrical system and converts the earth's magnetic lines of force into magnetic courses which the pilot converts into aircraft headings (see p. 161).

The instrument contains two bar magnets attached to a compass card. The compass card and magnets are mounted on a pivot points which allows the card to tilt up to 18 degrees. The entire assembly is contained in an airtight case filled with white acid-free kerosene which dampens oscillations and serves as a lubricating agent. At the rear of the compass case, a diaphragm is installed to allow for any expansion or contraction of the kerosene, thus preventing the formation of bubbles or possible bursting of the case. The compass also has two compensating magnetics located in the top of the case marked N-S and E-W. These adjustments are used by maintenance personnel to correct the cardinal headings for any slight magnetic disturbances within the cockpit. Deviation error that cannot be compensated out of the instrument is noted on the compass correction card.

B.   Magnetic Compass Errors:

1.   *Variation:* The magnetic compass points to magnetic north – not to true north. The angular difference between true and magnetic north is known as variation and changes for different locations on the earth. Lines connecting the points of equal magnetic variation are *Isogonic lines* and are plotted on aeronautical charts with variation shown in degrees east or west. A line connecting the points of zero variation is called the *Agonic line.* Variation must be considered when converting true courses, true headings, or true winds to magnetic direction (see inside back cover).

2.   *Deviation:* Deviation is the error in compass indications caused by magnetic disturbances originating within the aircraft. The magnitude of deviation varies with operation of different electrical equipment. As mentioned above, deviation error that cannot be compensated out of the compass should be noted on the compass correction card.

3.   *Magnetic Dip:* The tendency of the magnetic compass to point down as well as north is known as magnetic dip (dip error). This is responsible for the northerly and southerly turning errors as well as the acceleration and deceleration errors (see Chapter IX, p. 134: "Timed Turns and Use of the Magnetic Compass"). At the magnetic equator, the vertical component of the earth's magnetic field is zero and the magnetic compass is not affected by dip error. As the aircraft is flown from the magnetic equator, the effect of the vertical component of the earth's magnetic field becomes pronounced. Since the compass card's center of gravity is below the pivot point and the card is balanced in the kerosene, the magnetic compass does not tilt and follow the vertical component during wings level unaccelerated flight.

4.   *Oscillation Error:* Oscillation error is the erratic swinging of the compass card, which may be the result of turbu-

lence or rough pilot technique. During oscillation, the compass is affected by all of the dip errors.

Appendix D
ILLUSIONS IN FLIGHT

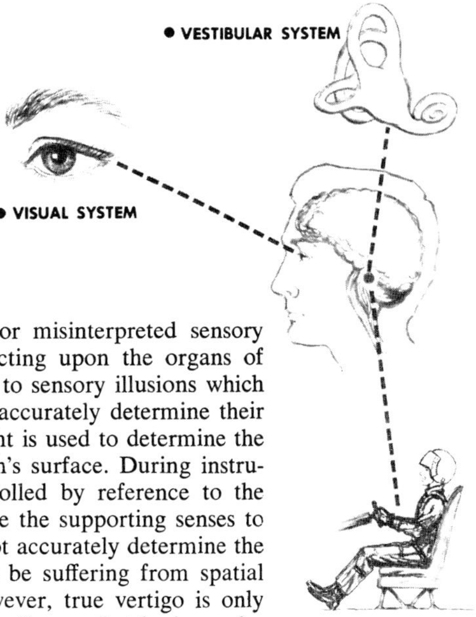

- **VESTIBULAR SYSTEM**

- **VISUAL SYSTEM**

During flight, illusions result from false or misinterpreted sensory impressions created by inflight forces acting upon the organs of equilibrium and balance. All pilots are susceptible to sensory illusions which may suddenly and markedly affect their ability to accurately determine their flight attitude. During visual flight, the sense of sight is used to determine the relationship between aircraft attitude and the earth's surface. During instrument flight, when aircraft attitude must be controlled by reference to the flight instruments, conflicts may evolve which cause the supporting senses to disagree with the sense of sight. When a pilot cannot accurately determine the location of the surface of the earth, he is said to be suffering from spatial disorientation, also commonly called vertigo. However, true vertigo is only the false sensation that space is revolving about the pilot, or that he is revolving in space. It is important to remember that sensory conflicts will occur regardless of a pilot's instrument experience or proficiency. However, the influence and result of the illusion will depend partly on a pilot's experience and training. By recognizing that the inputs from the supporting senses are false or not reliable, a pilot may suppress or ultimately learn to disregard these inputs to prevent conflict with what he sees on the aircraft instruments.

- **PROPRIOCEPTIVE SYSTEM**

Figure 2-1.
Organs of Equilibrium for Senses of Balance, Orientation, and Body Responses

ORGANS OF EQUILIBRIUM

Three of our sensory systems are especially important for maintaining equilibrium and balance. They are:
- The Vestibular (inner ear) System.
  Semicircular canals
  Otolith organs
- The Proprioceptive (muscle sense) System.
- The Visual System.

These sensory systems function adequately for the normal earthbound activities such as walking, running, jumping, falling, etc., but when man is subjected to the environment of air and space, the organs of equilibrium induce errors. Such errors cause illusions which may result in spatial disorientation or vertigo.

*Figure 2-2.   Vestibular (Inner Ear) System — Semicircular Canals Detect Rotations,
Otolith Organs Detect*

THE INNER EAR

TILTING

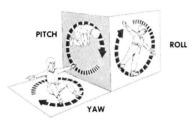

PITCH

ROLL

YAW

The otolith organs are stimulated
by gravity and linear accelerations

The semicircular canals are
stimulated by angular accelerations.

UPRIGHT—
● TRUE SENSATION

NO TURN—
no sensation
● TRUE SENSATION

TILT FORWARD—
● TRUE SENSATION

ACCELERATING TURN—
sensation of turning clockwise
● TRUE SENSATION

TILT BACKWARD—
● TRUE SENSATION

PROLONGED CONSTANT TURN—
no sensation of turning
● FALSE SENSATION

FORWARD ACCELERATION—
sensation of tilting backwards
● FALSE SENSATION

DECELERATING TURN—
sensation of turning counterclockwise
● FALSE SENSATION

CENTRIPETAL ACCELERATION—
sensation of upright
● FALSE SENSATION

Direction and Intensity of Gravity and G-Forces

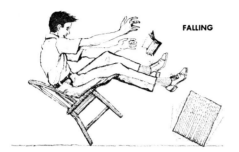

FALLING

Vestibular System

SEMICIRCULAR CANALS. The semicircular canals are filled with a fluid which moves relative to the canal walls when angular accelerations are applied to the head. The movement of the fluid causes bending of hair filaments in the canals, resulting in nerve impulses being sent to the brain. The pilot interpretation is that rotary motion is occurring. The three semicircular canals on each side are positioned at right angles to each other so that angular accelerations in any spatial plane can be detected; i.e., yaw, pitch, or roll. Since the response characteristics of the semicircular canal system are specific ·for ground-based operations, perceptual errors may be induced in flight because:
- A very small or very short-lived angular acceleration may not be perceived.
- The patterns of acceleration experienced in flight are quite different from those experienced on the ground, thus the response of the canals gives us erroneous information.

OTOLITH ORGANS. If these organs are subjected to linear or gravitational accelerations, the hair cell filaments penetrating the otolithic membrane bend. When the filaments are bent, nerve impulses travel along the vestibular nerve to the brain, providing information relating head position to true vertical (the direction of the pull of gravity). During flight, other forces are combined with the force of gravity. The direction of this combined or resultant force, which acts upon the otolith membrane, is almost never the direction of the true vertical. In fact, if the brain monitors the positions of the otolithic membranes, and determines from them which way is "down," the brain will be deceived a large portion of the time in flight.

Figure 2-3.   Proprioceptive System — The Seat-of-the-Pants Sense

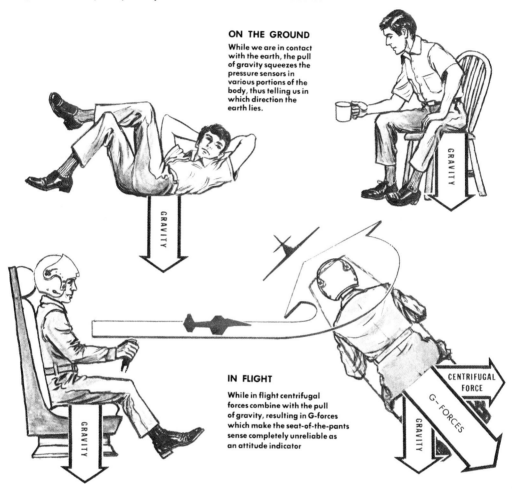

ON THE GROUND

While we are in contact with the earth, the pull of gravity squeezes the pressure sensors in various portions of the body, thus telling us in which direction the earth lies.

IN FLIGHT

While in flight centrifugal forces combine with the pull of gravity, resulting in G-forces which make the seat-of-the-pants sense completely unreliable as an attitude indicator

Proprioceptive System

The proprioceptive sensors, which are of major importance in equilibrium, are those that respond to pressure and stretch. They are buried in many body structures, including the skin, joints, and muscles; and the sensations they elicit when stimulated are the pressing feelings that a person experiences when he sits, or the sensations which enable him to know the position of his arms, legs, and body. This system is the so-called "seat of the pants" sense referred to in flying because some pilots believed they could determine which way was down by analyzing which portions of their bodies were subjected to the greatest amount of pressure.

Figure 2-4. The Visual System

The pilot must rely on the sense of sight to properly interpret his flight instruments.

Visual System

The pilot's eyes play perhaps the most important role in maintaining equilibrium. By experience, one learns the meaning of the horizon and learns to determine "up and down" from the position and attitude of objects within his visual field. The presence of a visual horizon makes it possible for a pilot to remain oriented, even under conditions which would cause illusions if only the vestibular and "seat of the pants" sensory systems were monitored. In flight, the visual system is the most reliable orientation sense, for it is only through this sense that the aircraft flight instruments can be properly interpreted.

SPATIAL DISORIENTATION

Mechanisms of the Illusions

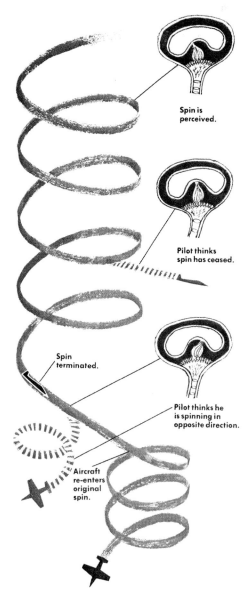

Spin is
perceived.

Pilot thinks
spin has ceased.

Spin
terminated.

Pilot thinks he
is spinning in
opposite direction.

Aircraft
re-enters
original
spin.

Figure 2-5.
The Graveyard Spin

GRAVEYARD SPIN. When the semicircular canals are stimulated by the angular acceleration produced by the spin entry, the pilot's first impression is accurate — that is, he perceives a spin. After about 10 to 20 seconds the fluid in the canals reaches a constant speed and the sensing mechanism returns to the resting position. Thereupon, the sensation of spinning is replaced by one of no rotary motion despite the fact the spin continues. If the spin is then terminated, an angular deceleration is produced which acts upon the semicircular canals to cause a sensation of spinning in the opposite direction. Suffering from the illusion of spinning in the opposite direction, the pilot may try to correct for his false impression by putting the aircraft back into the original spin.

GRAVEYARD SPIRAL. This maneuver is similar to the graveyard spin except the aircraft is in a descending turn rather than a stalled condition. The constant rate of turn causes the pilot to lose the sensation of turning after a period of time. The pilot, noting the loss of altitude, may pull back on the stick or perhaps add power in an attempt to gain back the lost altitude. Unless the pilot has first corrected the bank attitude, such actions can only serve to tighten a downward spiral. Once the spiral has been established, the pilot will suffer the illusion of turning in the opposite direction after he stops the turning motion of the aircraft. Under these circumstances an inexperienced pilot may take the wrong corrective action which results in re-establishment of the spiral.

CORIOLIS ILLUSION. When the body is in a prolonged turn, the fluid in those canals that were stimulated by the onset of the turn eventually reaches a constant speed. If the head is then tipped, this induces fluid movement in a second set of semicircular canals. The resulting sensation is one of rotation in the plane of the new position of the canal, even though no actual motion has occurred in that plane. Thus, abrupt head movements may cause a pilot to perceive maneuvers which he is not actually doing. If the pilot tries to correct for his illusion, he may put the aircraft in a very dangerous attitude. The coriolis illusion is probably the most deadly of all the illusions because of its overwhelming sensations and because it usually occurs during maneuvers that normally take place relatively close to the ground.

THE LEANS. This is the most common vestibular illusion and is caused by rolling or banking the aircraft after the pilot has a false impression of the true vertical. If the pilot is in a prolonged turn, the semicircular canals may perceive a roll to wings level as a turn in the opposite direction. This causes the pilot to lean in an attempt to assume what he thinks is a true vertical posture. The leans may also be caused by differences in roll rate. If a pilot establishes a very subtle roll to the left which does not stimulate the vestibular apparatus and then rolls rapidly to level flight, he may retain the false impression of only having rolled to the right. Again, the pilot may fly adequately in spite of this illusion, although he may lean to assume a false vertical posture.

Figure 2-6.
The Coriolis Illusion

If a pilot moves his head abruptly during a prolonged turn, the Coriolis Effect can cause an overwhelming illusion of change in aircraft attitude.

Figure 2-7.
The Leans

When an aircraft accelerates forward, inertia causes the otolithic membrane in his otolith organs to move. This results in the sensation of climbing, and may cause the pilot to dive in an attempt to compensate for illusory change of attitude.

Figure 2-8.
The Oculogravic Illusion

OCULOGYRAL ILLUSION. This illusion occurs when objects in the field of vision appear to move when the semicircular canals are stimulated. Such illusions can occur during the graveyard spin, the graveyard spiral, and during the coriolis illusion.

OCULOGRAVIC ILLUSION. This illusion creates the false sensation of change of attitude when the otolith organs are stimulated. Such an illusion can occur when a high-performance aircraft accelerates forward while in level flight and gives the pilot the sensation that he is in a nose-up attitude. If a pilot were to correct for this illusion, he might dive the aircraft into the ground. This illusion is often experienced during takeoff roll.

Figure 2-9.
Visual Illusion
(Blending of Earth and Sky)

Figure 2-10.
Visual Illusion
(False Vertical and Horizontal Cues)

BLENDING OF EARTH AND SKY. Sometimes pilots confuse ground lights with stars. In doing so, the possibility exists of flying into the ground because the perceived horizon is below the actual one. Sometimes pilots confuse unlighted areas of the earth with an overcast night sky. They are then likely to perceive certain ground features such as a seashore, as the horizon, and fly into the unlighted water or terrain above it.

FALSE VERTICAL AND HORIZONTAL CUES. Flying over sloping cloud decks or land that slopes gradually upward into mountainous terrain often compels pilots to fly with their wings parallel to the slope rather than straight and level. A related phenomenon is the disorientation caused by the aurora borealis, in which false vertical and horizontal cues generated by the aurora result in attitude confusion in pilots trying to fly formation or refuel at night in northern regions.

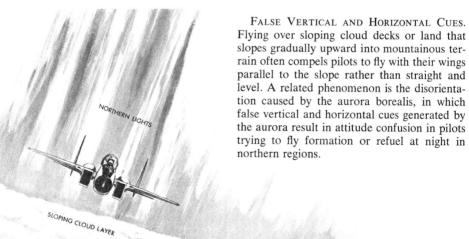

A static light, stared at
for several seconds in the
dark, will appear to move.

The Autokinetic Effect
is lessened by:

Figure 2-11.
Autokinesis

The greater the
brightness of
the light

The greater the
size of the light

The greater the
number of lights.

RELATIVE MOTION.   An adjacent automo-
bile creeping forward at a stop light can create
the illusion that our own vehicle is creeping
backwards. In formation flying, such illusions
are common.

AUTOKINESIS.   A stationary light, stared at
for several seconds in the dark, will appear to
move. This phenomenon can cause considerable confusion in pilots flying formation at
night. Increasing the brilliance, size, or number of lights, or causing the lights to flash on
and off will diminish the effect of the autokinetic phenomenon.

THE SEAT-OF-THE-PANTS SENSE.   This is
a misleading sense because during coordinated
flight the forces resulting from centrifugal force
and gravity are always toward the floor of the
aircraft. Thus, a pilot can never tell through
his pressure sensors which direction is the true
vertical.

Conditions Most Conducive to Spatial Disorientation Accidents and Incidents

When a pilot is extremely busy manipulating the cockpit controls, anxious, mentally stressed or fatigued, his proficiency on instruments and formation flying is decreased. Hypoxia, various medicines (particularly amphetamines and barbiturates), G stresses, temperature stresses, and emotional problems reduce the pilot's ability to resist spatial disorientation. Pilots of jet aircraft suffer from spatial disorientation more frequently than pilots flying propeller-driven aircraft. Pilots with less actual instrument time are more susceptible to spatial disorientation than the more experienced pilot. Many spatial disorientation accidents and incidents have been reported during the penetration turn, final approach, and climb-out after takeoff. This is when the coriolis illusions are the most devastating. Other very critical times are night or weather formation flights, the wingman losing sight of the lead in weather, or when a pilot flying in VMC (Visual Meteorological Conditions) suddenly enters IMC (Instrument Meteorological Conditions).

Inducing Spatial Disorientation

A number of maneuvers can be used to induce spatial disorientation. Each maneuver normally creates a specific reaction; however, any reaction resulting in a false sensation is effective.

The purpose of these maneuvers is to help pilots understand how susceptible the human system is to disorientation. The maneuvers demonstrate that interpretations of aircraft attitudes from bodily sensations are frequently false and unrealistic. The maneuvers also provide a better understanding of how disorientation relates to aircraft motion and head movement. They instill in the pilot a greater confidence in flight instrument interpretation by the sense of sight to determine the aircraft attitude.

The following spatial disorientation maneuvers are selected because of their relationship with normal instrument and/or turbulent flight. Other maneuvers, more violent and prolonged, may have a disorienting effect; however, they are not the type of maneuver or situation likely to be inadvertently encountered.

NOTE: The following maneuvers should be simulated and practiced only under direct supervision. They should not be accomplished in a single-place aircraft.

Spatial Disorientation Maneuvers

SENSATION OF CLIMBING WHILE TURNING.   This sensation can be induced by having the pilot close his eyes while the aircraft is in a straight and level attitude. The supervisory pilot should execute, with a relatively slow entry, a well-coordinated 90° turn using about 1½ positive Gs. While the aircraft is turning under the effect of positive G and with the pilot's eyes still closed, the supervisory pilot should ask the pilot his version of the aircraft attitude. The usual sensation is that of a climb. If the pilot so responds, have him open his eyes. He can then see that a slowly established coordinated turn produces a climb sensation from the action of centrifugal force (+G) on the equilibrium organs.

   Correlation Under Actual Instrument Conditions. If the aircraft enters a slight, coordinated turn in either direction while the eyes are diverted away from the instruments, the sensation of a nose-up attitude may occur. The instantaneous application of similar forces may create this same illusion without the aircraft actually turning.

   When a change of direction in any one of the three planes of motion occurs and the rate of angular acceleration in the turn is too little to stimulate the inner ear, the change in G forces caused by the turn is the only sensation perceived. Positive G is usually associated with a climb; negative G with a dive or nose over. This association is an unconscious habit developed through experience with G forces, as well as a conscious feeling of climbing or diving due to the effect of gravity on the inner mechanisms of the ear.

SENSATION OF DIVING DURING RECOVERY FROM A TURN.   This sensation can be created by repeating the turning procedure described above, except that the pilot keeps his eyes closed until the recovery from the turn is approximately one-half completed. While the recovery is being executed and with the pilot's eyes still closed, the supervisory pilot should note the pilot's version of the aircraft attitude. The usual response is that the aircraft is descending. This false sensation is apparent when the pilot opens his eyes while the aircraft is still recovering from the turn.

   Correlation Under Actual Instrument Conditions. If the eyes are diverted from the instruments during a turn under instrument conditions, a slow inadvertent recovery will cause the body to perceive only the decrease in positive G forces. This sensation causes the pilot to believe he has entered a descent.

FALSE SENSATIONS OF TILTING TO RIGHT OR LEFT.   This sensation may be induced from a straight and level attitude with pilot's eyes closed. The supervisory pilot should maintain wings level and use right rudder to produce a slight skid to the left. The usual sensation is that of being tilted to the right. This false sensation is the effect of side-to-side accelerative forces on the organs of equilibrium.

   Correlation Under Actual Instrument Conditions. If the eyes are momentarily diverted from the instruments as a skid to one side occurs, a false sensation of tilting the body to the opposite side may occur.

FALSE SENSATION OF REVERSAL OF MOTION.   This false sensation can be demonstrated in any one of the three planes of motion. The pilot should close his eyes while in straight and level flight. The supervisory pilot should roll the aircraft at a constant rate of 1° to 2° per second to a 30° to 45° bank angle. The roll should be stopped abruptly and the bank attitude held. The usual reaction is a sense of rapid rotation in the opposite direction. After this false sensation is noted, the supervisory pilot should have the pilot open his eyes and observe the attitude of the aircraft. The false sensations produced from stopping the roll abruptly may result in a strong urge to apply reverse aileron pressure for recovery. This sensation can also be demonstrated by abruptly ending a constant velocity yaw after 20 to 30 seconds duration.

Correlation Under Actual Instrument Conditions. If the aircraft rolls or yaws with an abrupt stop while the eyes are diverted from the instruments, a sensation of rolling or yawing to the opposite direction may occur. Therefore, the natural response to this false sensation would result in a re-entry or an increase of the original roll or yaw. This response is a common error in rolls or spins when the visual references are poor. The sense of sight is the only sense which should be relied upon for correct recovery techniques.

SENSATION OF DIVING OR ROLLING BEYOND THE VERTICAL PLANE. This maneuver should be started from straight and level flight while the pilot sits normally and either closes his eyes or lowers his gaze to the floor. The supervisory pilot should start a normal coordinated turn to between 30° and 45° of bank. As the aircraft is turning, have the pilot lean forward and turn his head to either side, then rapidly resume the normal upright position. The supervisory pilot should time the maneuver so that the turn is stopped just as the pilot resumes his normal position.

This maneuver usually produces an intense disorientation by giving the sensation of falling in the direction of roll and downward. The sensation is so strong and rapid that it may result in a quick and forcible movement upward and backward in the opposite direction. The marked physical response associated with this type of sensation can be very dangerous if it occurs at low altitude.

Correlation Under Actual Instrument Conditions. Severe spatial disorientation may result when the aircraft enters a turn while the pilot's head is moved down and sideways and then suddenly returned to the upright position. The usual reflex and almost uncontrollable urge to move physically in the opposite direction may be transferred to the aircraft controls. If this reflex is not controlled, it could easily cause exaggerated aircraft attitudes and further disorientation. Cockpit duties and/or distractions most likely to create this sensation under actual instrument conditions are changing radio frequencies, reaching for maps or charts, studying terminal instrument approach procedures, looking for obscure switches or controls, etc. The degree of disorientation and physical response depends upon the motion of the aircraft, the motion of the head, and the time element.

---------------------------**WARNING**---------------------------

Take extreme care to limit rapid head movements during descents and turns, particularly at low altitudes. Cockpit duties should be subordinate to maintaining aircraft control. If possible, delegate these duties to other crew members so that sufficient attention can be given to the attitude indicator and other flight instruments.

SENSATION OF CLIMBING. This maneuver may be demonstrated by starting from straight and level flight at the aircraft normal final approach airspeed. While the pilot closes his eyes, the supervisory pilot should increase the airspeed and maintain straight and level flight. During the latter part of the airspeed increase, the supervisory pilot should ask the pilot, whose eyes are still closed, what is his sensation of the aircraft attitude. The usual sensation perceived without visual reference is that the aircraft is climbing.

Correlation Under Actual Instrument Conditions. This sensation may be very strong during an instrument missed approach. The false sensation of an excessive climb is produced by the change in aircraft attitude and aircraft acceleration. This sensation may occur prior to the climb and after level off. The use of afterburners usually increases this illusion. The degree of disorientation and physical response depends upon the attitude change and the rate of aircraft acceleration.

MAINTAINING SPATIAL ORIENTATION

The false sensations of instrument flight are experienced by most pilots. They will become less susceptible to these false sensations and their effects as they acquire additional instrument experience. Although these sensations cannot be completely prevented, the pilot can and must suppress them by self-discipline, conscientious instrument practice, and experience.

The keys to suppressing spatial disorientation are:

• A pilot must learn to control his aircraft by relying on the sense of sight and the flight instruments.

• He must learn to ignore or control the urge to believe any false sensations perceived from the supporting senses.

Figure 2-12. Believe What the Flight Instruments are Telling About the Aircraft Attitude

Appendix E
INSTRUMENT APPROACH CHARTS

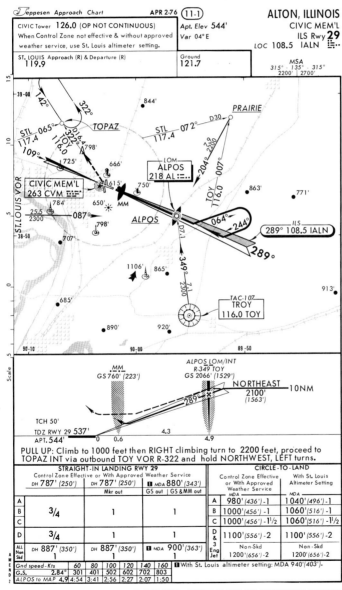

Jeppesen Approach Chart   APR 2-76   (11-1)

CIVIC Tower **126.0** (OP NOT CONTINUOUS)	*Apt. Elev* **544'**	**ALTON, ILLINOIS**
When Control Zone not effective & without approved weather service, use St. Louis altimeter setting.	*Var* **04° E**	CIVIC MEM'L ILS Rwy **29**
		LOC **108.5** IALN

ST. LOUIS Approach (R) & Departure (R) **119.9** | Ground **121.7** | MSA 315° - 135° - 315° 2200' | 2700'

PULL UP: Climb to 1000 feet then RIGHT climbing turn to 2200 feet, proceed to TOPAZ INT via outbound TOY VOR R-322 and hold NORTHWEST, LEFT turns.

STRAIGHT-IN LANDING RWY 29

Control Zone Effective or With Approved Weather Service

	DH **787'** (250')	DH **787'** (250')	▯ MDA **880'** (343')
		Mkr out	GS out | GS & MM out
A			
B	3/4	1	1
C			
D	3/4	1	1
ALL Non Skd	DH **887'** (350')	DH **887'** (350')	▯ MDA **900'** (363')
	1	1	1

CIRCLE-TO-LAND

	Control Zone Effective or With Approved Weather Service MDA	With St. Louis Altimeter Setting MDA
A	980' (436')-1	1040' (496')-1
B	1000' (456')-1	1060' (516')-1
C	1000' (456')-1½	1060' (516')-1½
D & 3 Eng Jet	1100' (556')-2	1100' (556')-2
	Non-Skd 1200' (656')-2	Non-Skd 1200' (656')-2

Gnd speed-Kts	60	80	100	120	140	160	▯ With St. Louis altimeter setting: MDA 940' (403').
G.S. 2.84°	301	401	502	602	702	803	
ALPOS to MAP 4.9	4:54	3:41	2:56	2:27	2:07	1:50	

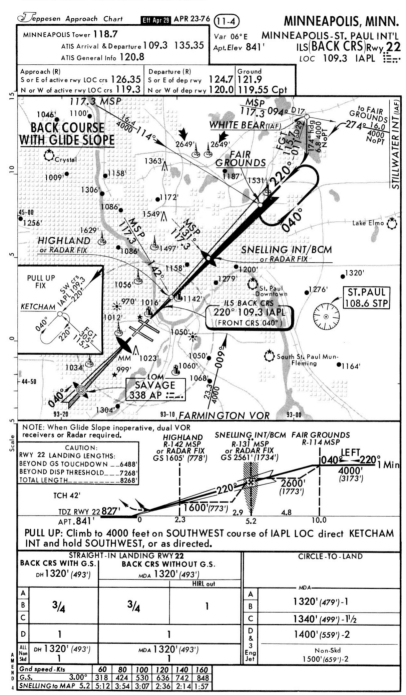

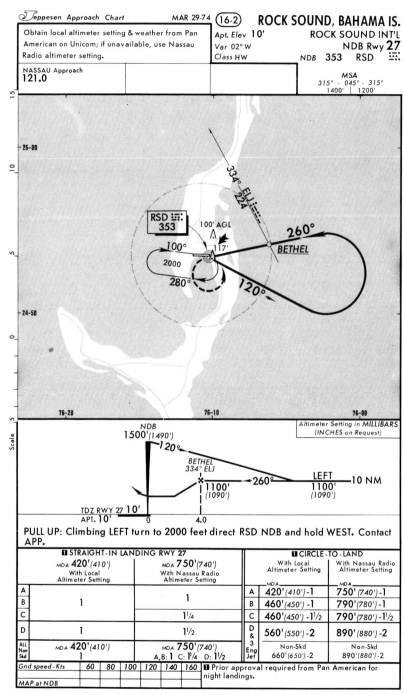

Jeppesen Approach Chart MAR 29-74 (16-2) **ROCK SOUND, BAHAMA IS.**

Obtain local altimeter setting & weather from Pan American on Unicom; if unavailable, use Nassau Radio altimeter setting.	*Apt. Elev* 10' *Var* 02° W *Class* HW	ROCK SOUND INT'L NDB Rwy **27** *NDB* 353 RSD ⠿
NASSAU Approach **121.0**		*MSA* 315° - 045° - 315° 1400' 1200'

RSD ⠿
353

100' AGL
∧
100° 117'
2000
280°
260°
BETHEL
120°

334° ELJ
22A

NDB
1500'(1490')
120°

BETHEL
334° ELJ
✳ ←260° LEFT 10 NM
|1100' 1100'
(1090') (1090')

TDZ RWY 27 10'
APT. 10'   0   4.0

Altimeter Setting in MILLIBARS
(INCHES on Request)

PULL UP: Climbing LEFT turn to 2000 feet direct RSD NDB and hold WEST. Contact APP.

	■ STRAIGHT-IN LANDING RWY 27		■ CIRCLE-TO-LAND		
	MDA **420'**(410') With Local Altimeter Setting	*MDA* **750'**(740') With Nassau Radio Altimeter Setting		With Local Altimeter Setting	With Nassau Radio Altimeter Setting
				MDA	*MDA*
A	1	1	A	420'(410')-1	750'(740')-1
B			B	460'(450')-1	790'(780')-1
C		1¼	C	460'(450')-1½	790'(780')-1½
D	1	1½	D & 3 Eng Jet	560'(550')-2	890'(880')-2
ALL Non Skd	*MDA* **420'**(410') 1	*MDA* **750'**(740') A,B: 1 C: 1¼ D: 1½		Non-Skd 660'(650')-2	Non-Skd 890'(880')-2
Gnd speed-Kts	60 80 100 120 140 160		■ Prior approval required from Pan American for night landings.		
MAP at NDB					

Jeppesen Approach Chart **Eff May 20** MAY 14-76 (11-3)

ST. LOUIS, MO.
LAMBERT-ST. LOUIS INT'L
LOC (BACK CRS) Rwy 6
LOC 110.3 ISTL

ST. LOUIS Tower 118.5 120.05
ATIS 110.3 120.45

Apt. Elev 589'
Var 05°E

Approach (R)	Departure (R)	Ground
298°-116° 125.15	298°-116° 119.9	121.9
117°-297° 126.5	117°-297° 124.9	119.5Cpt

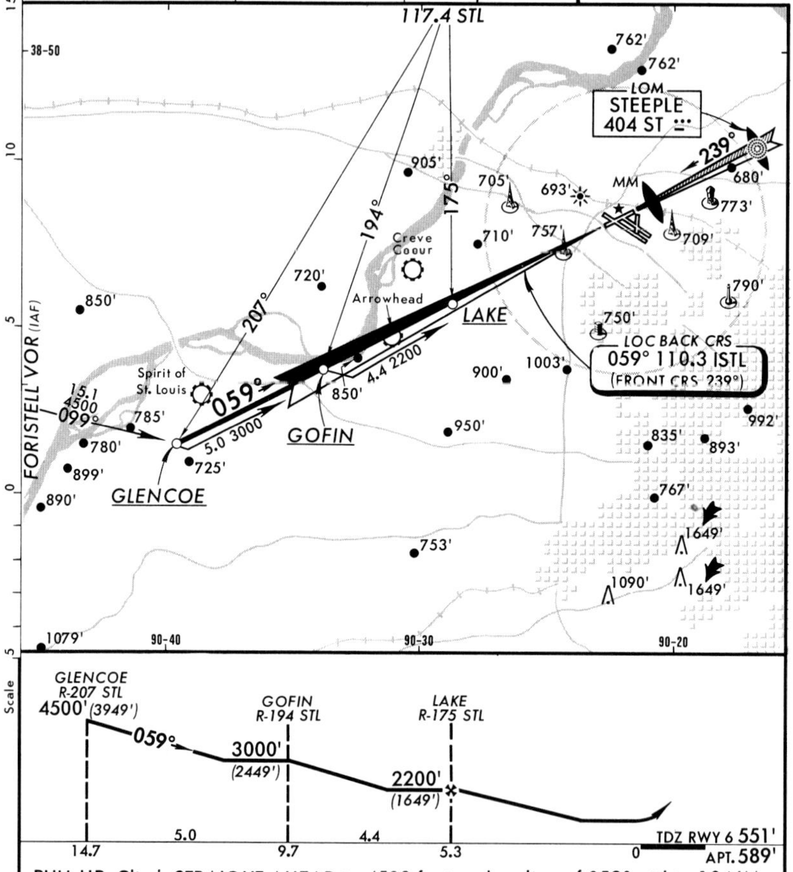

PULL UP: Climb STRAIGHT AHEAD to 4500 feet on heading of 059° within 10 NM.

STRAIGHT-IN LANDING RWY 6 MDA 1020'(469')		ALS out
A	3/4	1
B	3/4	1
C	3/4	1
D	1	
ALL Non Skd	MDA 1020'(469') 1	

CIRCLE-TO-LAND	MDA
A	1040'(451')-1
B	1060'(471')-1
C	1060'(471')-1½
D & 3 Eng Jet	1140'(551')-2
	Non-Skd 1240'(651')-2

Gnd speed-Kts		60	80	100	120	140	160
LAKE INT to MAP	5.3	5:18	3:59	3:11	2:39	2:17	1:59

AMEND 21

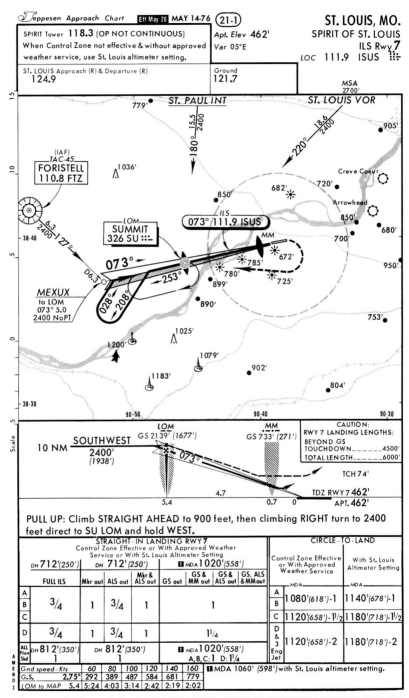

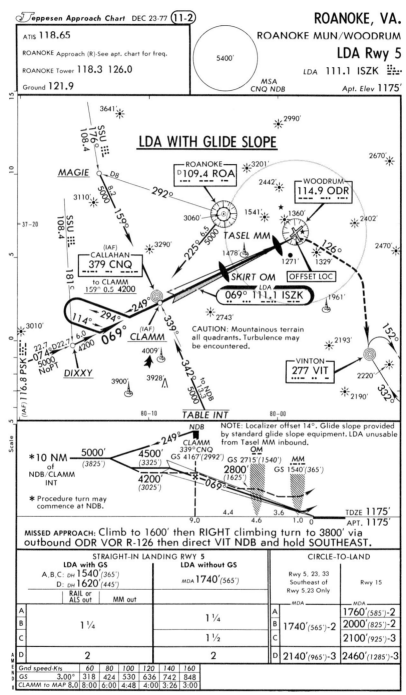

ROANOKE, VA.
ROANOKE MUN/WOODRUM

ATIS 118.65

ROANOKE Approach (R)·See apt. chart for freq.

LDA Rwy 5

ROANOKE Tower 118.3 126.0

LDA 111.1 ISZK

Ground 121.9

5400'

MSA
CNQ NDB

Apt. Elev 1175'

3641'   2990'

LDA WITH GLIDE SLOPE

2670'

SSU
176°
108.4

ROANOKE
D109.4 ROA   3201'

MAGIE   D8

WOODRUM
114.9 ODR

2442'

292°

3110'   5000 8.2

159°   3060'   1541'   1360'   2402'

37-20

SSU
108.4

(IAF)

225° 6.5
5000

TASEL MM

2470'

CALLAHAN
379 CNQ

3290'

1478'   1271' 1329'

126°

181°

to CLAMM
159° 0.5 4200

SKIRT OM   OFFSET LOC

LDA
069° 111.1 ISZK   1961'

3010'   114°   294°   249°

(IAF)
CLAMM   339°

069°   CAUTION: Mountainous terrain
all quadrants. Turbulence may
be encountered.

2743'   2193'

152°

22.7 D22.7 6.0
074°   4200   4009'

5000
NoPT

DIXXY   3900'   3928'   342°
5000 to NDB
13.3

VINTON
277 VIT

2220'

332°

2190'

TABLE INT

80-10   80-00

Scale

NDB   NOTE: Localizer offset 14°. Glide slope provided
by standard glide slope equipment. LDA unusable
from Tasel MM inbound.

249°   CLAMM
339°CNQ

OM

MM

*10 NM
of
NDB/CLAMM
INT   5000'
(3825')   4500'
(3325')   GS 4167'(2992')   GS 2715'(1540')   GS 1540'(365')

2800'
(1625')

4200'
(3025')   069°

* Procedure turn may
commence at NDB.   4.4   4.6   3.6   1.0 0   TDZE 1175'
APT. 1175'

9.0

MISSED APPROACH: Climb to 1600' then RIGHT climbing turn to 3800' via
outbound ODR VOR R-126 then direct VIT NDB and hold SOUTHEAST.

	STRAIGHT-IN LANDING RWY 5			CIRCLE-TO-LAND	
	LDA with GS	LDA without GS			
	A,B,C: DH 1540'(365') D: DH 1620'(445')	MDA 1740'(565')		Rwy 5, 23, 33 Southeast of Rwy 5,23 Only	Rwy 15
	RAIL or ALS out	MM out			
A			1¼	MDA	MDA
B	1¼			1740'(565')-2	1760'(585')-2
C			1½		2000'(825')-2
D	2		2		2100'(925')-3
				2140'(965')-3	2460'(1285')-3

Gnd speed-Kts	60	80	100	120	140	160
GS 3.00°	318	424	530	636	742	848
CLAMM to MAP 8.0	8:00	6:00	4:48	4:00	3:26	3:00

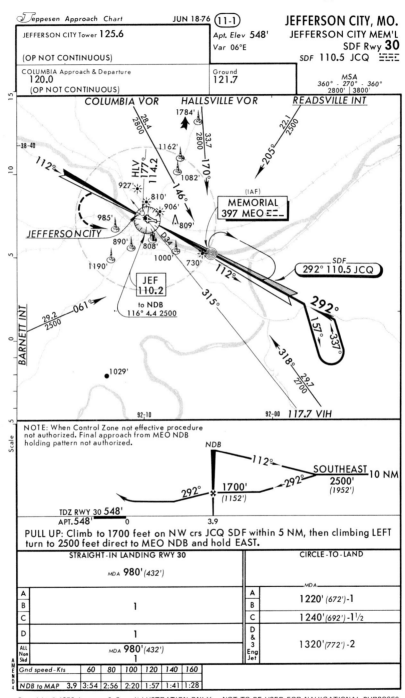

Jeppesen Approach Chart — Eff May 20 — MAY 14-76 — (13-1)

PHOENIX, ARIZ.

PHOENIX Tower (Runway 8L-26R) 118.7	(Runway 8R-26L) 120.9	Apt. Elev 1128' PHOENIX SKY HARBOR INT'L
	ATIS Arr 121.2 Dep 124.3	Var 14°E VOR Rwy **26L**
		Class VORTAC VOR 115.6 PHX

Approach (R) & Departure (R)
PHX R-310 to R-059 **119.2** PHX R-145 to R-264 **124.1**
PHX R-060 to R-100 **120.4** PHX R-265 to R-309 **126.8**
PHX R-101 to R-144 **124.9**

Ground 121.9
118.1 Cpt

MSA

280°-010°	010°-100°	100°-190°	190°-280°
5900'	6100'	4200'	5600'

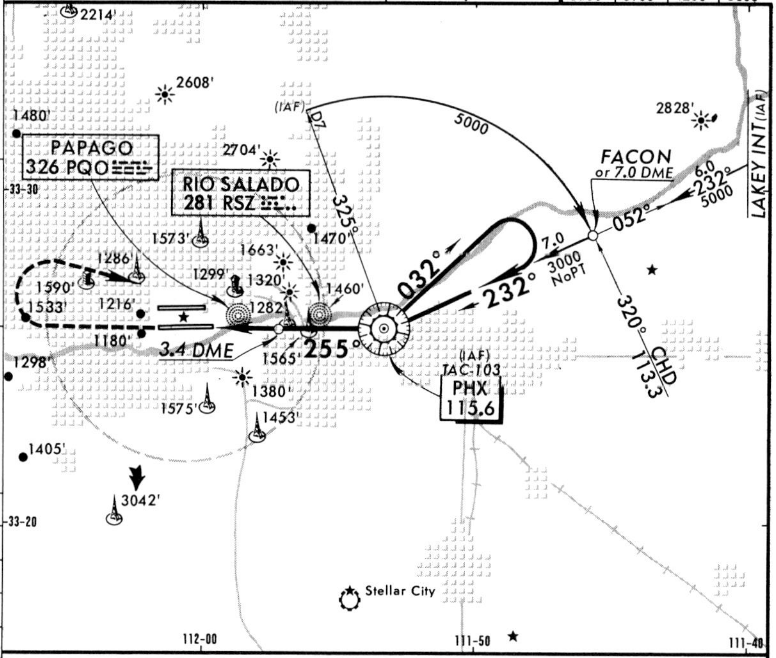

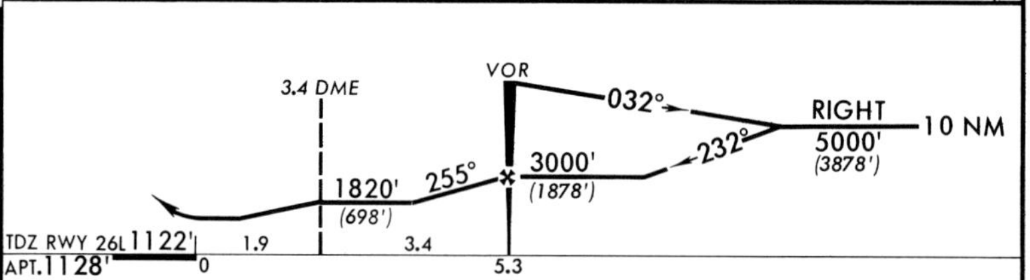

PULL UP: Climb STRAIGHT AHEAD to 3000 feet, climbing RIGHT turn to 5000 feet to PHX VOR.

	STRAIGHT-IN LANDING RWY 26L		CIRCLE-TO-LAND	
	MDA 1560' (438') With 3.4 DME	MDA 1820' (698') Without 3.4 DME	With 3.4 DME MDA	Without 3.4 DME MDA
A	1	1	1600' (472') -1	1820' (692') -1
B	1	1	1600' (472') -1	1820' (692') -1
C	1	1¼	1600' (472') -1½	1820' (692') -1½
D	1	1½		
D & 3 Eng Jet			1880' (752') -2	1880' (752') -2
ALL Non Skd	MDA 1560' (438') 1	MDA 1820' (698') A, B: 1 C: 1¼ D: 1½		

AMEND 18

Gnd speed-Kts		60	80	100	120	140	160
VOR to MAP	5.3	5:18	3:59	3:11	2:39	2:17	1:59

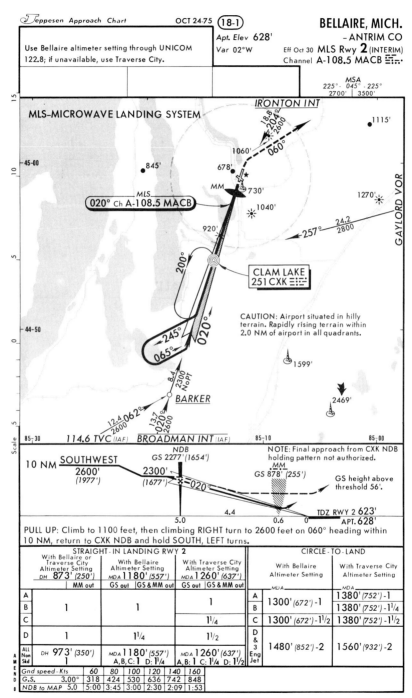

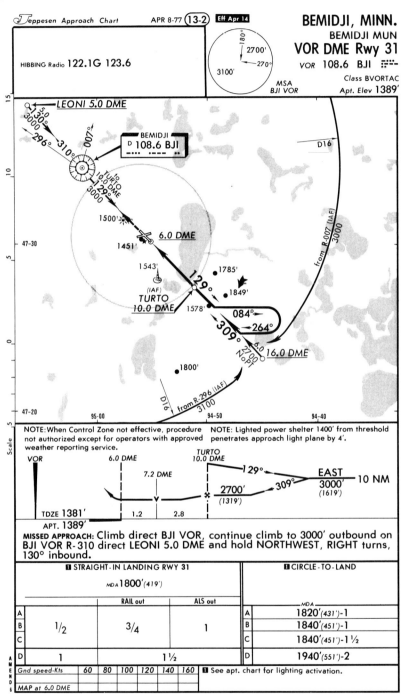

Jeppesen Approach Chart   APR 8-77 (13-2)   Eff Apr 14

HIBBING Radio 122.1G 123.6

BEMIDJI, MINN.
BEMIDJI MUN
VOR DME Rwy 31
VOR 108.6 BJI

MSA
BJI VOR

Class BVORTAC
Apt. Elev 1389'

2700'
270°
3100'
180°

LEONI 5.0 DME

BEMIDJI
D 108.6 BJI

D16

from R-007 (IAF)
3000

296° 310° 007°
130°
3000'

TURTO
10.0 DME
3000

1500'
6.0 DME
1451'
1543'
TURTO
(IAF)
10.0 DME
129°
1785'
1849'
1578'
084°
264°
309°
16.0 DME
2700' NoPT
1800'
from R-296 (IAF)
3100

D16

47-30
47-20
95-00   94-50   94-40

NOTE: When Control Zone not effective, procedure not authorized except for operators with approved weather reporting service.

NOTE: Lighted power shelter 1400' from threshold penetrates approach light plane by 4'.

VOR   6.0 DME   7.2 DME   TURTO 10.0 DME   129°   EAST 3000' (1619')   10 NM
2700' (1319')   309°
TDZE 1381'   1.2   2.8
APT. 1389'

MISSED APPROACH: Climb direct BJI VOR, continue climb to 3000' outbound on BJI VOR R-310 direct LEONI 5.0 DME and hold NORTHWEST, RIGHT turns, 130° inbound.

	STRAIGHT-IN LANDING RWY 31				CIRCLE-TO-LAND
	MDA 1800' (419')				MDA
		RAIL out	ALS out		
A				A	1820' (431')-1
B	1/2	3/4	1	B	1840' (451')-1
C				C	1840' (451')-1 1/2
D	1	1 1/2		D	1940' (551')-2
Gnd speed-Kts	60	80	100	120	140	160		See apt. chart for lighting activation.
MAP at 6.0 DME								

Appendix F
GLOSSARY OF AERONAUTICAL TERMS

This glossary defines the aeronautical terms and abbreviations used throughout the book. In addition, it includes the definitions of more than 100 terms intended for pilot and controller communications excerpted from the new Pilot/Controller Glossary published by the Department of Transportation. The Federal Aviation Agency considers these terms (printed in **bold**) as the most misunderstood terms used in Air Traffic Control and it is hoped that these operational definitions will eliminate any existing confusion and enable both users and operators of the National Airspace System finally to speak the same language.

Abeam: An aircraft is "abeam" a fix, point or object when that fix, point or object is approximately 90 degrees to the right or left of the aircraft track. Abeam indicates a general position rather than a precise point.

Abort: To terminate a preplanned aircraft maneuver; e.g., an aborted takeoff.

Acknowledge: Let me know that you have received and understand my message.

ADF: Automatic Direction Finder — refers to the low/medium frequency radio receiver in the aircraft. The ADF pointer indicates your relative bearing to the station (see Appendix B, p. 215).

Advise Intentions: Tell me what you plan to do.

Affirmative: Yes.

Air Route Traffic Control Center/ARTCC/CENTER: A facility established to provide air traffic control service to aircraft operating on

IFR flight plans within controlled airspace and principally during the enroute phase of flight. When equipment capabilities and Controller workload permit, certain advisory/assistance services may be provided to VFR aircraft.

Air Traffic Clearance/ATC Clearance/Clearance: An authorization by air traffic control, for the purpose of preventing collision between known aircraft, for an aircraft to proceed under specified traffic conditions within controlled airspace.

Airspeed: Velocity of an aircraft stated in miles per hour or knots (see Appendix C, p. 230).

Airway: Air route designated between two navigation stations on the earth's surface.

Altitude: The height of a level, point or object measured in feet Above Ground Level or from Mean Sea Level (see Appendix C, p. 226).

Altitude Readout/Automatic Altitude Report: An aircraft's altitude, transmitted via the Mode C transponder feature, that is visually displayed in 100-foot increments on a radar scope having readout capability.

Altitude Restrictions Are Cancelled: Adherence to previously imposed altitude restrictions is no longer required during a climb or descent.

ANDS: Accelerate north/decelerate south OR anticipate north/delay south. ANDS is a word you can use to remember the northerly turn and acceleration errors of the magnetic compass (see p. 134).

Approach Speed: The recommended speed contained in aircraft operating manuals used by pilots when making an approach to landing. This speed will vary for different segments of an approach as well as for aircraft weight and configuration.

Arc: A circle of constant radius around a VORTAC station. When used in conjunction with a DME approach, the track over the ground of an aircraft flying at a specified distance (nautical miles) around the station until intercepting the final approach course.

ASR: Airport Surveillance Radar — radar providing the position of your aircraft by azimuth and range data without elevation data. It is designed for a range of 50 miles and is used by terminal approach and departure control.

ATC: Air Traffic Control — any federal facility engaged in the direction and control of aircraft in controlled airspace.

ATC Advises: Used to prefix a message of noncontrol information when it is relayed to an aircraft by other than an air traffic controller.

ATC Clears: Used to prefix an ATC clearance when it is relayed to an aircraft by other than an air traffic controller.

ATC Requests: Used to prefix an ATC request when it is relayed to an aircraft by other than an air traffic controller.

Back Course: The "back side" of an ILS localizer course — the electronic extension of the runway centerline proceeding in the opposite direction from the Front Course. Many Back Courses provide an additional non-precision approach for the airport.

Bearing: The horizontal direction to or from any point, usually measured clockwise from true north, magnetic north or some other reference point through 360 degrees.

Below Minimums: Weather conditions below the minimums prescribed by regulation for the particular action involved, e.g., landing minimums, takeoff minimums.

Blue: The left half of the **blue/yellow** color arc on the bottom of the VOR display.

Braking Action (Good, Medium or Fair, Poor, Nil): A report of conditions on the airport movement area providing a pilot with a degree/quality of braking that he might expect. Braking action is reported in terms of good, medium (or fair), poor or nil.

CDI: Course Deviation Indicator — the left/right needle on the VOR display.

Center: The ATC facility responsible for the enroute phase of IFR operations; the full name is Air Route Traffic Control Center.

Circling Approach: Any instrument approach where the active runway is aligned more than 30 degrees away from the final approach course, or where a normal rate of descent from the minimum IFR altitude to the runway cannot be accomplished.

Circle to Runway (Runway Number): Used by ATC to inform the pilot that he must circle to land because the runway in use is other than the runway aligned with the instrument approach procedure. When the direction of the circling maneuver in relation to the airport/runway is required, the Controller will state the direction (eight cardinal compass points) and specify a left or right downwind or base leg as appropriate; e.g., "Cleared VOR Runway 36 approach circle to Runway 22" or "Circle northwest of the airport for a right downwind to Runway 22."

Clear Of Traffic: Previously issued traffic is no longer a factor.

Clearance: See Air Traffic Clearance.

Clearance Limit: The fix, point, or location to which an aircraft is cleared when issued an air traffic clearance.

Clearance Void If Not Off By (Time): Used by ATC to advise an aircraft that the departure clearance is automatically cancelled if takeoff is not made prior to a specified time. The pilot must obtain a new clearance or cancel his IFR flight plan if not off by the specified time.

Cleared As Filed: Means the aircraft is cleared to proceed in accordance with the route of flight filed in the flight plan. This clearnace does not include the altitude, SID, or SID transition.

Cleared Direct: An ATC instruction which means to track from your present position to the designated fix.

Cleared for Stright-in Approach: Proceed direct to the appropriate radio facility and complete the published approach *without* executing a procedure turn.

Cleared For (Type Of) Approach: ATC authorization for an aircraft to execute a specific instrument approach procedure to an airport; e.g., "Cleared for ILS runway 36 approach."

Cleared For Approach: ATC authorization for an aircraft to execute any standard or special instrument approach procedure for that airport. Normally, an aircraft will be cleared for a specific instrument approach procedure (see Instrument Approach Procedure).

Cleared For Take-Off: ATC authorization for an aircraft to depart. It is predicated on known traffic and known physical airport conditions.

Cleared For The Option: ATC authorization for an aircraft to make a touch-and-go, low approach, missed approach, stop and go, or full stop landing at the discretion of the pilot. It is normally used in training so that an instructor can evaluate a student's performance under changing situations.

Cleared Through: ATC authorization for an aircraft to make intermediate stops at specified airports without refiling a flight plan while enroute to the clearance limit.

Cleared To Land: ATC authorization for an aircraft to land. It is predicated on known traffic and known physical airport conditions.

Climb To VFR: ATC authorization for an aircraft to climb to VFR conditions within a control zone when the only weather limitation is restricted visibility. The aircraft must remain clear of clouds while climbing to VFR.

Compass Locator: A non-directional low-frequency radio beacon co-located with the outer marker. Converts an OM (outer marker) into a LOM (locator outer marker).

Compass Rose: A circle graduated in degrees, printed on some charts or marked on the ground at an airport. It is used as a reference to either true or magnetic direction.

Conflict Alert, Advise You Turn Right/Left Heading (Degrees) and/or Climb/Descend To (Altitude) Immediately: See Radar Safety Advisory.

Contact:
1. Establish communication with (followed by the name of the facility and, if appropriate, the frequency to be used).
2. A flight condition wherein the pilot ascertains the attitude of his aircraft and navigates by visual reference to the surface.

Contact Approach: A short-cut to a published instrument approach procedure wherein an aircraft on an IFR flight plan, operating clear of the clouds with at least one mile visibility and having received an ATC authorization, may deviate from the prescribed instrument approach procedure and proceed to the destination airport by visual reference to the ground.

Controlled Airspace: Airspace designated as the continental control area, control area, control zone, or transition area within which some or all aircraft may be subject to air traffic control.

Correction: An error has been made in the transmission and the correct version follows.

Course: The intended direction of flight in the horizontal plane referenced to either true or magnetic north. All courses on IFR charts are magnetic.

Cross (Fix) At (Altitude): Used by ATC when a specific altitude restriction at a specified fix is required.

Cross (Fix) At Or Above (Altitude): Used by ATC when an altitude restriction at a specified fix is required. It does not prohibit the aircraft from crossing the fix at a higher altitude than specified; however, the higher altitude may not be one that will violate a succeeding altitude restriction or altitude assignment.

Cross (Fix) At Or Below (Altitude): Used by ATC when a maximum crossing altitude at a specific fix is required. It does not prohibit the aircraft from crossing the fix at a lower altitude; however, it must be at or above the minimum IFR altitude.

Cruise: Used in an ATC clearance to authorize a pilot to conduct flight at any altitude from the minimum IFR altitude up to and including the altitude specified in the clearance. The pilot may level off at any intermediary altitude within this block of airspace. Climb/descent within the block is to be made at the discretion of the pilot. However, once the pilot starts descent and reports leaving an altitude in the block he may not return to that altitude without additional ATC clearance. Further, it is approval for the pilot to proceed to and make an approach at destination airport and can be used in conjunction with:
1. An airport clearance limit at locations with a standard/special instrument approach procedure. The FARs require that if an instrument letdown to an airport is necessary the pilot shall make the letdown in accordance with a standard/special instrument approach procedure for that airport, or
2. An airport clearance limit at locations that are within/below/outside controlled airspace and without a standard/special instrument approach procedure. Such a clearance is NOT AUTHORIZATION for the pilot to descend under IFR conditions below the applicable minimum IFR altitude nor does it imply that ATC is exercising control over aircraft in uncontrolled airspace; however, it provides a means for the aircraft to proceed to destination airport, descend and land in accordance with applicable FARs governing VFR flight operations. Also, this provides search and rescue protection until such time as the IFR flight plan is closed (see Instrument Approach Procedure).

Delay Indefinite (Reason If Known) Expect Approach/Further Clearance (Time): Used by ATC to inform a pilot when an accurate estimate of the delay time and the reason for the delay cannot immediately be determined; e.g., a disabled aircraft on the runway, terminal or center area saturation, weather below landing minimums.

DF: Direction Finding — emergency headings (steer) to the airport provided by a Flight Service Station equipped with DF equipment. A DF steer is a disoriented IFR pilot's last resort.

D.G.: Directional Gyro — a gyro stabilized, non-direction seeking, heading indicator which must be periodically set to the aircraft's magnetic compass.

DH: Decision Height — the height at which a decision must be made during an ILS or PAR approach to either continue the approach or to execute a missed approach. This point on the glide slope is determined by the altimeter reading.

DME: Distance Measuring Equipment — an airborne navigational aid which interrogates a VORTAC and measures the aircraft's distance from a navaid in nautical miles. Some DME equipment can also provide the aircraft's groundspeed and time-to-station (see p. 217).

EAC: Expect Approach Clearance — the time at which it is expected that an approach clearance will be issued to an arriving aircraft that is holding. EAC is associated with a *terminal area delay* and when issued to an aircraft, provides time for Controllers to clear the airspace ahead in the event of a communications failure.

EFC: Expect Further Clearance — the time at which it is expected that an additional clearance will be issued to an aircraft that is holding. EFC is associated with an *enroute delay* and when issued to an aircraft, provides time for Controllers to clear the airspace ahead in the event of a communications failure.

En Route Air Traffic Control Services: Air traffic control service provided aircraft on an IFR flight plan, generally by centers, when these aircraft are operating between departure and destination terminal areas. When equipment capabilities and controller workload permit, certain advisory/assistance services may be provided to VFR aircraft.

ETA: Estimated Time of Arrival.

ETD: Estimated Time of Departure.

ETE: Estimated Time Enroute.

Execute Missed Approach: Instructions issued to a pilot making an instrument approach which means continue inbound to the missed approach point and execute the missed approach procedure as described on the Instrument Approach Procedure Chart, or as previously assigned by ATC. The pilot may climb immediately to the altitude specified in the missed approach procedure upon making a missed approach. No turns should be initiated prior to reaching the missed approach point. When conducting an ASR or PAR approach, execute the assigned missed approach procedure immediately upon receiving instructions to "execute missed approach."

Expect (Altitude) At (Time) or (Fix): Used to inform a pilot when to expect the specified altitude. In the event of a two-way radio communication failure before receiving an enroute altitude assignment within the highest route structure filed, the aircraft should begin climb to the expected altitude at the time or fix specified in the clearance.

Expect Approach Clearance (Time)/EAC: The time at which it is expected that an arriving aircraft will be cleared to commence an approach for landing. It is issued when the aircraft clearance limit is a designated Initial, Intermediate, or Final Approach Fix for the approach in use and the aircraft is to be held. If delay is anticipated, the pilot should be advised of his EAC at least 5 minutes before the aircraft is estimated to reach the clearance limit.

Expect Further Clearance (Time)/EFC: The time at which it is expected that additional clearance will be issued to an aircraft. It is issued when the aircraft clearance limit is a fix not designated as part of the approach procedure to be executed and the aircraft will be held. If delay is anticipated the pilot should be advised of his EFC at least 5 minutes before the aircraft is estimated to reach the clearance limit.

Expect Further Clearance Via (Airways, Routes or Fixes): Used to inform a pilot of the routing he can expect if any part of the route beyond a short range clearnace limit differs from that filed.

FAF: Final Approach Fix — the last radio fix over which final approach (IFR) to an airport is executed. A report is always required when passing the FAF inbound.

Final: Commonly used to mean that an aircraft is on the final approach course or is aligned with a landing area.

Final Approach: The flight path of an aircraft which is inbound to the airport on an approved final instrument approach course, beginning at the final approach fix and extending to the airport or the point where the circling for landing or missed approach is executed.

Final Approach Course: A straight line extension of a localizer, a final approach radial/bearing, or a runway centerline, all without regard to distance.

Fix: A definite geographical position, determined either by the intersection of bearings from two radio navigation stations, by radar or by the use of DME in conjunction with the VOR.

Flight Level: A level of constant atmospheric pressure related to a reference datum of 29.92 inches of mercury. Each is stated in three digits that represent hundreds of feet. For example, flight level 250 represents a barometric altimeter indication of 25,000 feet; flight level 255, an indication of 25,500 feet.

Flight Service Station/FSS: Air Traffic Service facilities within the National Airspace System (NAS) which provide preflight pilot briefing and enroute communications with VFR flights, assist lost IFR/VFR aircraft, assist aircraft having emergencies, relay ATC clearances, originate, classify, and disseminate Notices to Airmen, broadcast aviation weather and NAS information, receive and close flight plans, monitor radio NAVAIDS, notify search and rescue units of missing VFR aircraft, and operate the national weather teletypewriter systems. In addition, at selected locations, FSSs take weather observations, issue airport advisories, administer airman written examinations, and advise Customs and Immigration of transborder flight.

Fly Heading (Degrees): Informs the pilot of the heading he should fly. The pilot may have to turn to, or continue on, a specific compass direction in order to comply with the instructions. The pilot is expected to turn in the shorter direction to the heading, unless otherwise instructed by ATC.

Glide Path, (On/Above/Below): Used by ATC to inform an aircraft making a PAR approach of its vertical position (elevation) relative to the descent profile. The terms "slightly" and "well" are used to describe the degree of deviation; e.g., "slightly above glidepath." Trend information is also issued with respect to the elevation of the aircraft and may be modified by the terms "rapidly" and "slowly;" e.g., "well above glidepath, coming down rapidly" (see PAR Approach).

Glide Slope: An electronic signal which provides vertical guidance during a precision approach, and which activates the horizontal needle on the ILS display.

Go Ahead: Proceed with your message. Not to be used for any other purpose.

Go Around: Instructions for a pilot to abandon his approach to landing. Additional instructions may follow. Unless otherwise advised by ATC, a VFR aircraft or an aircraft conducting visual approach should overfly the runway while climbing to traffic pattern altitude and enter the traffic pattern via the crosswind leg. A pilot on an IFR flight plan making an instrument approach should execute the published missed approach procedure or proceed as instructed by ATC; e.g., "Go Around" (additional instructions, if required).

HAA: The height of the MDA above the published airport elevation. This is published in conjunction with circling minimums.

HAT: The height of the DH or MDA above the highest elevation in the touchdown zone. This is published in conjunction with straight-in minimums.

Have Numbers: Used by pilots to inform ATC that they have received runway and wind information only.

Heading: The magnetic direction in which an aircraft is pointed.

Holding: A predetermined maneuver which keeps an aircraft within a specified airspace while awaiting further clearance.

Holding fix: A specified fix used as a reference point in establishing and maintaining the position of an aircraft while holding.

How Do You Hear Me?: A question relating to the quality of the transmission or to determine how well the transmission is being received.

Ident: A request for a pilot to activate the aircraft transponder identification feature. This will help the controller to confirm an aircraft identity or to identify an aircraft.

If Feasible, Reduce Speed To (Speed): See Speed Adjustment.

If No Transmission Received For (Time): Used by ATC in radar approaches to prefix procedures which should be followed by the pilot in event of lost communications.

IFR: Instrument Flight Rules — see FAR 91.33. The abbreviation IFR is universally used as a label for all instrument operations.

ILS: Instrument Landing System — a combination of electronic components which furnish an aircraft horizontal and vertical guidance to a missed approach point near the runway.

Immediately: Used by ATC when such action is required to avoid an imminent situation.

Increase Speed To (Speed): See Speed Adjustment.

Instrument Approach Procedure/IAP/Instrument Approach: A series of predetermined maneuvers for the orderly transfer of an aircraft under instrument flight conditions from the beginning of the initial approach to a landing, or to a point from which a landing may be made visually. It is prescribed and approved for a specific airport by competent authority.

I Say Again: The message will be repeated.

Knot: An expression of speed equal to 1 nautical mile per hour.

LDA: Localizer Directional Aid — a standard ILS localizer which is offset more than 3 degrees from the runway.

LOC: Localizer — an electronic extension of the runway centerline which provides horizontal guidance (left-right information) during an ILS approach.

LOM: Compass Locator at the outer marker.

Lost Communications/Two-Way Radio Communications Failure: Loss of the ability to communicate by radio. Aircraft are sometimes referred to as NORDO (No Radio). Standard pilot procedures are specified in FAR Part 91. Radar controllers issue procedures for pilots to follow in the event of lost communications during a radar approach, when weather reports indicate that an aircraft will likely encounter IFR weather conditions during the approach.

Low Altitude Alert, Advise You Climb Immediately To (Altitude): See Radar Safety Advisory.

Maintain:
    1.   Concerning altitude/flight level, the term means to remain at the altitude/flight level specified. The phrase "climb and" or "descend and" normally precede "maintain" and the altitude assignment; e.g., "descend and maintain 5000." If a SID procedure is assigned in the initial or subsequent clearance, the

altitude restrictions in the SID, if any, will apply unless otherwise advised by ATC.

2. Concerning other ATC instructions, the term is used in its literal sense; e.g., maintain VFR.

Make Short Approach: Used by ATC to inform a pilot to alter his traffic pattern so as to make a short final approach.

MAP: Missed Approach Point — the point at which a missed approach must be executed expressed in time or distance from the final approach fix, or as an altitude on the glide slope, if the runway environment is not in sight.

Marker Beacon: A highly directional radio transmitter used to indicate distance from the runway on an ILS approach. The outer and middle markers are both marker beacons and are received in the aircraft by panel-mounted lights which illuminate to indicate passage over them.

Mayday: The international radiotelephony distress signal. When repeated three times, it indicates imminent and grave danger and that immediate assistance is requested. (See PAN) (Refer to AIM Part 1.)

MCA: Minimum Crossing Altitudes — the lowest altitudes an aircraft may safely cross certain radio fixes when proceeding in the direction of a higher minimum enroute IFR altitude.

MDA: Minimum Descent Altitude — the lowest altitude, expressed in feet above mean sea level, to which descent is authorized on final approach or during circling-to-land maneuvering in the execution of a standard instrument approach procedure where no electronic glide slope is provided.

MEA: Minimum Enroute Altitude — the lowest altitude between two radio fixes which assures acceptable navigational signal coverage and meets obstruction clearance requirements between those fixes.

Microwave Landing System/MLS: An instrument landing system operating in the microwave spectrum which provides lateral and vertical guidance to aircraft having compatible avionics equipment.

Missed Approach:
1. A maneuver conducted by a pilot when an instrument approach cannot be completed to a landing. The route of flight and altitude are shown on instrument approach procedure charts. A pilot executing a missed approach prior to the Missed Approach Point (MAP) must continue along the final approach to the MAP. The pilot may climb immediately to the altitude specified in the missed approach procedure.
2. A term used by the pilot to inform ATC that he is executing the missed approach.
3. At locations where ATC radar service is provided the pilot should conform to radar vectors, when provided by ATC, in lieu of the published missed approach procedure.

MM: Middle Marker — a highly directional radio beacon located about one-half mile from the end of the runway on an ILS approach. A distance indicator, it transmits an audible signal of high pitched alternate dots and dashes. If marker beacon lights are installed in the aircraft, the *amber light will flash* in conjunction with the sound. The middle marker does *not* indicate the missed approach point!

MOCA: Minimum Obstruction Clearance Altitude — the specified altitude in effect between radio fixes on VOR/LF airways, and off-airway routes on route segments, which meets obstruction clearance requirements for the entire route segment and which assures acceptable navigational signal coverage only within 22 nautical miles of a VOR.

MRA: Minimum Reception Altitude — the lowest altitude required to receive adequate signals to determine specific VOR/VORTAC fixes.

MSA: Minimum Safe (Sector) Altitude — the lowest altitude within 25 nautical miles of an approach fix which guarantees 1,000 feet obstacle clearance. Expressed as one altitude for all directions or as several altitudes for different sectors around the fix, the MSA is printed on the upper right hand corner of Jeppesen approach plates (see Appendix E).

NAS Stage: The enroute ATC system's radar, computers and computer programs, Controller plan view displays (PVDs/Radar Scopes), input/output devices, and the related communications equipment which are integrated to form the heart of the automated IFR air traffic control system. This equipment performs Flight Data Processing (FDP) and Radar Data Processing (RDP). It interfaces with automated terminal systems and is used in the control of enroute IFR aircraft.

Nautical Mile: One minute of latitude (measured vertically on all navigation charts); all distances in IFR charts are indicated in nautical miles; all DME displays read nautical miles.

NDB: See Non-Directional Beacon.

Negative: "No" or "Permission not granted" or "That is not correct."

Negative Contact: Used by pilots to inform ATC that:
1. Previously issued traffic is not in sight. It may be followed by the pilot's request for the Controller to provide assistance in avoiding the traffic.
2. They were unable to contact ATC on a particular frequency.

No Gyro Approach/Vector: A radar appraoch/vector provided in case of a malfunctioning gyrocompass or directional gyro. Instead of providing the pilot with headings to be flown, the Controller observes the radar track and issues control instructions "turn right/left" or "stop turn" as appropriate.

Non-directional Beacon/Radio Beacon/NDB: An L/MF or UHF radio beacon transmitting nondirectional signals whereby the pilot of an aircraft equipped with direction finding equipment can determine his bearing to or from the radio beacon and "home" on or track to or from the station. When the radio beacon is installed in conjunction with the Instrument Landing System marker, it is normally called a Compass Locator.

Non-precision Approach: A standard instrument approach procedure in which no electronic glide slope is provided.

Numerous Targets Vicinity (Location): A traffic advisory issued by ATC to advise pilots that targets on the radar scope are too numerous to issue individually.

OM: Outer Marker — a highly directional radio beacon located 4 to 7 miles from the runway which is usually the final approach fix on an ILS or localizer approach. A distance indicator, it transmits an audible signal of continuous low-pitched dashes. If marker beacon lights are installed in the aircraft, the *blue light will flash* in conjunction with the sound.

Omni: An abbreviation for "Very High Frequency Omni-directional Radio Range," also known as VOR.

On Course:
1. Used to indicate that an aircraft is established on the route centerline.
2. Used by ATC to advise a pilot making a radar approach that his aircraft is lined up on the final approach course.

Out: The conversation is ended and no response is expected.

Over: My transmission is ended; I expect a response.

PAN: The international radio-telephony urgency signal. When repeated three times indicates uncertainty or alert, followed by nature of urgency.

PAR: Precision Approach Radar — a precision approach predicated upon voice instructions issued to the pilot by the Controller as he observes the aircraft's azimuth, distance, and elevation on radar. Known as a GCA (Ground Controlled Approach) at military airfields.

Pilot's Discretion: When used in conjunction with altitude assignments, means that ATC has offered the pilot the option of starting climb or descent whenever he wishes and conducting the climb or descent at any rate he wishes. He may temporarily level off at any intermediary altitude. However, once he has vacated an altitude he may not return to that altitude.

Precision Approach: A standard instrument approach procedure in which an electronic glide slope is provided. The only precision approach operationally available for civilian use is the Instrument Landing System (ILS).

Procedure Turn: A maneuver used to reverse course in order to establish the aircraft inbound on the approach course. The maneuver is generally used in non-radar environments or when you arrive over the approach fix headed away from the runway.

Procedure Turn Altitude: The altitude at or above which your course reversal turn must be executed. This altitude must be maintained until reintercepting the approach course inbound.

Radar: Radio Detection and Ranging (see Appendix B, p. 217).

Radar Contact:
    1.   Used by ATC to inform an aircraft that it is identified on the radar display and radar service may be provided until radar identification is lost or radar service is terminated. When a pilot is informed of "radar contact" he automatically discontinues reporting over compulsory reporting points.
    2.   The term an air traffic controller uses to inform the transferring Controller that the target being transferred is identified on his radar display.

Radar Contact Lost: Used by ATC to inform a pilot that radar identification of his aircraft has been lost. The loss may be attributed to several things including the aircraft merging with weather or ground clutter, the aircraft flying below radar line of sight, the aircraft entering an area of poor radar return or a failure of the aircraft transponder or ground radar equipment.

Radar Safety Advisory: A radar advisory issued by ATC to radar identified aircraft under their control if an aircraft is observed to be at an altitude which, in the Controller's judgment, places the aircraft in unsafe proximity to terrain, obstructions or other aircraft. The Controller may discontinue the issuance of further advisories if the pilot advises he is taking action to correct the situation or has the other aircraft in sight.

1. Terrain/Obstruction Advisory — A radar advisory issued by ATC to aircraft under their control if an aircraft is observed at an altitude which, in the Controller's judgment, places the aircraft in unsafe proximity to terrain/obstructions; e.g., "Low Altitude Alert, advise you climb immediately to three thousand."

2. Aircraft Conflict Advisory — A radar advisory issued by ATC to aircraft under their control if an aircraft not under their control is observed at an altitude which, in the Controller's judgment, places both aircraft in unsafe proximity to each other. With the alert, ATC will offer the pilot an alternate course of action when feasible, e.g., — "Conflict Alert, advise you turn right heading zero niner zero" or "climb to eight thousand immediately."

The issuance of a radar safety advisory is contingent upon the capability of the Controller to observe an unsafe condition. The course of action provided will be predicated on other traffic under ATC control. Once the advisory is issued, it is solely the pilot's prerogative to determine what course of action, if any, he will take.

Radar Service Terminated: Used by ATC to inform a pilot that he will no longer be provided any of the services that could be received while under radar contact. Radar service is automatically terminated and the pilot is not advised in the following cases:

1. When the aircraft cancels its IFR flight plan.
2. At the completion of a radar approach.
3. When an arriving aircraft receiving Stage I, II, or III service is advised to contact the tower.
4. When an aircraft conducting a visual approach is advised to contact the tower.
5. When an aircraft vectored to a final approach course for an instrument approach has landed or the tower has the aircraft in sight, whichever occurs first.

Radar Vector: A heading issued to an aircraft to provide navigational guidance by radar.

Radial: A magnetic outbound course transmitted (radiating) from a VOR/VORTAC/TACAN navigation facility.

Radio Compass: Same as ADF.

Readback: Repeat my message back to me.

Reduce Speed To (Speed): See Speed Adjustment.

Relative Bearing: The number of degrees that an ADF pointer is displaced *clockwise* from the nose (top index of the ADF dial) of the aircraft. A relative bearing (RB) indicates the location of the beacon "relative" to the nose of the aircraft and is read directly off the ADF dial under the head of the pointer.

Report: Used to instruct pilots to advise ATC of specified information, e.g., "Report passing Hamilton VOR."

Request Full Route Clearance/FRC: Used by pilots to request that the entire route of flight be read verbatim in an ATC clearance. Such request should be made to preclude receiving an ATC clearance based on the originally filed flight plan when a filed IFR flight plan has been revised by the pilot, company, or operations prior to departure.

Resume Normal Navigation: Used by ATC to advise a pilot to resume his own navigational responsibility. It is issued after completion of a radar vector or when radar contact is lost while the aircraft is being radar vectored.

RMI: Radio Magnetic Indicator — a navigation instrument which displays the aircraft's heading at the top of a rotating card (exactly like an open-faced directional gyro), and indicates the aircraft's magnetic course to the appropriate stations by means of pointers mounted on this card that are connected electronically to the VOR and/or ADF receivers.

Roger: I have received all of your last transmission. It should not be used to answer a question requiring a yes or no answer (see Affirmative, Negative).

Runway Environment: The runway threshold, approved lighting aids, or other markings identifiable with the runway. Having the runway environment in sight is one of the requirements for descending below DH or MDH on any approach.

RVR: Runway Visual Range — visibility measured in hundreds of feet by a photoelectric sensor called a "transmissometer." This device, which is located adjacent to the runway, computes the pilot's in-flight visibility and transmits the information to the tower Controller who can advise the pilot of any variable conditions during his approach.

Say Again: Used to request a repeat of the last transmission. Usually specifies transmission or portion thereof not understood or received, e.g., "Say again all after ABRAM VOR."

Say Altitude: Used by ATC to ascertain an aircraft's specific altitude/flight level. When the aircraft is climbing or descending, the pilot should state the indicated altitude rounded to the nearest 100 feet.

Say Heading: Used by ATC to request an aircraft heading. The pilot should state the actual heading of the aircraft.

SDF: Simplified Directional Facility — an instrument approach procedure with a localizer like final approach course that may vary in width between 6 degrees and 12 degrees depending upon the installation and be offset somewhat from the runway heading.

SID: Standard Instrument Departure — a published departure clearance designed to reduce communication time. Each SID is named and numbered and directs you to an enroute fix via the routing designated in the clearance.

Sidestep Maneuver: A visual maneuver accomplished by a pilot at the completion of an instrument approach to permit a straight-in landing on a parallel runway not more than 1200 feet to either side of the runway to which the instrument approach was conducted.

Speak Slower: Used in verbal communications as a request to reduce speech rate.

Speed Adjustment: An ATC procedure used to request pilots to adjust aircraft speed to a specific value for the purpose of providing desired spacing. Speed adjustments are always expressed as indicated airspeed and pilots are expected to maintain a speed of plus or minus 10 knots of the specified speed.

Squawk (Mode, Code, Function): Activate specific modes/codes/functions on the aircraft transponder, e.g., "Squawk Three/Alpha, Two one zero five, Low."

Standby: Means the controller or pilot must pause for a few seconds, usually to attend to other duties of a higher priority. Also means to "wait" as in "stand by for clearance." If a delay is lengthy, the caller should re-establish contact.

STAR: Standard Terminal Arrival Route — a published arrival clearance designed to reduce communication time. Each STAR is named and numbered and directs you into the terminal area via the routing designated in the clearance.

Stepdown Fix: An intermediate point between the Final Approach Fix and the Missed Approach Point that, when identified by the pilot, will enable him to descend to lower minimums on the approach.

Stop Altitude Squawk: Used by ATC to inform an aircraft to turn-off the automatic altitude reporting feature of its transponder. It is issued when the verbally reported altitude varies 300 feet or more from the automatic altitude report.

Stop Squawk (Mode or Code): Used by ATC to tell the pilot to turn specified functions of the aircraft transponder off.

Straight-in Approach: An instrument approach wherein the final approach is begun without first having to execute a procedure turn, the final approach course is aligned within 30 degrees of the runway and a normal descent from the minimum IFR altitude can be accomplished.

Target: The indication shown on a radar display resulting from a primary radar return or a radar beacon reply.

TAS: True Airspeed.

That Is Correct: The understanding you have is right.

Track: The actual flight path of an aircraft over the surface of the earth.

Traffic Advisories: Advisories issued to alert a pilot to other known or observed IFR/VFR air traffic which may be in such proximity to his aircraft's position or intended route of flight to warrant his attention. Such advisories may be based on:
1. visual observation from a control tower,
2. observation of radar identified and nonidentified aircraft targets on an ARTCC/Approach Control radar scope, or,
3. verbal reports from pilots or other facilities.

Controllers use the word "traffic" followed by additional information, if known, to provide such advisories, e.g., "Traffic, 2 o'clock, one zero miles, southbound, fast moving, altitude readout seven thousand five hundred."

Traffic advisory service will be provided to the extent possible depending on higher priority duties of the Controller or other limitations, e.g., radar limitations, volume of traffic, frequency congestion or controller workload. Radar/nonradar traffic advisories do not relieve the pilot of his responsibility for continual vigilance to see and avoid other aircraft. IFR and VFR aircraft are cautioned that there are many times when the Controller is not able to give traffic advisories concerning all traffic in the aircraft's proximity; in other words, when a pilot requests or is receiving traffic advisories, he should not assume that all traffic will be issued.

Traffic In Sight: Used by pilots to inform a controller that previously issued traffic is in sight.

Transmitting In The Blind/Blind Transmission: A transmission from one station to other stations in circumstances where two-way communication cannot be established, but where it is believed that the called stations may be able to receive the transmission.

Unable: Indicates inability to comply with a specific instruction, request, or clearance.

Under The Hood: Indicates that the pilot is using a hood to restrict visibility outside the cockpit while simulating instrument flight. An appropriately rated pilot is required in the other control seat while this operation is being conducted. (Refer to FAR Part 91.)

Vector: A heading issued to an aircraft to provide navigational guidance by radar.

Verify: Request confirmation of information; e.g., "verify assigned altitude."

Verify Specific Direction Of Takeoff (or Turns After Takeoff): Used by ATC to ascertain an aircraft's direction of takeoff and/or direction of turn after takeoff. It is normally used for IFR departures from an airport not having a control tower. When direct communication with the pilot is not possible, the request and information may be relayed through an FSS, dispatcher, or by other means.

VFR: Visual Flight Rules — see FAR Part 91.33. The abbreviation VFR is universally used as a label for all non-instrument operations.

Visibility: The horizontal distance at which targets of known distance are visible over at least half of the horizon. It may be measured and reported by a ground observer, a transmissometer (RVR) or a pilot.

Visual Approach: A short-cut to a published instrument approach procedure wherein an aircraft on an IFR flight plan, operating in VFR conditions and having received an air traffic control authorization, may deviate from the prescribed instrument approach procedure and proceed to the airport of destination by visual reference to the ground.

VOR/Very High Frequency Omnidirectional Range Station: A ground-based electronic navigation aid transmitting very high frequency navigation signals, 360 degrees in azimuth, oriented from magnetic north. Used as the basis for navigation in the National Airspace System. The VOR periodically identifies itself by morse code and may have an additional voice identification feature. Voice features may be used by ATC or FSS for transmitting instructions/information to pilots (see Appendix B, p. 214).

VORTAC: A VOR station co-located with TACAN (Tactical Air Navigation) ground transmitting equipment that provides DME and azimuth data to military aircraft. For civilian operations, a VORTAC simply denotes a VOR station that generates DME range information.

VOT: Very High Frequency Omnitest — a ground facility which radiates a test signal to check VOR receiver accuracy. The system is limited to ground use only.

WILCO: I have received your message, understand it, and will comply with it.

Words Twice:
1. As a request: "Communication is difficult. Please say every phrase twice."
2. As information: "Since communications are difficult, every phrase in this message will be spoken twice."

Yellow: The right half of the **blue/yellow** color arc on the VOR display.

Zulu Time: Greenwich Mean Time — Zulu time means the same thing as, and is frequently abbreviated as, "Z" time.

Bibliography

Aero Publishers Inc., *Federal Aviation Regulations for Pilots.* Fallbrook, Calif., 1982.

Andresen, Jack, *Fundamentals of Aircraft Flight and Engine Instruments.* New York: Hayden, 1969.

Bendix Corporation, *Flying the VOR,* pilot's manual. Fort Lauderdale, Florida: Bendix Avionics Division, December 1968.

British Light Aviation Centre, *B.L.A.C. Manual of Flying and Ground Training.* London: British Light Aviation Centre Ltd., 1969.

Buck, Robert N., *Flying Know-How.* New York: Delacorte Press, 1975.

Culver, Henry H. Jr., "Pilot's *Dial-a-Panel* Navigation Trainer." St. Louis, Missouri: Flight Information Publications, 1982.

Dommasch, Sherby, and Connolly, *Airplane Aerodynamics,* 4th ed. New York: Pitman, 1967.

Federal Aviation Agency, *Air Traffic Control Procedures Manual,* AT7110.65. Washington, D.C.: U.S. Government Printing Office, January 1976.

————— , *Airman's Information Manual.* Washington, D.C.: U.S. Government Printing Office, August 1982.

————— , *Flight Instructor's Handbook,* AC61-16A. Washington, D.C.: U.S. Government Printing Office, 1969.

————— , *Flight Training Handbook,* AC-61-21A. Washington, D.C.: U.S. Government Printing Office, 1980.

————— , *IFR Pilot Exam-O-Grams.* Washington, D.C.: U.S. Government Printing Office, March 1974.

————— , *Instrument Flying Handbook,* AC-61-27C. Washington, D.C.: U.S. Government Printing Office, 1980.

Ferrara, John M., *Every Pilot's Guide to Aviation Electronics.* Heightstown, New Jersey: El Jac Publishing Corp., 1974.

Hall, J. S., *Radar Aids to Navigation.* New York: McGraw-Hill, 1947.

Heflin, W. A. (ed.), *The United States Air Force Dictionary.* Maxwell Air Force Base, Ala.: Air University Press, 1956.

Hoyt, John R., *As the Pro Flies.* New York: McGraw-Hill, 1959.

Jeppesen and Co., *Instrument Rating Course,* Mach 2. Denver, Colo., 1980.

Kershner, W. K., *The Instrument Flight Manual.* Ames, Iowa: Iowa State University Press, 1981.

Langewiesche, Wolfgang, *Stick and Rudder.* New York: Whittlesey House, 1944.

Lyon, Thoburn C., *Practical Air Navigation.* Denver, Colo., Jeppesen, 1972.

Murchie, Guy, *Song of the Sky.* New York: Ziff-Davis, 1979.

Pan American Navigation Service, Inc., *The Instrument Rating,* 19th ed., Zweng Manual. N. Hollywood, Calif., 1969.

Radio Corp. of America, *Distance Measuring Equipment,* AVQ-75, Pilot's Handbook, March 1965.

Safford, Edward L., *Aviation Electronics Handbook.* Blue Ridge Summit, Pa.: TAB Books, 1975.

Sawyer School of Aviation, *Instrument Flight Workbook.* Phoenix, Arizona, 1969.

Sickle, N. D. Van, *Modern Airmanship,* 5th ed. New York: Van Nostrand, 1980.

Stever, Guyford H., and James J. Haggerty, *Flight.* LIFE Science Library (international ed.). Amsterdam, Holland: TIME Inc., 1966.

Taylor, Richard L., *Instrument Flying.* New York: Macmillan, 1972.

United States Air Force, *Air Navigation,* Volumes I and II, AFM 51-40. Washington, D.C.: U.S. Government Printing Office, 1960.

_____ , *Dead Reckoning, Computers,* AFM 51-12. Washington, D.C.: U.S. Government Printing Office, May 1959.

_____ , *Instrument Flying,* AFM 51-37 (Revised). Washington, D.C.: U.S. Government Printing Office, 1973.

United States Navy, *Aerodynamics for Naval Aviators,* NAVAIR 00-80T-80. Washington, D.C.: U.S. Government Printing Office, January 1965.

Weems, P. V. H., *Air Navigation,* 4th ed. Annapolis, Md.: Weems System of Navigation, 1955.

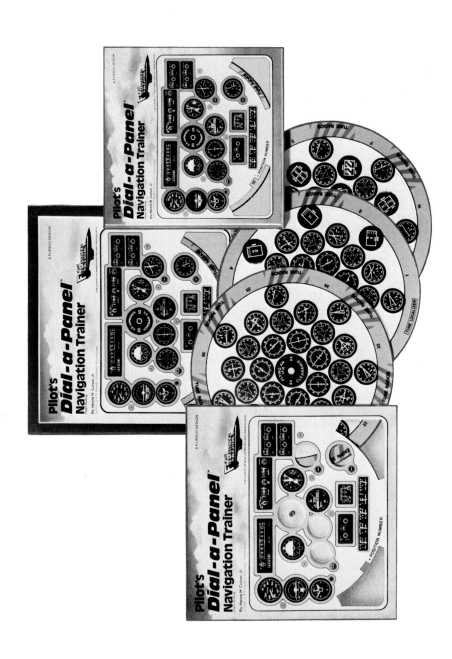

Introducing: *Dial-a-Panel*™

Henry H. Culver, Jr., a *Gold Seal* instrument flight instructor and the author of this bestselling book, has developed a very ingenious alternative to the electronic simulator: his unique "Pilot's *Dial-a-Panel* Navigation Trainer." Designed specifically for commercial/instrument students, *Dial-a-Panel* is an inexpensive procedural trainer that offers a complete home-study course in advanced VFR and IFR radio navigation (including RNAV), animated on a large, easy-to-read control panel with adjustable flight instruments and pre-set nav displays. Its fun, easy format encourages you to regularly practice and review every aspect of attitude flying and radio navigation, and it is the first of a new generation of non-powered "smart" training aids that teaches you radio navigational procedures in your home exactly the same way that they are taught in the airplane; i.e., by your interpretation of the instruments. This sophisticated "programmed panel" concept of instruction, which is integrated into the circuitry of expensive, electronic simulators, is now successfully animated by *Dial-a-Panel* through the use of its innovative rotating disc, visual navaid equipment. The versatility of this equipment enables you not only to set the needle indications on all of the flight instruments, but also to rotate one of twenty-four, numbered discs within the simulated panel and to interpret successive groups of programmed, navigation instruments as they swing into view. Simply dial a panel change and "fly" the different in-flight problems, clearances and approaches which are presented in the comprehensive 248 page training manual. By enabling you to learn the fundamentals of navigation as well as to explore the practical applications of this knowledge, the "Pilot's *Dial-a-Panel* Navigation Trainer" effectively bridges the gap between the classroom and the cockpit and gives you such a realistic interaction with your instrument panel that it is literally your personal flight simulator for radio navigation. The *Dial-a-Panel* folder and instrument discs are constructed of a durable, high density cardboard that is plastic coated and all hardware is made of spring steel and brass. Kit dimensions: 10½" x 10½" x1½"; weight: 3½ lbs; price: $49.95.

- Complete, programmed home-study course in advanced VFR and IFR radio navigation that includes all necessary enroute and approach charts (conforms with the new FAA *Instrument Flying Handbook:* AC 61-27C).

- Step-by-step solutions to in-flight navigational problems animated on a realistic panel with adjustable flight instruments and pre-set nav displays.

- Comprehensive review of the entire course including a final check-ride that incorporates an IFR clearance that you can actually fly.

☀NEW PRODUCT   *FLYING BOOK NEWS SELECTION!*

Dial-a-Panel™

There's no other simulator like it! The "Pilot's *Dial-a-Panel* Navigation Trainer" is a sophisticated, new, visual training aid that offers a
complete course in advanced VFR and IFR radio navigation, animated on a
large, easy-to-read control panel with adjustable flight instruments and pre-
set nav displays. Designed specifically for commercial/instrument students, its unique construction allows you to rotate one of twenty-four,
numbered discs (see disc No. 19 below) within the simulated panel and to
interpret successive groups of programmed, navigation instruments as they
swing into view. Simply dial a panel change and "fly" the different in-flight
problems, clearances and approaches which are presented in the comprehensive, 248 page training manual. The "Pilot's *Dial-a-Panel* Navigation
Trainer" gives you such a realistic interaction with your instrument panel
that it is literally your personal flight simulator for radio navigation.

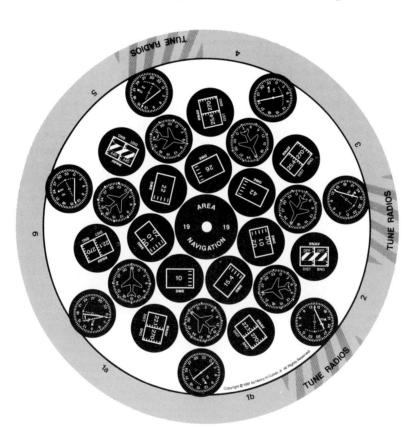

IFR POCKET SIMULATOR PROCEDURES

P. O. Box 16616
St. Louis, Missouri 63105

Please send me _____ copy(ies) of **IFR Pocket Simulator Procedures** at $19.95†
plus $1.25 shipping for one (1) book **or** $35.95 *postpaid* for two (2) books.
Enclosed is my check for $ _____. Make checks payable to Flight Information
Publications Co.

Name _____

Address _____

City _____ State _____ Zip _____

† *Residents of Missouri add 4½% sales tax.*

DIAL-A-PANEL NAVIGATION TRAINER

P. O. Box 16616
St. Louis, Missouri 63105

Please send me _____ kit(s) of the **"Pilot's Dial-a-Panel Navigation Trainer"**
at $49.95† plus $2.50 shipping for one (1) kit **or** $89.95 *postpaid* for two (2) kits.
Enclosed is my check for $ _____. Make checks payable to Flight Information
Publications Co.

Name _____

Address _____

City _____ State _____ Zip _____

† *Residents of Missouri add 4½% sales tax.*

GIVE A

POCKET SIMULATOR

TO A PILOT FRIEND

Ask for *IFR Pocket Simulator Procedures* at your
local airport pilot shop. If for some reason the book
is unavailable, use the reverse side of this page to
order directly from the publisher.

GIVE A

Dial-a-Panel™

TO A PILOT FRIEND

Ask for the "Pilot's *Dial-a-Panel* Navigation Trainer"
at your local airport pilot shop. If for some reason
the training aid is unavailable, use the reverse side
of this page to order directly from the publisher.

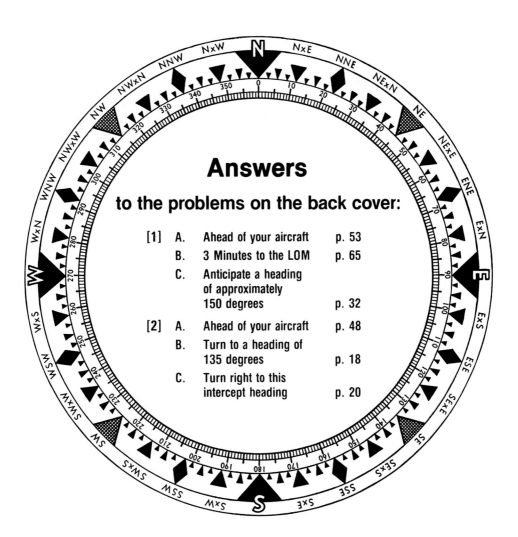

Answers

to the problems on the back cover:

[1] A. Ahead of your aircraft   p. 53

     B. 3 Minutes to the LOM   p. 65

     C. Anticipate a heading of approximately 150 degrees   p. 32

[2] A. Ahead of your aircraft   p. 48

     B. Turn to a heading of 135 degrees   p. 18

     C. Turn right to this intercept heading   p. 20